Zoë January 1996
. from Robert. -

Dictionary of Medical Folklore

The Wordsworth
Dictionary of Medical Folklore

Carol Ann Rinzler

Wordsworth Reference

This edition published 1994 by Wordsworth Editions Ltd,
Cumberland House, Crib Street, Ware, Hertfordshire SG12 9ET.

Copyright © 1979, 1991 by Carol Ann Rinzler.

All rights reserved. This publication may not be
reproduced, stored in a retrieval system,
or transmitted, in any form or by any means, electronic,
mechanical, photocopying, recording or otherwise,
without the prior permission of the publishers.

ISBN 1-85326-323-0

Printed and bound in Finland by UPC Oy.

This book is dedicated to
T. George Harris, Joel Gurin
and Linda Troiano,
with gratitude for
their continuing enthusiasm
and intellectual curiosity

Contents

Contents

A Note
to the Reader

The information about medical folklore, medicines and medical conditions in this book is drawn from historical sources or from sources considered current at the time the book was written. Names and titles are current as of the date of the studies and comments to which they are linked.

The material in this book is for your information only. It is not medical advice and should never be used in place of your own doctor's advice or without his or her consent. Because your doctor is the person most familiar with your personal medical history, he or she is also the person best qualified to advise you on medical matters.

Please note that some of the product names listed in this book are registered trademarks.

Some of the material in this book has appeared in *American Health, Country Living, Family Circle, Hippocrates, Ladies' Home Journal* and *Moxie.*

Preface

No matter how sophisticated we grow, most of us still believe, however surreptitiously, in magic, and most of the magic we believe has to do with medicine.

Is there a place anywhere on earth where people have grown up without a storehouse of magical medical advice? I doubt it.

We may call these bits and pieces of advice "old wives' tales" and publicly sneer at the naïveté of those who quote them, but who among us is absolutely certain, one hundred percent, that an apple a day does *not* keep the doctor away or that we cannot avoid colds simply by keeping our feet dry?

Like most writers, I am an inveterate collector of newspaper and magazine clippings. Which means that at home, in the doctor's office, in someone else's living room, it's a cinch to spot the magazines I've already read. They're the ones with the slightly moth-eaten look.

My passion for clipping, though, is definitely not matched with an equal passion for filing. I really envy writers who keep their clippings neatly filed. Years ago, I read that Theodore White (or was it Arthur Schlesinger, Jr.?) actually traveled with an expandable alphabetized folder so he could put things in their proper places right from the start. That's my idea of real class, but it's not the way I do things.

What I do is this: I toss all my clippings into a large manila envelope on the back of my desk and every other month or so, when the envelope is full enough to topple over, I sort through the clippings to see if anything of interest floats to the top.

Because I have always been interested in medicine and nutrition, pretty much everything I clip falls into one of these two broad categories. Around 1974, during one of my tedious sorting sessions, I noticed that I was beginning to accumulate a nice little collection of clippings about medical and nutritional old wives' tales. Some of the clippings seemed to prove one tale or another true; some, false.

Clearly, though, there was something incubating in those manila envelopes. The first tangible result was an article on 50 of the more common medical old wives' tales that ran in *Glamour* in April 1975.

After that, I sort of assumed that the collection of medical myths would just end up decently buried in the file drawer where I store checking material for completed articles.

But to my surprise, the pile of clippings kept growing. Day after day, I would come across nifty snippets in the newspapers, magazines and books that made their way across my desk. Within two years, I had a stack of full manila envelopes. I certainly couldn't throw them out, and if I didn't put them in some sort of order they would probably have spread clear across the room. So I put together a proposal for the first edition of *The Dictionary of Medical Folklore,* which was published in 1979.

And (would you believe it?), as soon as the book was in hard cover, that manila envelope of clippings began to fill up again.

Eventually, it produced enough new information to fill six years' worth of columns in *American Health,* plus articles for a few other magazines. But over the years, medical research continued to advance, invalidating or clarifying some of the information in the 534 entries in the original *Dictionary.*

At the beginning of 1990, it seemed to be time to update the *Dictionary* to bring medical folklore into line with current medical science. Deb Brody, my editor at *Facts On File,* liked the idea, and, as one presidential candidate who shall be nameless once sort of said about another, "There we go again."

I have had a wonderful time during my sixteen years tracking down medical folklore.

You have to admire, for a start, the sheer persistence of it all. Medical folklore existed long before there were modern doctors or mass-produced modern medicines, and it may yet outlive them all because the indisputable fact is that a lot of it really works.

True, some medical folklore is pleasant fiction, like the idea that keeping your feet dry will keep you from catching cold. (It won't, of course, if you come in contact with a cold virus to which you are susceptible.)

It's also true that some medical folklore is based on a misinterpretation of the facts, like the idea that catching a chill means catching a cold. In reality, the chill is an early symptom of the cold, not its cause.

But a significant proportion of the things your mother or your grandmother told you is right on target for reasons we are only now beginning to understand.

For example, drinking sugared tea really will soothe a sore throat because (as science now knows) consuming sweet foods triggers the almost instantaneous release of natural painkillers called endorphins in the brain. Swallowing a teaspoon of sugar may stop your hiccups because the rough crystals irritate the lining of your mouth and interrupt the glottal spasms that are one element of hiccups. Spicy foods help a cold because they make your mucous membranes secrete liquids that help you clear out mucous when you blow your nose.

What makes American medical folklore particularly fascinating is that it comes from so many different sources around the world. The French brought dandelion tea, a natural mild diuretic. Middle Europeans carried along some garlic, which we now know contains antibiotic compounds, as an all-around protective. The Chinese brought ginseng, which, while it won't enable you to live forever, does contain some substances similar to estrogens. The English were wrong when they told us to put cobwebs on an open wound to stop the bleeding, but they were right in sharing with Native Americans the knowledge that a tea brewed from the bark of the willow tree could lower a fever and ease aches and pains.

All of those are in this book.

But every time I think I have it all, I find another medical old wives' tale to chase. So I have no doubt that you will find that one of your favorite pieces of medical folklore is still missing from my collection. If I'm right, I'd certainly like to hear about it. You can send me a note c/o Facts On File, 460 Park Avenue South, New York, New York 10016, and I will do my best to track it down for any future edition of this book.

In the meantime, enjoy. And don't forget to feed your cold and starve your fever. Or is it the other way around?

Carol Ann Rinzler

Acknowledgements

Over the past decade, literally dozens of people have been kind enough to take the time to answer my questions about one or more pieces of medical folklore. I am immensely grateful to this group of generous people, including Dr. John Adriana, Dr. Harry Arnold, Dr. Steven Aron, Jóseph P. Bark, M.D., Dr. Sam Baron, Dr. Berryl Benacerraf, Page Blankingship, Barry Bowman, Dr. Roger Brodkin, Dr. Charles Brown, Dr. John Calkins, Dr. Mary A. Carsakadon, Dr. Alfonse Cinotti, Bonnie S. Dean, Eliot C. Dick, Ph.D., Raymond Dionne, D.D.S., Dr. Richard L. Dobson, Dr. R. Gordon Douglas, Dr. Alan Dundes, James Duke, Ph.D., Dr. Johanna Dwyer, Dr. Enayat Elahi, Dr. David N.F. Fairbanks, Marianne Gillette, Dr. Arthur Gold, Dr. Sherwood L. Gorbach, Thomas R. Gossel, Ph.D., Dr. Cecil Hart, Murray Hamlet, D.V.M., Dr. Robert I. Henkin, Karen Helton, D.V.M., Dr. Elliott Hershmann, Dr. J. Owen Hendley, John Hierholzer, Ph.D., Dr. James Hillard, Dr. Roger Hubbard, Dr. Milton Ingerman, Arthur I. Jacknowitz, Dr. Thomas Kantor, Dr. John Kinsella, Dr. Richard Knutsen, Dr. Guinter Kuhn, Dr. David Levitsky, Walter H. Lewis, Ph.D., Dr. Basil Lucak, Merrill Mitler, Ph.D., Dr. Brian Morgan, Joan Morimando, Alfred C. Olson, Ph.D., Dr. Kevin O'Toole, Robert J. Pandina, Ph.D., Dr. Floyd Pennington, Dr. Robert Provine, Dr. Rees B. Rees, Dr. J. Murdoch Ritchie, Dr. Daniel Runyan, Dr. Alan Shalita, Dr. Edgar B. Smith, Dr. Seymour Solomon, Dr. Hamilton Southworth, Dr. Mark Y. Stoeckel, Julie Stock, Dr. James S. Strain, Dr. Richard Taylor, Dr. Michael Thorpy, Varro E. Tyler, Ph.D., Dr. Robert L. Warner, Dennis Zawie, D.V.M., Dr. Irwin Ziment and Gail Zimmerman.

Introduction

Most people are more likely to receive home remedies for minor illnesses than to go to a doctor for modern medical treatment. These treatments are sometimes unpleasant, usually harmless, yet occasionally quite beneficial. Sometimes, the old way really does work best. Likewise, some of our grandmothers' sayings ("I know it's going to rain because I feel it in my bones)", turn out to be true. Yet as many others turn out to be exactly what we expected: old wives' tales with great interest as folklore but no value as medical treatment. No one should accept medical folklore just because on one occasion it seemed to work – or reject it as always worthless where modern health care is easily available.

As with most things, the truth lies somewhere in between. By examining how medical folklore originates and what has been scientifically learned about it, Carol Ann Rinzler has provided a balanced view of these issues in this book.

In the past, finding cures was largely a matter of trial and error. The observation that chewing on willow leaves relieves pain was perfectly valid long before it was discovered that willow leaves contain salicylates, the same ingredient that gives aspirin its anaesthetic and anti-inflammatory properties. Of course, many home remedies are not remedies at all – and Ms Rinzler expertly separates fact from legend. She has made great efforts to gather the latest research findings, and she presents the information in clear, understandable summaries of each topic. Most important, she is careful to point out that serious medical problems should not be treated with home remedies alone, and that even the most well-founded home remedy won't work if the wrong condition is being treated.

If you have some favorite health belief or home remedy, you can read this book to discover its origin and how it works (or why it doesn't). If you've been the recipient of some folk "wisdom" that made you feel worse, this book will explain why. And if you're just curious about folk treatments and remedies, you'll read this book cover to cover to absorb its copious and easily understood information.

Michael D. Jensen, M.D.
Mayo Clinic
Rochester, Minnesota

A

ACNE

Acne is an adolescent problem. It is true that most cases of acne begin during adolescence and that most people with acne are teenagers. In fact, according to data compiled by the National Center for Health Statistics, three out of every four American teenagers have at least a mild case of acne.

During adolescence, acne is linked to an increase in the production of the male hormone testosterone that makes the sebaceous (oil) glands in the skin larger. Everyone, both male and female, produces some male and female hormones, but males produce more testosterone and they produce it more rapidly at puberty. Therefore, they are more likely than females to have severe acne during adolescence.

However, some cases of acne do not begin until a person reaches his or her late twenties or early thirties. This kind of acne, known as adult acne, seems to target women more often than men. It, too, is linked to hormone production, so it often appears right before a woman's menstrual period when estrogen production slows and clears up afterwards when it starts to rise again.

Pregnancy cures acne. During pregnancy, a woman secretes higher levels of estrogen. Because an increased body level of estrogen seems to relieve or prevent acne, a woman's acne may get better when she is pregnant—as well as when she is taking oral contraceptives.

Sunbathing cures acne. In very moderate doses, sun exposure may help dry up superficial acne eruptions. But any sunburn can damage skin, and long exposure to the sun or strenuous exercising in the sun may make acne worse by stimulating the production of sebum, the oily exudate from the sebaceous glands that may plug a pore to create the blemish called a blackhead. Blackheads may be contaminated by bacteria that can break down the walls of the surrounding skin cells, creating an opportunity for infection. If this happens, the blackhead turns into the highly visible infection known as a pimple.

Perspiration causes acne. Perspiration is harmless, but the accompanying increase in sebum production may block pores and cause acne infections. (See above)

Acne is caused by bacteria. No. Acne is triggered by hormone production. But if you poke at the hormonally triggered bumps, you may injure the skin and contaminate the wound with the bacteria that live naturally on your hands and skin. The result: infected pimples.

Spicy foods make your skin break out. No. Eating very spicy foods stimulates perspiration. That's why people who live in hot places such as India favor spicy foods such as curries. The perspiration produced by eating these foods evaporates on the skin, creating a temporary cooling effect. But spices also stimulate the production of sebum, and perspiration plus sebum may equal blackheads.

See also CHOCOLATE, FRIED FOODS, NATURAL FOOD, TUNA FISH.

AGING

Memory loss is inevitable as we get older. Not necessarily. As we get older the most common loss of memory is a selective one: We tend to have difficulty remembering the most recent things we learned and may not be able to recall what happened in the past 24 hours yet have no trouble remembering things that happened years ago. The most charitable explanation for this is that the older we get, the more things we have to think about and the less able we are to add entries to the encyclopedia in our brain for easy reference. The problem can be ameliorated with the lists and mnemonic devices people always use to make sure they don't forget important events.

Brain power declines naturally as we get older. Again, the answer is not necessarily. Eating well and exercising regularly seem to help maintain brain function in healthy older people. Poor nutrition is a common problem among older people who live alone and simply forget to eat regularly. Or, the natural reduction in the acuity of the sense of taste that comes with getting older may diminish interest in food. But healthy people who maintain their interest in food as they get older also seem to maintain their mental abilities.

At the University of New Mexico School of Medicine in 1983, a study of 260 healthy adults age 60 to 94 showed that the ones who ate a varied, nutritious diet performed best on memory and thinking tests. A program of regular exercise also helps by improving the flow of oxygen to the brain.

That is not to say that some people do not lose memory and mental acuity as they get older, usually because of a specific medical condition such as a brain tumor or one of the dementing illnesses such as Alzheimer's disease. Alzheimer's causes a loss of brain capacity, including a loss of memory power, because it destroys cells in the layer of gray matter (cerebral cortex) covering the brain and in other brain areas. Although Alzheimer's commonly appears in people older than 50, it is by no means either inevitable or universal. In fact, the newest research suggests that there may be a hereditary or genetic component to the illness.

We all get fat as we get older. Well, maybe heavier. There's no doubt about the reality of middle-age spread. What's happening owes something to gravity, of course, but more to the natural body changes that occur as we get older.

With age, our metabolism slows. All of us, male and female alike, need fewer calories to maintain exactly the same weight. According to the National Research Council, which sets the recommended dietary allowances (RDAs) for specific nutrients and energy (calories), the average 35-year-old, 160-pound man and 35-year-old, 125-pound woman need about 11 calories per pound just to run their basic body systems (heart, brain, lungs, kidneys). At age 60+, they need about two calories fewer per pound to perform these functions. Remember, this is a basic calorie allowance just to run the body systems. All the work done in a normal day—housework, school work, walking, thinking, exercise—requires additional calories.

As a result, if we continue to live at the same pace and eat the same amount of food, we'll gain some weight naturally as we age. If we slow down our work a bit, and continue to eat the same amount of food, we'll gain more weight. Moderate exercise programs and watching what you eat may help keep things in line, but you'll be fighting nature every step of the way.

Muscles turn to fat as we get older. No. Muscles are muscles, and fat is fat, two entirely different kinds of tissue. The problem is that as we get older, the protein content of the body drops, while the fat content increases. As a result, we do naturally end up with less muscle tissue, more fat.

In 1990, though, researchers at the Medical College of Wisconsin in Milwaukee published the results of study suggesting that giving synthetic human growth hormone to elderly people whose bodies are deficient in the natural hormone might help maintain muscle tissue. In the study, a treatment group of 12 healthy men age 51 to 81 were given weekly injections of human growth hormone; a control group of 10 men received placebo injections. At the end of six months, the men who got the hormone had an 8.8% increase in lean body mass, including muscle tissue, and a 14.4% decline in fatty tissue. Because treatment with human growth hormone may cause such side effects as high blood pressure, diabetes and heart disease, the researchers caution that the study, which applies only to people whose bodies do not produce enough human growth hormone on their own, is strictly experimental.

Older people grow 'long in the tooth.' True. With age, we are all likely to lose some of the bone in our jaws, either to periodontal disease or to osteoporosis. Losing this bone causes the gum tissue to draw back further up on the teeth. Even if we manage to hold onto the bone, the fact is that our gums, like our other body tissues, tend to shrink with age. Either way, the inevitable result is that our teeth look longer.

Everyone loses his or her teeth with age. If you expect to, the chances are good that you will. It is a self-fulfilling prophecy because people who think that tooth loss is inevitable usually don't get good dental and periodontal care. Maybe that's why dental statistics show that there are some 25 million people in this country who don't have a tooth left in their heads. Another 25 million have lost at least half their teeth, and it is rare to find someone who makes it past 30 without at least one extraction.

There's no reason why that should be so. Human teeth are strong enough to last as long as we live, so long as we keep them clean and healthy. The most important causes of tooth loss are decay or periodontal disease, and in almost all cases the American Dental Association stresses the fact that cooperation between dentist, periodontist and patient might save teeth. The only exceptions are our "wisdom teeth," the large back molars that are legacies from our ancestors who had larger jaws. Today, these teeth are often removed because they no longer fit comfortably into our smaller, more evolved jaws.

See also EXERCISE, GLAUCOMA, SEXUAL POTENCY.

AIR-CONDITIONING

Exposure to air-conditioning causes colds. The only thing that causes you to catch cold is exposure to the cold virus. But there are two ways in which air-conditioning might trigger a physical or an allergic reaction that may mimic the symptoms of a cold.

First, the swift change in temperature you experience when you go from a warmer environment into the cold of an air-conditioned room may cause the mucous membrane lining of your nasal passages to swell temporarily so that it "weeps" a liquid discharge. This physical phenomenon is called vasomotor rhinitis. People suffering from vasomotor rhinitis may sneeze, cough and generally exhibit all the symptoms of a cold, but the symptoms are likely to disappear when the cause of swelling is avoided. The second example of how exposure to air-conditioning can make you appear to have a cold involves an allergic reaction to the dust, mold and other allergens an air conditioner may spray into the room it is cooling. If you are sensitive to these allergens, you are likely to develop a runny nose and reddened eyes when you are in such an air-conditioned room. In the winter, steam heat, which can cause dust and mold to rise off the radiator into the air, may trigger the same type of reaction.

ALCOHOLIC BEVERAGES

Alcohol makes you sexy. It is true that liquor lowers inhibitions, but it also interferes with the ability to attain and sustain an erection. Many a would-be seducer has found himself in an embarrassing predicament after attempting to drink his date into a compromising situation.

In vino, veritas. Too much liquor may lower the psychological barriers that inhibit us from being indiscrete, or at least impolite. When we drink more than we can effectively metabolize (the amount varies from person to person), some of us become pugnacious, loquacious, or just plain teary, and end up saying things we would never say while sober. Whether or not what we say is true is another story.

Alcohol makes you witty. No. But you may feel as if it does. When you drink too much you lose your ability to perceive your actions clearly. Under the influence of alcohol, you may talk louder and faster. But that doesn't make you witty, only noisy. Alcohol may also make you ruder. In a study at the University of California, Irvine, researchers found that people who have had several drinks may forget to listen—or actually may not hear—when other people talk.

Men hold their liquor better than women do. On average, this is true. The fact that men are able to drink more without showing it was once thought to be due to the fact that a man's body is 60% to 70% water; a woman's only 50% to 60%. The extra liquid in the male body was believed to dilute alcohol more effectively so that a man would show fewer signs of intoxication if he matched a woman drink for drink.

In 1990, however, researchers at the Mount Sinai School of Medicine and the Bronx Veterans Affairs Medical Center in New York discovered a more thoroughly scientific explanation. Women, it appears, have a smaller amount of gastric alcohol dehydrogenase, an enzyme in the stomach that metabolizes alcohol. As a result, more pure alcohol moves from the stomach into the intestines and from there into the bloodstream, where it makes its way to the liver and the brain. Thus, if a woman and a man of the same weight both consume the same amount of alcohol, say, two moderate drinks, the woman is more likely to show signs of impairment.

Men and woman who abuse alcohol reduce the amount of the enzyme, but women are affected more dramatically. Male alcoholics lose *some* of their ability to metabolize alcohol, but women who abuse alcohol may end up with virtually no effective enzyme at all. When they drink, one of the researchers reported, it is as though they were injecting alcohol directly into their veins.

Never mix whiskey and wine in one night. Actually, you can even mix the two in one drink, such as a Manhattan (a cocktail made with whiskey plus vermouth, a wine), and still come out all right so long as you know your limits. The real point is that too much of either or both in combination will do you in.

Whiskey and water is a milder drink than whiskey and soda. Sort of. Water dilutes the alcohol, slowing its absorption into your bloodstream. Soda also dilutes the whiskey, but it moves it faster past your stomach into the small intestine and into the bloodstream. As a result, you really may feel the effects of a Scotch and soda faster than the effects of a Scotch and water.

Alcoholic beverages give you only 'empty calories.' Not quite. Surprising though it may seem, according to the U.S. Department of Agriculture, alcoholic beverages do supply small but measurable amounts of specific nutrients.

	Nutrients per Serving			
	Beer (regular) 12 oz	Wine (red) 3.5 oz	Wine (white) 3.5 oz	Whiskey (86 proof) 1.5 oz
Calories	150	75	80	105
Carbohydrates (g)	13	3	3	trace
Calcium (mg)	14	8	9	trace
Iron (mg)	0.1	0.4	0.3	trace
Sodium (mg)	18	5	5	trace
Thiamin (mg)	0.02	0	0	trace
Riboflavin (mg)	0.09	0.03	0.01	trace
Niacin (mg)	1.8	0.1	0.1	trace

Source: U.S. Department of Agriculture, *Nutritive Value of Foods.* Washington, D.C.: U.S. Government Printing Office, 1981

No matter how much you drink, it won't affect your liver so long as you maintain a decent diet. False. In general, the amount of damage done to your liver by alcohol consumption is in direct proportion to the amount of alcohol you drink and length of time you have been drinking. Although excessive use of alcohol may decrease appetite and/or interfere with the absorption of nutrients, exactly how it damages the liver remains to be shown. Scientists do know, however, that women are more susceptible to liver damage from drinking (see above) and that liver disease caused by alcohol may occur among more than one member of a family. Both items suggest that genetic factors, as well as diet and general health, may influence a body's reaction to alcohol.

Liquor is a natural sleeping pill. It is true that drinking alcohol makes some people sleepy, but drinking at bedtime is no prescription for a good night's sleep.

Consuming alcoholic beverages may interfere with normal sleep patterns, either shortening the periods of REM (rapid eye movement) sleep during which dreaming occurs or, conversely, making a person dream more intensely. The first effect explains why some people who drink at bedtime wake up restless and irritable; the second, why other bedtime drinkers suffer from nightmares.

See also ALCOHOL ABUSE, BRANDY, CHAMPAGNE, COLDS, COLOR BLINDNESS, GIN, HANGOVER, MARTINIS, WINE.

ALCOHOLISM

Alcoholism is inherited. Maybe. Recent research suggests that although there may indeed be a genetic component to alcoholism, that is only one part of the problem.

There is no evidence to support the suggestion that there is a gene for "alcoholism." But there is some indication that some people do inherit a genetic inability to metabolize alcohol properly. These people may also be most vulnerable to other conditions such as psychological problems (causing them to use alcohol as a "feel-good" medicine) and behavioral conditioning (growing up in a family in which people continually abused alcohol) that may lead them into alcohol abuse.

ALOE

The juice of the aloe plant heals cuts, nicks, scrapes, and minor burns. Aloe gel, the clear, slick liquid that oozes out from the aloe when you break a leaf of the plant, is a folk remedy that seems to work, although nobody knows exactly why. Dozens of laboratory tests have proven that the gel will soothe small injuries; An aloe plant provides a ready, effective remedy for minor scrapes, cuts and burns, but serious burns require serious medicine, up to and including skin transplants.

Caution: If you are allergic to plants, you'll want to check with your doctor before using aloe.

ANEMIA

Women are more likely than men to suffer from anemia. True, so long as what we are talking about is the the form of anemia caused by iron deficiency. Women of child-bearing age lose blood each month at menstruation, and thus are more likely than men to be deficient in hemoglobin, the pigment in red blood cells that carries oxygen to every cell in the body.

Eating almonds cures anemia. Well, you could say that it helps. Like many other old-fashioned remedies for what used to be known as "female weakness," this one is based on a food rich in iron. According to the U.S. Department of Agriculture, there are 6.1 milligrams (mg) of iron in a cup of chopped raw almonds. This is about 41% of the Recommended Dietary Allowance (RDA) for a woman of child-bearing age (15 mg). By comparison, a cup of chopped raw pecans provides 2.6 mg iron; a cup of roasted peanuts, 3 mg; and a cup of roasted cashews, 5.3 mg.

See also SKIN COLOR.

ANTIBIOTICS

Take antibiotics with milk so the medicine will not upset your stomach. It depends on the antibiotic. All antibiotics are designed to kill bacteria, but they may not discriminate between helpful microorganisms and the ones that make you ill. That means that when you take an antibiotic, it may wipe out the bacteria that live naturally in your intestinal tract, where they help to break down food so you can get the nutrients from it. As a result, you may develop an upset stomach, diarrhea or constipation. Taking your medicine with milk won't make much difference because it won't replace the bacteria your antibiotic eliminates. With some drugs, milk can be positively counterproductive. The calcium in milk and milk products binds with tetracyclines (Achromycin, Aureomycin, Declomycin, Terramycin, Vibramycin, among others) and carries them out of your body before they can affect the bacteria that are making you sick.

Other antibiotics, which are not affected by plain milk, may interact with specific milk products. For example, penicillins are inhibited by blue cheese. In short, it makes sense to ask your doctor about food-and-drug interactions whenever you take any drug, not just antibiotics.

Never take antibiotics with acidic foods. Once again, it depends on the antibiotic. Acidic beverages, such as fruit juices and carbonated sodas, may inactivate some antibiotics, notably erythromycin. On the other hand, the tetracyclines (see above) are potentiated (made stronger) when taken with acid foods.

Avoid alcoholic beverages when you're on antibiotics. A good rule. Some antibiotics do interact with alcoholic beverages. For example, if you drink while you're taking metronidazole (Flagyl, Metizole) or a sulfa drug such as sulfamethoxazeole (Gantanol, Bactrim, Septra) or sulfisoxazole (Gantrisin, Azo-gantrisin), you may experience a reaction similar to the one you would experience if you drank after taking disulfiram (Antabuse), a drug used to prevent alcohol abusers from drinking. Disulfiram prevents your liver from metabolizing (decomposing) alcohol. As a result, the level of unmetabolized alcohol in your body increases, causing an extremely uncomfortable series of symptoms that may include heated flushing, a throbbing headache, chest pains and shortness of breath, sweating and vomiting. A severe disulfiram reaction may lead to convulsions, or even death.

Store all your antibiotics in the refrigerator. A bad idea. The dampness in the refrigerator may damage tablets and capsules. Storing the pills in your bathroom medicine chest is not much better because the dampness in a bathroom is also likely to damage them. Nor should medicine be stored near a radiator (too warm) or near a window (too bright). The safest place? A cool (room temperature), dry closet or chest out of direct sunlight. If you have small children in the house, keep all medicine in a locked cabinet to prevent accidental ingestion.

Just to be safe, take antibiotics when you have a cold. Antibiotics work against bacteria; they won't lay a finger on the viruses that cause colds. Some doctors give them anyway to prevent secondary infections in older people or people whose immune systems have been compromised by a second illness. Others believe that it is best to hold off from taking antibiotics until the secondary infection appears, so as to avoid possible side effects from the antibiotics and reduce the growth of antibiotic-resistant bacteria. However, in the end, whether to administer antibiotics is a decision that must be made by your doctor.

APPENDICITIS

Swallowing fruit seeds causes appendicitis. No way. Although surgeons who remove inflamed appendixes often do find small bits of matter inside, they rarely (if ever) find fruit seeds because an accidentally swallowed cherry pit or watermelon seed generally goes straight through your intestinal tract.

That doesn't mean it's a good idea to wolf down seeds and pits. Some, such as apple seeds and the seeds inside an apricot, or peach pit, contain amygdalin, a naturally occurring chemical that breaks down into hydrogen cyanide in your stomach. There have been reports of adults being poisoned after eating several apple seeds; for a small child, eating several apple seeds might be lethal.

A pain in the lower right side of your abdomen means appendicitis. It may, but so can a pain in the upper right side of the abdomen. In fact, the pain of appendicitis may be "referred" to a point as far away as your right shoulder. The better way to diagnose appendicitis is with a blood test (an increased number of white blood cells indicates infection) to confirm the classic symptoms: pain, nausea and/or vomiting and a rigid abdomen.

Appendicitis is a boy's disease. There's some truth in this. Statistics compiled by the American College of Surgeons show that 78% of all appendectomies are performed on people younger than 40. After age 40, the risk goes down dramatically. Fewer than 15% of all cases of appendicitis occur in people past 40, less than 8% in people older than 60.

According to *Harrison's Principles of Internal Medicine,* a well-known standard medical textbook, the person most likely to develop an infected appendix is a young man between puberty and age 24. Why appendicitis is more common among young people or why boys are at higher risk than girls is a question still to be solved.

APPLES

An apple a day keeps the doctor away. It couldn't hurt. Apples are a low calorie, low sodium, no fat, no cholesterol snack food. They are also high in fiber. The flesh of one medium apple provides 1.07 grams pectin, a soluble food fiber that appears to lower serum cholesterol. The apple also has 2.03 grams lignin and cellulose, insoluble food fibers that help bulk up stool, help prevent constipation, and, according to the American Cancer Society, may reduce your risk of colon cancer.

Apples also provide boron, a nutrient that increases the body's absorption of calcium and may protect against osteoporosis. In 1989, researchers at the U.S.D.A. Agricultural Research Service in Grand

Forks, North Dakota, estimated that adults need about 3.0 mg boron a day, an amount easily obtained from two fresh apples. In 1989, scientists at the Hirosaki University School of Medicine in Japan reported that people who eat three or more apples a day seem less likely to develop high blood pressure as they get older even if they consume (as most Japanese do) a diet rich in high sodium foods such as soy sauce.

Last but not least, apples store well. They will stay fresh and crisp for months in a cool dry cellar, providing fresh fruit all winter long. That may be why they have been considered health food for hundreds of years. The International Apple Institute in McLean, Virginia, says that our familiar "apple-a-day" rhyme (which has been popular in the United States since the 19th century) is almost certainly descended from an Olde English verse that runs, "Ate an apfel/avore gwain bed/makes the doctor/beg his bread."

An apple is nature's toothbrush. Alas, no. While apples are loaded with fiber and nicely low in calories, chomping on them won't clean the surface of your teeth or scrub away the food particles between teeth or edging under your gums. It's true that snacking on an apple is healthier for your teeth than eating a hot fudge sundae or even raisins (whose sticky flesh clings to your teeth, providing a perfect medium for the bacteria that cause cavities), but when it comes to cleaning teeth, apples are no substitute for regular flossing and brushing.

See also APPENDICITIS

ARTHRITIS

Acidic foods or chocolate or milk products or foods from the nightshade family cause arthritis. Consuming alfalfa or fish oil or vinegar and honey or fasting or eliminating meat from your diet cure it. The idea that certain foods can provoke or relieve symptoms of rheumatoid arthritis has always hovered in a kind of never-never land of myth and magic. Although several studies had shown that people with arthritis often feel better after fasting, there was none to prove a relationship between specific foods and arthritis pains or to show that arthritis could be affected by food allergies.

Now there is. In 1987, researchers of the University of Florida College of Medicine found that a small minority (5%) of people with arthritis have a definite increase in symptoms when they consume milk, milk products and foods such as cakes and cookies in which milk is a "hidden" ingredient. (The studies concentrated on adults, who comprise 80% of the patients with rheumatoid arthritis. There is no information yet on whether children with rheumatoid arthritis suffer the same symptoms when they drink milk.)

The researchers say that the idea that food allergies can trigger arthritis symptoms is entirely "logical and potentially enlightening." Eating a food to which you are allergic can cause your body to produce antigens and antibodies, chemicals known to trigger inflammatory reactions. The opposite occurs when you eat cold water fish such as salmon that contain omega-3 polyunsaturated fatty acids. Omega-3 fish oils contain chemicals that inhibit inflammation. Some studies suggest that omega-3 fish oils can alleviate the symptoms of rheumatoid arthritis, but this remains unproven.

It's best to get your fish oils from real foods, not capsules. According to the *Tufts University Diet & Nutrition Letter*, studies have shown that fish oil supplements may lower the levels of HDLs, the protective lipoproteins (fat and protein particles) that help carry cholesterol out of your body, as well as cause digestive problems such as belching and loose stool.

As for the other foods on this list of causes and cures, the Arthritis Foundation turns thumbs down on alfalfa, which can be toxic to humans, and says there is not a whit of proof that "acid foods," chocolate or foods from the nightshade family will trigger your arthritis or that consuming vinegar and honey or giving up meat will cure it.

See also BEE STINGS.

ASAFETIDA

Hang a bag filled with asafetida around your neck to ward off colds. Well, it certainly will keep other people (and their colds) far away. Asafetida, also known as devil's dung, is the gum from the stalk of a plant native to Turkey and Afghanistan. It smells like garlic, and like garlic it has long been used to ward off colds, but there is absolutely no evidence to suggest that it works.

ASPIRIN

Taking aspirin with cola drinks can make you tipsy. The coca leaf and the kola nut are two of the raw ingredients used to create the flavor of the *original* cola beverage Coca-Cola.

The coca leaf is the source of cocaine, which was not a prohibited substance when the recipe for Coca-Cola was invented by John S. Pemberton, an Atlanta pharmacist in 1886. As a result, lots of people, including some serious scientists, have speculated that the formula, reputed to have packed quite a punch, contained cocaine. The introduction of the "wonder drug" aspirin after the First World War, followed by Prohibition, led to the popular misconception that combining aspirin and Coke could produce the effects once achieved by legal drinking. Today, of course, we know there is no coke in Coke. Cola makers still use coca leaves to flavor their products, but the leaves are purified and all traces of cocaine removed.

But cola drinks still contain a potent stimulant: caffeine. Two 10-ounce glasses of caffeinated cola contain approximately as much caffeine as 1 cup of regular coffee. What makes that interesting is that caffeine and aspirin, rather than making you high, are the *sine qua non* of non-prescription headache remedies. The aspirin soothes the pain; the caffeine helps constrict engorged (swollen) blood vessels that make your head ache and also gives you a little emotional lift. At least one major commercial analgesic, Anacin, has made its reputation on the effectiveness of this combination. The home remedy version is two aspirin with a cup of regular coffee or a glass of caffeinated cola.

'Take two aspirin and call me in the morning'. Some people interpret this as the doctor's way of avoiding patient consultations late at night, but in many cases it really does make good medical sense. If you have a fever, it is usually higher in the evening than in the morning. If you are in pain, that, too, is often worse at night when the distractions of the day are gone. Aspirin attacks on both fronts. It is an antipyretic, a drug that reduces fever, and it relieves pain. By lowering fever and reducing discomfort, aspirin may make it possible for you to get a good night's sleep, which will make you feel much better by morning, when you can call to thank your doctor for her sage advice. (See caution on following page.)

Aspirin cures a cold. Study after study has shown with depressing regularity that while aspirin may relieve the aching muscles and headache that often accompany a cold or flu, it does nothing at all to change the course of the disease. But taking aspirin while you have your cold may increase the likelihood of your giving the cold to your friends.

In 1975, researchers at the University of Illinois Medical Center in Chicago gave 45 healthy volunteers nose drops containing viruses that cause the common cold. Once the volunteers caught cold, the researchers treated 25 of them with aspirin and gave the rest a placebo. Taking regular samples of the volunteers nasal secretions, the researchers found that the people who were taking aspirin were more likely than the people taking the placebo to have viruses in their nasal drippings. Because taking the aspirin made them feel good enough to go about their daily routines, they were more likely to spread their colds to others.

In addition, children who take aspirin while they have a viral illness may be at risk of developing Reye's Syndrome, a relatively uncommon but serious condition that can cause brain damage and damage to the nervous system.

Caution. Always check with your doctor before giving aspirin to any child who is ill.

Gargle with aspirin to relieve a sore throat. Only if you swallow the gargle. Aspirin is less efficiently absorbed through the membrane lining of your mouth and throat so it is unlikely to provide sufficient pain relief. In addition, it is irritating and may make your throat even more sore.

To cure a toothache, hold an aspirin against the gum until the tablet dissolves. The problem here is similar to the one you have when trying to relieve a sore throat by gargling with aspirin: The drug is not well-absorbed through the tissues in your mouth. Worse yet, there is the real possibility that holding an aspirin against the gum tissue will injure the gum.

Generic brands of aspirin are as effective as brand name products. It depends. Regardless of the name on the label, all "regular-strength" plain aspirin contains precisely the same amount of the active ingredient, acetylsalicylic acid, plus enough filler to bulk it up into the familiar round tablet. The filler may affect the tablet's performance in your stomach. The faster it dissolves, for example, the faster the aspirin in the tablet moves into your bloodstream to alleviate your pain. Thus, you may find that different brands of aspirin perform differently in your body.

All aspirin tablets deteriorate over time, particularly when they are exposed to air, but a poorly made container, brand name or generic, speeds this degeneration by allowing air into the bottle. Badly made aspirin tablets, brand name or generic, may crumble in the container; an imperfect tablet may give you less than the full five grain dose of aspirin. All in all, it's the quality standards by which the aspirin is made, not the name on the bottle, that determines the value of the product.

Crumbled aspirin is stale. Not necessarily. As noted above, crumbling is more often the result of packing problems. A better test of freshness is to sniff the aspirin bottle. A vinegary or ammonia-like scent indicates that the tablets have deteriorated and are no longer fully effective as painkillers. Throw them out.

If you take aspirin on a regular basis, eventually you will need larger and larger doses to relieve the same amount of pain. False. Over time, you begin to build up a tolerance to certain painkillers such as codeine and morphine, so that you need larger amounts to do the same job. But you never develop a tolerance to aspirin. No matter how often you take it, your body never demands a larger dose for the same amount of pain. This is a major reason for aspirin's long-standing popularity as a palliative for people with chronic, but controllable, pain.

Aspirin substitutes are as good as aspirin. It depends on the substitute—and what you want it to do. Aspirin is a painkiller that also reduces fever and inflammation. Acetaminophen (Tylenol) relieves fever and pain, but not inflammation; nonsteroidal anti-inflammatory drugs such as ibuprofen (Advil) and naproxen (Anaprox, Naprosyn) relieve pain and inflammation but not fever. Aspirin and the NSAIDs are effective against the inflammation of arthritis; acetaminophen is not.

Aspirin substitutes are less toxic than aspirin. False. Aspirin, acetaminophen and the nonsteroidal anti-inflammatory drugs (NSAIDs) may all cause allergic reactions. All may trigger abnormal bleeding, although acetaminophen and some NSAIDs are less likely than the others to cause gastric ulcer. Long-term use of any of these analgesics, particularly the NSAID ibuprofen, may cause kidney damage or exacerbate existing kidney disease; long-term use or overdose of acetaminophen may cause potentially fatal liver damage.

ASTHMA

Giving a chihuahua to a child who has asthma will cure the asthma. This piece of medical folklore is most popular in the southern half of the United States, straight across the country from the piney woods of Georgia to the sun-drenched provinces of southern California. The people who think it's true believe that the chihuahua "takes away" the child's asthma.

Of course they're wrong. What's really happening here is that people have put two facts together and come to the wrong conclusion. Fact number one is that childhood asthma often fades, or at least becomes less debilitating, as you get older. Fact number two is that small dogs, such as Yorkshire terriers, toy poodles and chihuahuas, have tiny tracheas that may collapse as the dogs age. According to the Animal Medical Center in New York, the rings of cartilage that compose the trachea then vibrate with every breath, and the dogs may find it difficult to breathe. Medical folklore interpreted this respiratory distress as the dog's having "taken away" the asthma from its master.

ATHLETE'S FOOT

Athlete's foot comes from swimming pools. It can, but it doesn't have to come to you. "Athlete's foot" is the popular name for a fungal infection, *Tinea pedis,* which thrives in warm, damp places like the floor near a pool or in a locker room shower. If you walk barefoot on one of these surfaces and there are small cracks in the skin, the fungus may invade. Keep your feet clean, dry and covered with sandals or swim shoes, and you are likely to evade the athlete's foot fungus no matter how many swimming pools you visit.

Wearing sneakers gives you athlete's foot. Any shoe that keeps your feet hot and damp increases your risk of developing athlete's foot. Sneakers, with their rubber soles and occasionally nonporous tops, can prevent perspiration inside the shoe from evaporating, so that your feet stay wet. Eventually, the continually wet skin on your feet may crack, making you even more susceptible to the athlete's foot fungus. Ventilated sneakers and shoes reduce the risk by allowing air to circulate inside the shoe.

See also BAKING SODA, COTTON SOCKS, SUNLIGHT.

B

BACKACHE

Sleeping without a pillow will make a bad back better. Not necessarily. Some people whose backache stems from muscle spasms in the upper back or the neck may feel better sleeping on a flat surface, but others with the ubiquitous lower back pain can worsen the condition by leaving neck and shoulders unsupported. Check with your doctor before chucking your pillow.

BAD BREATH

Drink strong black coffee to sweeten your breath. The 1868 edition of *The Dispensatory of the United States*, a contemporary guide to medicines and remedies, credits coffee with the power to eliminate "offensive and noxious effluvia from decomposing animal and vegetable substances." Presumably, that includes the stuff that gets stuck between your teeth each time you eat.

But modern science has yet to prove the case. If drinking coffee does seem to sweeten your breath, it may be that it works as a mouthwash, flushing away bits of food or smelly substances such as the sulfur compounds that give onions and garlic their distinctive aroma or, perhaps, by masking the odor of these foods and chemicals with a more pleasant one.

BAKING SODA

Baking soda is a natural antacid. True. Baking soda (chemical name: sodium bicarbonate) is a naturally basic (alkaline) material that can neutralize the excess acid that causes "heartburn" after you've eaten too much or eaten foods that disagree with you. However, baking soda does have some potential side effects of its own. It is high in sodium, and it can form insoluble chemical complexes with certain nutrients such as iron and drugs such as tetracycline antibiotics, aspirin, barbiturates and digitalis. As a result, your body cannot absorb and use these drugs.

Baking soda is a natural dentifrice. True. Sodium bicarbonate, an effective mild abrasive that can remove discoloration and debris on the surface of the tooth, is an approved ingredient in many brand name dentrifices and can be used, on its own, as an inexpensive dental cleaner made by mixing a small amount of powder with just enough water to make a workable mush. *Caution:* Before switching to baking powder as a dentrifice, it is a good idea to check with your own dentist or periodontist. If you have notable gum recession, for example, the baking soda paste may be too abrasive for exposed surfaces at the base of the tooth. Never use baking soda to scrub dentures lest the powder scratch and damage the surface of the false teeth.

Baking soda is a natural underarm deodorant. True. Human beings have two kinds of sweat glands, eccrine glands and apocrine glands. Eccrine glands, found all over the body, are the ones that secrete perspiration, the dilute solution of water and salts that evaporates on the skin, cools us down and helps regulate body temperature. Apocrine glands, found in the armpit, around the nipples and navel, and in the genital area, do not release perspiration and have no cooling function. Instead, apocrine glands secrete a milky substance containing fatty acids. When the bacteria that live naturally on the skin digest these fatty acids, they produce the unpleasant smell we call body odor. Baking soda, which is basic (alkaline), inactivates (neutralizes) those fatty acids and eliminates the odors. But baking soda is not an antiperspirant, so it won't keep underarms dry.

Baking soda cures athlete's foot. Alas, no. In fact, the fungus that causes athlete's foot may actually flourish in the basic (alkaline) environment created when you dust your toes with dry baking soda or pat on a paste of baking soda and water.

A pinch of baking soda in the cooking water keeps green vegetables from turning brown when you heat them. True. Chlorophyll, one of the pigments that give green vegetables their color, is sensitive to acids. When you heat the vegetables in water, the chlorophyll reacts with the acids in the water or in the vegetables themselves to form pheophytin, a brown pigment that makes the vegetables olive drab. Adding baking soda to the cooking water makes the water basic (alkaline) and prevents the reaction. But it also robs the vegetables of water-soluble vitamins such as thiamine and vitamin C. The more baking soda you use and the longer you cook the vegetables, the greater the loss of vitamins will be.

See also MOSQUITO BITES.

BALDNESS

'No boy ever gets bald, no woman and no castrated man.' That's what Aristotle said, and to a large degree modern science has proven him right. Both men and women have male and female hormones, but male hormones predominate in a man's body and female hormones in a woman's. True male pattern baldness (the ordinarily irreversible loss of hair unrelated to any illness or medical condition) is an inherited characteristic linked to the male hormones. It generally begins as thinning at the front of the head or in a circle on the top, sometimes as early as the teenage years, when puberty floods a boy's body with the male hormone testosterone. Eunuchs castrated before puberty never experience this surge of male hormones and virtually never lose their hair as they grow older.

A healthy woman may experience a kind of pattern hair loss at the front of her head when she approaches menopause and her ovaries' production of estrogen declines, but it is not likely to be as dramatic as a man's or to leave her totally bald in any one area. In rare cases, a woman may develop a condition known as virilism. Its symptoms, which include a deepening voice, increased muscle mass, more facial hair, and baldness, are caused by an overproduction of male hormones.

A tight ponytail can make you bald. Or at least, it can give you a bald spot, because constantly pulling the hair back tight from the face may eventually pull out some hairs around the hairline. Loosen the ponytail or wear your hair down and the hair will almost certainly grow back.

Being pregnant makes you bald. Hair goes through a natural cycle of growth and rest. The growth part of the cycle is known as the anogen phase; the resting part is called the telogen phase. Hair in the telogen phase is constantly being shed and immediately replaced by hair in the anogen phase. During pregnancy, however, there is a temporary increase in the number of hairs in the telogen phase and thus a sudden increase in the number of hairs being shed. As a result, a pregnant woman's hair may temporarily look thinner than normal, but once the baby is delivered, the natural hair growth cycle resumes and the hair fills in again.

Taking vitamins prevents baldness. It's true that hair loss may be one side effect of a nutritional problem, such as crash dieting, malnutrition or iron deficiency or long-term, larger-than-normal doses of vitamin A, but there is absolutely no evidence to suggest that any single vitamin or mineral prevents normal male pattern baldness.

Massaging your scalp prevents baldness. No, but it does feel wonderful.

BALSAM

The sap of the balsam tree soothes a cough. True. But not straight from the tree. According to *The Merck Index*, the standard guide to chemical substances, Balsa tolu, the sap of the *Toluifera balsamum*, a tree native to South America, is the source of a substance that may be medically extracted and purified for use in cough remedies as an expectorant. Expectorants increase the secretion of liquid from the mucous membranes lining of the throat and bronchi, making it easier to cough up mucus.

The sap of the balsam tree heals wounds. Again the answer is yes, but not right from the tree. According to *The Merck Index*, Balsam peru, the sap of the *Toluifera pereirae*, which grows in forests near the Pacific coast of Central America, may be purified for use in human and veterinary skin medications designed to treat skin ulcers and other wounds.

BATHS, HOT

If you take a hot bath while you are pregnant, it will bring on a miscarriage. Highly unlikely. However, not every woman who thinks she is pregnant because her period is late is really pregnant. If the period is on its way, it is not inconceivable that a hot bath might stimulate the flow. If that were to happen, someone who thought she was pregnant—but really wasn't—might mistakenly think she had a miscarriage.

A hot bath at bedtime prevents insomnia. Not necessarily. Both very cold baths and very hot baths may be stimulating. And while a medium warm soak may untie knotted muscles and relax the entire body, some people find that it just sets them up for another energetic go at whatever was causing the tension in the first place. In short, this is a very personal remedy that works for some of the people some of the time.

See also SHOWERS.

BED REST

Resting in bed will cure what ails you. Not necessarily. Bed rest is of indisputable value in certain situations, like when you've got a broken leg, and snuggling under the covers when you have a bad cold or flu can help you feel better—and may be all you have energy to do. But too much of this good thing can be hazardous to your health. According to experts at the Mayo Clinic in Rochester, Minnesota, prolonged bed rest—one or two weeks or more—can cause constipation, stiff muscles and joints, even lung congestion and blood clots in your legs, which is why surgeons now insist on their patients' getting up and out of bed as fast as possible after surgery. To avoid overdosing on bed rest during a cold or flu, you may want to do some mild stretching or walking during the day—if you can.

BEE STINGS

Bees sting sweet people. This saying, sometimes used to comfort a shrieking child who's just been stung, does have some truth to it, but the attractant is a sweet flavor or aroma, not a sweet disposition. Bees, hornets, wasps and ants are all drawn to sweet-tasting, sweet-smelling people. Hair spray, perfume, aftershave and even some scented sunblocks and tanning products are like catnip to these insects—who also are attracted to bright colors and, believe it or not, flowery printed fabrics. To reduce the risk of being stung by bees, experts suggest avoiding these products when you're outside. Keep all food tightly covered, and check the children to see that they're not wandering around coated with ice cream, jam or other goodies that appeal to a bee as much as they do to you.

Perfume draws bees. True. See above.

Bee stings sting, but otherwise they're a minor annoyance. True, unless you happen to be allergic to the venom, in which case the sting can trigger an overwhelming, potentially fatal allergic reaction known as anaphylactic shock. If you know you're allergic to bee venom, ask your doctor about an insect sting emergency kit that contains a syringe filled with epinephrine, a drug that counters the effect of the histamine your body releases when you are exposed to something to which you are allergic. Epinephrine quickly restores blood circulation, relieves itching and swelling, and relaxes the smooth muscles of your air passages so that you can breathe freely. It also relieves cramping by relaxing the muscles that control your bladder and gastrointestinal tract.

Caution: Head straight for the emergency room if you have any symptoms of anaphylactic shock such as headache, shortness of breath, or gastric upset after being stung by a bee or any other insect.

Bee stings cure arthritis. No doubt anyone coping with the immediate pain caused by the venom the bee injects when it stings is likely to forget, at least for a while, the deeper pain of arthritis. But to date there is no evidence to show that deliberately allowing yourself to be stung by bees will relieve arthritic pain or inflammation.

See also MUD, TEA.

BIRTH CONTROL

A woman cannot become pregnant if she does not have an orgasm. False. Ordinarily, a man must achieve orgasm in order to release quantities of sperm sufficient to impregnate his partner. But whether or not a woman reaches orgasm during intercourse has absolutely no affect on her chances of becoming pregnant because it is ovulation, not orgasm, that triggers the release of a mature egg from her ovary into her reproductive tract. All that counts is that the egg be available and the sperm be able to reach it.

Sneezing at the moment of orgasm prevents a woman from becoming pregnant. This is a myth that dates back at least as far as the Romans, who believed that a woman's squatting and sneezing at orgasm or right after intercourse could prevent conception. Another Roman birth control method: sneezing while leaping backward seven times after intercourse. People who believed these old wives' tales thought that the contractions of the abdominal muscles caused by sneezing could push sperm out of the vagina. They were wrong: Sneezing—no matter when or how—is not an effective form of birth control.

Douching with an acid solution such as vinegar and water after intercourse prevents pregnancy. No. Although acid solutions can make the vagina inhospitable to sperm, no douche is considered a reliable means of birth control.

Cola drinks are effective contraceptive douches. No. *Caution:* It is extremely dangerous to use a carbonated solution, such as a soft drink, as a douche. The endometrium (the lining of the uterus) is covered with open blood vessels. If a carbonated douche is forced into the vagina under pressure, as from a douche apparatus, it can move through the cervix into the uterus. It is conceivable that air from the liquid might enter one of the blood vessels on the uterine lining and cause a potentially fatal air embolism.

See also BREAST-FEEDING, MENSTRUATION, VIRGINS.

BIRTH DEFECTS

A man's age when he becomes a father has no effect on whether or not his baby will be born with birth defects. False. Men stay fertile longer than women, but they are not immune to changes in sperm that may contribute to birth defects in the babies they father. According to researchers at the University of British Columbia in Canada, while older women have a higher risk of producing a baby with a defect due to the absence or duplication or mutation of an entire chromosome, older fathers have an increased risk of producing babies with a defect due to the mutation of a single gene. Single-gene defects, such as achrondoplasia (a form of dwarfism that can be detected pre-natally via sonography), Apert's syndrome (a pointed head and the fusion of four fingers into one mass, also detectable by sonogram) and Marfan syndrome (a group of skeletal and vascular defects that cannot be detected before the baby is born), are about five times more common among babies whose fathers are older than 40 than among babies whose fathers are in their twenties, regardless of how old the mother is.

See also DOWN'S SYNDROME, GERMAN MEASLES (RUBELLA), PRE-NATAL INFLUENCES.

BITES

See DOG BITES.

BLACK EYE

A raw steak is the best first aid treatment for a black eye. The discoloration known as a "black eye" is caused by bleeding from tiny broken blood vessels just under the skin. First, the hemoglobin (red pigment) in the spilled red blood cells loses oxygen and turns dark blue. Next, the oxygen-deficient hemoglobin breaks down into its component green and yellow pigments. Finally, the cells decompose and are reabsorbed by your body, at which point all the unusual colors disappear and your skin looks normal again.

If you apply a cold dressing to an injury as soon as it occurs, you may be able to keep the bruise from blossoming. The cold constricts the tiny broken blood vessels and stops the bleeding. A chilled, raw steak right from the refrigerator is okay as a cold dressing. In addition, it is a fine example of folk medicine that advises using like (a raw bloody steak) to cure like (a raw, maybe bloody injury). But a plain ice bag, five minutes on, five minutes off, is probably more effective and certainly a lot cheaper. Neither the steak nor the ice bag will have any effect once the bruise has already appeared.

See also BRUISES.

BLISTER

Breaking a blister can be fatal. If you are older than, say, 40, you have almost certainly heard the cautionary tale of Calvin Coolidge's son who, in 1924, developed a blister on his heel while playing tennis, broke the blister and subsequently died. Of course, it is clear that what he succumbed to was not the broken blister but the subsequent infection that could not be controlled in an age before antibiotics were readily available.

There is no reason to puncture a blister that doesn't hurt and doesn't interfere with walking; it will eventually dry up and disappear on its own. However, if you absolutely must speed things along, the *Mayo Clinic Health Letter* cautions to keep the injury clean. Their advice is to wash your hands and the blistered area with warm soapy water; swab the blister with an antiseptic such as iodine or 70% rubbing alcohol; use a sterile needle to puncture the blister in several places, allowing the fluid to drain while leaving the skin on top of it intact; cover the spot with an antibiotic ointment and gauze pad; check each day for redness, swelling, pus or heat and see your doctor right away if these or any other signs of infection appear.

Cover a blister with adhesive tape. A bad idea. When you remove the tape, you may tear off the top of the blister, leading to all the complications listed above.

BLOOD

Blood is thicker than water. Actually, human blood is just about the same density as seawater (it is more dense than fresh water). The real meaning of this saying, though, has less to do with chemistry than with family ties, which it assumes to be stronger than the ties between friends or casual acquaintances.

Your blood thickens in the winter and thins in the spring. No. In fact, the truth may be just the opposite, that blood is slightly more dense in the summer when your body loses more water through perspiration and you need to drink more in order to avoid becoming dehydrated. In any event, your ability to stay warm when it's cold out or cool when it's warm is determined not by the density of your blood but by a complex relationship between your pineal gland, a small pine-cone shaped body in your brain, and your autonomic nervous system, which governs all the functions your body performs more or less without your thinking about them: breathing, blood circulation, digestion, and the like.

When you are cold, your autonomic nervous system helps conserve heat by constricting the small blood vessels just under your skin so that less blood flows up from the warm center of your body to the cold surface of your skin. This keeps you warm by cutting down the amount of chilled blood circulating back into the center of your body. In hot weather, the process is reversed. Now the autonomic nervous system dilates blood vessels under your skin so that blood from the center of your body, when it is cooler than the air outside, can circulate up to your skin and cool you down. In addition, the autonomic nervous system promotes perspiration, which acts like your own personal air conditioner, evaporating and cooling the skin.

Aristocrats have blue blood. This obviously false notion is often thought to have originated in caste-conscious medieval Spain, where the nobles studiously avoided the hot Spanish sun. Thus, their skin remained pale with their veins showing clearly through. The veins looked blue against the skin, so the blood inside was presumed to be blue as well. Out in the fields, however, the peasants were either sunburned or they were naturally dark-skinned Moors. Either way, their veins did not look blue against their skin. And that's how this piece of folklore was born.

Bloodstains can never be entirely removed. The idea that bloodstains are permanent arises from their psychological, not their physical, impact. Spilling blood is a highly emotional act, no matter how it happens. When foul play is involved, the impact is even greater and the culprit himself is apt to feel, like Lady Macbeth, that "all the perfumes of Arabia will not sweeten this little hand."

But of course they will. In fact, the simplest way to get rid of bloodstains on white washable fabrics is to bleach them out with chlorine bleach. Colored washable fabrics may respond to simple soaking with detergent and cool water. Dried blood stains can be removed by softening the clot with oil (mineral oil or any vegetable oil will do) and then sponging it away with plain warm water.

See also HEMOPHILIA, WINE.

BLOOD PRESSURE

Your correct blood pressure should be your age plus 100. Not true. And, the older you get, the less true it becomes. Blood pressure is the pressure in our arteries, commonly described in terms of two numbers that look like this: 130/80. The first figure, systolic pressure, tells you the amount of force, measured (in millimeters of mercury) exerted against artery walls during systole, when your heart contracts (beats) and pushes blood out into the aorta, the large artery leading away from the heart. The second figure, the diastolic pressure, measures force exerted against artery walls when your heart is in diastole, resting between beats.

Your systolic pressure can be affected by your environment. If you are excited or scared, it is likely to go up. Systolic pressure readings are commonly higher when your blood pressure is taken in your doctor's office, rather than when it is taken in your own home. Your diastolic pressure is generally less likely to vary with the circumstances.

The idea that your systolic pressure should equal your age plus 100 probably comes from the generally observable fact that blood pressure rises with age. Although there are cultural groups, such as the

Andean Indians of Chile, who do not experience this phenomenon, among healthy people in the industrial West, a person whose blood pressure was 120/80 at age 20, may have a reading of 140/80 at age 40, which seems to fit the "plus 100" rule.

Nonetheless, high blood pressure in adults is generally defined as pressure equal to or higher than 140/90 for extended periods of time, so the rule inevitably runs into trouble as you pass the mid-century mark. A 60-year old person with blood pressure that registers 160/90 through repeated readings over several weeks is considered to have high, not normal, blood pressure.

BLUES, HOLIDAY

People are more likely to be depressed around holiday time. Modern medical folklore has it that the holidays trigger an instant rise in the number of people suffering from the blues. But statistical studies have consistently shown that the Christmas/New Year's holiday season is actually associated with a lower incidence of suicides and admissions to psychiatric hospitals.

For example, starting in 1977, researchers at Duke University charted the number of visits to a 24-hour psychiatric emergency service around the Christmas/New Year's holidays over a period of seven years. Their study, released in 1984, showed that the number of emergency psychiatric visits and admissions went down in the weeks before Christmas, and then rose again starting the week after Christmas. Their conclusion: The idea of a "Christmas depression" isn't entirely mythological (some people do find it hard to cope with all that forced hilarity), but it isn't inevitable, either. In fact, lots of other people who you'd expect to be depressed actually get a pleasant, if temporary, lift from the hopeful holiday spirit.

BODY CELLS

All the cells in your body are replaced every seven years. Your body is a virtual hive of activity in which body cells die and are replaced every day of your life. The idea that it would take seven years to complete a full turnover owes more to the magic inherent in the number seven than to physical reality.

Red blood cells last about six months. Skin cells are replaced every three to four weeks. According to Kenneth Jon Rose, author of *The Body in Time,* the lining of your digestive tract (stomach and intestines) is replaced every three days, and your liver cells live about five months. The hairs on your head grow out and are replaced every two to five years (providing, of course, you aren't balding). On the other hand, while men make new sperm cells every day, if you are a woman, all the egg cells you will ever carry in your ovaries are in place by the day you are born. Those you use when you become pregnant or lose by ovulating without becoming pregnant, are never replaced.

Until recently, the same was true of spinal cord nerve cells destroyed by injury or illness. Nerves in other parts of your body may grow back together if severed, thanks to non-nerve cells called Schwann's cells, but there are no Schwann's cells in the spinal cord, which is why injuries there have always been so devastating. Lately, however, researchers at the University of Zurich, Switzerland, using antibodies that block chemicals that inhibit nerve growth, have been able to encourage regeneration of the severed spinal cords of laboratory rats. The experimental antibodies, which originated in mice, cannot be used on human beings, but their existence opens the way to a better understanding of how nerve cells work and may eventually lead to similar products for human beings.

BODY PAINTING

Covering a person's entire body with paint gilt can cause death by suffocation. This is balderdash, but it was so attractively packaged by author Ian Fleming in his James Bond novel *Goldfinger* that virtually everyone who read the book or saw the Sean Connery movie almost certainly believes it to be true. Logic, however, will tell you that a person breathes not through his skin but through his mouth, nose, throat and lungs. So long as these air passages remain open, suffocation is impossible.

That is not to say that covering your entire body with paint or gilt is a good idea. Not only do paint and gilt irritate your skin, paint contains potentially toxic solvents that can be absorb through your skin, which is why professional painters wear overalls and gloves. Third, blocking your pores may interfere with your ability to cool your skin through perspiration. If you are overheated, that can lead to hyperthermia (a higher-than-normal body temperature). Skip the body and do your painting on paper, canvas or the walls.

BONES

'I can feel it in my bones.' More precisely, you can feel it in your joints and body tissues. Some people are exquisitely sensitive to

changes in atmospheric pressure. They get advance warning of impending changes in the weather because of the way their joints and body tissues respond to changes in atmospheric pressure.

Think of the pressure the atmosphere exerts on the body as a kind of girdle. When air pressure drops and the girdle is loosened, body tissues swell and bulge ever-so-slightly outward. You may feel bloated and clothes will actually be tight. It's just the opposite when the air pressure rises. Body tissues are squeezed ever-so-slightly inward, so you are likely to feel trim and fit.

In people with arthritis, the changes in the tissues around joints triggered by changes in atmospheric pressure may be extremely painful. People with respiratory allergies may find their nasal tissues drippy every time the air pressure drops. And those who are overweight may need a whole different set of clothes for low pressure days.

See MILK.

BRANDY

Brandy is good for the heart. All alcoholic beverages, including brandy, are sedatives. Many people find them calming. They are also vasodilators, agents that relax the muscles in the walls of your peripheral blood vessels (the blood vessels near the surface of your skin and in your arms and legs), allowing them to expand so that blood flows through more easily. Finally, a 1987 study from Harvard University found that low-to-moderate consumption of alcohol beverages appears to increase blood levels of two components of high-density lipoproteins (HDL), the ''good'' cholesterol in blood known to protect against coronary heart disease. But this study has been challenged on the grounds that the HDL components increased by alcohol consumption are not the ones that ward off heart disease.

In any event, a moderate amount of any kind of spirits, wine or brew would have the same effects, but brandy, Cognac (brandy made in the Charente and Charent-Maritime departments of France near Bordeaux) and Armagnac (brandy made in the southwestern region of France once part of Gascony), are, well, so civilized. To meet the standards set in *The National Formulary,* a catalog of all the drugs and medicines permitted to be sold in the United States, brandy must have been distilled from healthy ripe grapes (no other fruit allowed), contain between 48% to 54% alcohol (96 proof to 108 proof) and have been aged in wooden barrels for not less than two years.

A sip of brandy takes the chill off. Yes, but only temporarily, and any other alcoholic beverage would do as well. Alcohol dilates the blood vessels just under your skin, bringing more warm blood up from the center of your body. This may cause a flush, or rosy coloring of the skin, accompanied by an immediate sensation of warmth. But when the blood comes up to the surface, it is chilled, and when it circulates back into the center of your body and through your organs, it will chill them, too.

If you drink your brandy indoors, where it is warm, this see-sawing of body temperatures will stabilize quickly. But if you take a nip while you are out in the cold, as at a football game, you will eventually end up chillier than you were when you began.

BREAKFAST

Breakfast is the most important meal of the day. Eating habits, like sleep patterns, are pretty much an individual affair, so attempts to make people conform to neat formulas like this one about breakfast usually fail. As long as you get the proper amount of nutrients every day, it really doesn't much matter when you get them. So how come most people are hungry in the morning? Easy. We all respond to the ticking of an internal clock that signals hunger at various times during the day. One of the clearest hunger signals is a drop in temperature. Most people have a lower body temperature when waking up, so they feel hungry then. Others, who maintain a warmer body temperature when waking from a long night's sleep, will start to feel hungry slightly later in the day, perhaps around noon. Not surprisingly, people who start eating early in the day often stop earlier, too. Given their choice, these people may prefer a heavy lunch to a hearty evening dinner.

BREAST-FEEDING

Breast feeding prevents pregnancy. Nursing a newborn baby does tend to delay the return of regular menstruation after delivery, but it is by no means a completely reliable means of birth control.

Human breast milk is the perfect food for human babies. The balance of fats and carbohydrates in human breast milk is better suited than cow's milk to the needs of human babies. In addition human breast milk is an excellent source of iron (human infants absorb iron about ten times more efficiently from human milk than from cow's milk).

But breast milk is not a totally perfect food. For example, it has no vitamin D. If a breast-fed baby does not get vitamin D supplements or sufficient exposure to the sun, which creates vitamin D in the fatty layers of the body right under the skin, she may develop rickets, the disease caused by a vitamin D deficiency. In addition, some women's milk may be deficient in zinc, a mineral that helps us grow and fight infections.

A breast-fed baby gets 'immunities' in its mother's milk. True. Colostrum, the fluid that fills the breast immediately after birth, before the milk appears, contains substances known as immunological factors that help an infant fight infection. In 1988, researchers at McGill University in Montreal and at the University of Texas Medical Branch in Galveston announced the results of separate studies suggesting that proteins in breast milk may also stimulate the babies' own immune systems, encouraging various types of white blood cells to produce protective antibodies.

And, as if that weren't enough to recommend nursing a newborn, consider this: According to a study of 9,000 infants released in 1989 by researchers at the Johns Hopkins School of Public Health, breast-fed babies use their mouth muscles more effectively when getting milk from the breast and they are less likely than bottle-fed babies to end up with crooked teeth.

Breast-feeding prevents breast cancer. Preliminary results of studies at the Harvard School of Public Health comparing breast cancer patients with women who do not have the disease suggest that breast-feeding may protect against pre-menopausal breast cancer, perhaps by interrupting ovulation, or by changing a woman's hormonal balance, or by affecting the physical structure of the ducts in the breast where cancers are most likely to develop. This protective effect remains to be proven.

Breast-feeding causes breast cancer. There is absolutely no evidence to suggest that nursing causes breast cancer. Nor is there any evidence to suggest that a woman might be able to "pass" cancer on to her baby when she nurses.

Women who nurse their infants lose calcium from their bones. A 1989 study at Walter Reed Army Medical Center in Bethesda, Maryland, has hinted that women who feed their infants exclusively on breast milk for six months may lose significant amounts of mineral from the bones of the lower hips and spine even if they consume adequate amounts of calcium. In 1990, a study at the University of California at Santa Cruz found that women who breast-fed their babies for long periods of time with less than two years between deliveries were more likely than others to develop osteoporosis late in life.

These reports are preliminary and remain to be proven. Women who plan to nurse for long periods of time should consult their doctors to plan a diet high enough in calcium to protect both mother and child.

BRUISES

Press a half-dollar against a barked shin to prevent a bruise. This works on the same principle as putting a raw steak on a black eye. If you catch the injury fast enough and the half-dollar or steak is cold enough, it may cause damaged small blood vessels just under the skin to constrict, thus slowing the bleeding under the skin that creates the dark mark known as a bruise. As with steak on a black eye, the half-dollar on the shin is less effective than an ice compress, although neither will work once the bruise has developed.

See also BLACK EYE.

BUTTER

Butter a burn to prevent scarring. A bad idea. Butter covers the burn and keeps the skin from cooling down. Additives such as salt or flavors may irritate the injured skin. And if your burn requires medical attention, your doctor will have to scrape off the grease to reach the injury, a painful process at best.

The American Red Cross suggests first-aid treatment based on the severity of the burn.

First degree burns, such as those caused by mild sunburn, minor contact with a hot object such as a pot handle, or minor scalding from hot water or steam, may cause redness and mild swelling or pain. The best-known first aid for a first degree burn is to plunge the injured area into cold (not icy) water to relieve pain and, perhaps, prevent swelling.

Second degree burns, such as a very deep sunburn, or the burns caused by flash fires or contact with hot liquids, can turn the skin red or mottled. Or the surface may be wet with fluids oozing from damaged tissues underneath. Blisters and swelling may develop over several days. Again, the Red Cross's recommended first aid is to immerse the burned area in cold water and then apply clean cloth dressings that have been soaked in icy water and then wrung out. If the burn is painful or blistered, see your doctor.

Third degree burns, which can result from contact with an open flame, immersion in hot water or contact with electricity, destroy tissues deep below the surface of the skin. The result may be whitened or, more commonly, a charred appearance, plus loss of fluids due to the destruction of protective skin layers. Third degree burns are a medical emergency that require immediate medical attention. For more detailed instructions, call your doctor, your local emergency service, or dial the police emergency number, 911.

C

CALORIES

Calories don't count. They do, of course, but they don't always add up the same way.

If you take in more calories than your body needs to perform its normal activities, you will store the unused calories as fat. It takes about 3,500 unused calories to add one pound of fat to your body. If you eat just 200 calories a day more than you can use up, you will probably gain one pound in 17 days. That much is fairly obvious. A more subtle point, however, is that different people need different amounts of calories to do the same amount of work.

For example, the average man's body has proportionally more muscle than the average woman's; the average woman's body has proportionally more fat. Because muscle uses more energy than fat, a man's resting energy expenditure (REE), the number of calories he needs simply to run his body systems when he is completely at rest, is about 10% higher than a woman's. In real life, this means that a 140-pound man can hold his weight steady while eating about 10% more than a 140-pound woman who is the same age and does the same amount of physical work. (Your total energy requirement for the day is your REE plus enough calories to cover what you need for the work you do.)

The National Research Council's Food and Nutrition Board, which puts together the recommended dietary allowances (RDA) for specific nutrients, has established formulas by which you can determine approximately how many calories you can consume each day without gaining weight.

Begin by dividing your weight in pounds by 2.2 to get your weight in kilograms. Now use the following equations to find your REE:

Women	Age 10–18	(12.2 x weight in kg) + 746
	Age 18–30	(14.7 x weight in kg) + 496

	Age 30–60	(8.7 x weight in kg) + 829
	Age 60+	(10.5 x weight in kg) + 596
Men	Age 10–18	(17.5 x weight in kg) + 651
	Age 18–30	(15.3 x weight in kg) + 679
	Age 30–60	(11.6 x weight in kg) + 879
	Age 60+	(13.5 x weight in kg) + 487

Now multiply your REE by the appropriate "activity factor" listed below:

Light activity (House-cleaning, child care, golf, sailing, table tennis)	Men 1.6 Women 1.5
Moderate activity (Weeding, cycling, skiing, tennis)	Men 1.7 Women 1.6
Heavy activity (Heavy digging, mountain climbing, football)	Men 2.1 Women 1.9

Remember: Every body is different. These figures are only averages and may not work precisely for you.

Toast has fewer calories than plain bread. Alas, no. If it's the same slice of bread, it's got the same number of calories. But it may be less nutritious than untoasted bread. The change of color ("browning") that occurs when bread is exposed to heat changes the chemical structure of various amino acids, particularly lysine, creating forms of the amino acids that are harder for your body to absorb. This means, of course, that toasting reduces the protein value of the bread. According to researchers at Kansas State University, steaming food or cooking it in a microwave oven in dishes that have not been treated to promote browning makes the food look less attractive but keeps its nutritional value intact. Steamed toast, anyone?

See also CHINESE FOOD.

CANCER

A blow on the breast (or anywhere else) causes cancer. There is absolutely no connection whatsoever between any ordinary injury, no matter how bad a bruise it leaves, and your developing a cancer at the site later on.

A lump in your breast means cancer. On the contrary, a certain amount of lumpiness in the breast is normal and likely to increase with age. As many as 80% of all breast lumps are benign tumors such as fibroadenomas (fibrous tissue that compress the ducts in the breast) or the fluid-filled cysts characteristic of cystic mastitis. Because the remaining 20% of all breast lumps may turn out to be malignant, any lump that does not disappear within a week after a woman's menstrual period ends should be evaluated by her doctor. Men, who account for about 1% of the cases of breast cancer in the United States, should seek medical attention for any lump in the breast.

Everything causes cancer. Or, as some people say, too much of anything causes cancer. Either way, it's just not true. A perusal of any standard guide to chemical substances will show that there are hundreds, if not thousands, of chemicals that do not cause cancer no matter what the dose or the exposure.

Cancer is contagious. The idea that cancer is contagious rests on the assumption that it is caused by a virus. This is true of feline leukemia, a form of cancer that may be passed from cat to cat (but not to human beings), and adult T-cell leukemia (ATL), a rare form of leukemia endemic in southwestern Japan, as well as areas of the Caribbean and Central America. ATL is caused by the human T-cell leukemia virus (HTLV). Like the virus that causes AIDS, the virus that causes ATL can be spread through sexual contact, sharing contaminated needles or transfusion of contaminated blood. The occurrence of two other cancers, cancer of the cervix and cancer of the penis, appears to be linked to exposure to a human papilloma virus (HPV) transmitted from person to person through sexual contact. As of this writing, no other cancers are believed to be linked to viruses or considered even potentially contagious.

Cancer runs in families. Certain cancers, such as pre-menopausal cancer of the breast, colon cancer and small-cell lung cancer, do seem to appear more frequently among certain families or ethnic groups. In each case, however, what passes from generation to generation is not the cancer itself, but a genetic or physical anomaly that raises the individual's risk of cancer (but doesn't guarantee the disease).

Women whose close relatives (mother, sister) develop breast cancer before reaching menopause are considered to be at higher-than-normal risk for breast cancer themselves, but exactly what genetic or physical factors will trigger their cancer or how to prevent it remains a mystery.

The inherited susceptibility to cancers of the colon and rectum seems to involve an exceedingly complicated series of chemical changes in the body that leads to the loss of protective anti-cancer genes, known as anti-oncogenes, on several different chromosomes. The inherited predisposition to small-cell lung cancer appears to involve the loss of only two anti-oncogenes on only two chromosomes, one from each parent. So long as one anti-oncogene remains functional, the individual remains free of lung cancer. When both genes are "turned off," perhaps by smoking, the cancer appears. At present, although there seems to be some relationship between diet and colon cancer and the relationship between smoking and lung cancer is clear, there is still no clear-cut way to monitor or intervene protectively in these genetic changes.

See also BREAST-FEEDING, CATS, CIRCUMCISION, COFFEE, FLUORIDATION, FRIED FOODS, MENOPAUSE, VITAMIN A, VITAMIN C.

CANKER SORES

Canker sores are caused by too much acid in the system. No. Canker sores, also known as apthous ulcers, are one of your body's reactions to stress. More prosaically, they may also be caused by an injury such as a scratch from brushing or flossing your teeth. Eating citrus fruits, chocolate, nuts and aged cheese has been known to trigger canker sores and fever blisters in susceptible people, but eliminating these foods from your diet won't cure or keep them from popping up in the future whenever you're stressed out.

Note: Canker sores are *not* herpes infections. One way to tell the two apart is to see where they appear. A canker sore usually shows up on the tongue or the inside of the cheek. A herpes infection in the mouth ("cold sore" "fever blister") is more likely to occur on the gums or the roof of your mouth.

Rinsing with baking soda, milk of magnesia or any other antacid can relieve the pain of a canker sore. True. But not because they settle your stomach or relieve that elusive acid in your system. What's happening here is really much simpler and more logical. The basic (alkaline) antacid neutralizes the acid secretions of the bacteria or viruses that gather at the site of the canker sore, making the site less painful. You can rinse with a solution of antacid dissolved in warm water or simply paint the baking soda or antacid right on the sore. Either way, the relief will be instantaneous.

Note: Not every whitish sore in your mouth is a canker sore or a fever blister. If your sore does not heal within a week to 10 days, see your dentist to rule out the possibility that the sore is an early oral cancer.

Gentian violet cures a canker sore. No. Canker sores eventually heal by themselves. Any dentist who recommends smearing gentian violet on a canker sore is simply humoring you by responding to your demand that he, for heaven's sake, do something.

Alum cures a canker sore. No. Canker sores hurt because the infection exposes sensitive nerve endings in your mouth. Alum, an astringent once popular in pickling recipes, is an astringent that temporarily stuns nerve endings into submission so the sore stops hurting for a while. But it won't cure the canker sore.

CANNED FOODS

It's dangerous to leave canned foods in the can once the can has been opened. When a sealed can is opened, oxygen flows in. In the presence of oxygen, acid foods such as orange juice will react with the metal inside the can, darkening its surface and, perhaps, darkening the food. The acid/oxygen/metal reaction is unaesthetic but essentially harmless. However, if the can was been sealed with lead, when it is exposed to oxygen the food will begin to absorb lead from the seal, and this reaction is potentially dangerous to anyone who plans to eat the canned food. Although very few cans are sealed with lead these days, the safest course is simply to take canned food out of the can as soon as the can is opened.

See also FOOD POISONING.

CARROTS

Carrots are good for your eyes. Absolutely. Like other deep green or yellow vegetables, carrots are rich in carotenoids, pigments such as beta-carotene that are known as precursors of vitamin A.

(True vitamin A, known as retinol, is found only in foods of animal origin such as liver and eggs.)

Your body converts carotenes with vitamin A activity to 11-*cis* retinol, the essential chemical in rhodopsin, a protein found in rods, the cells in your eyes that allow you to see when the light is dim. Rhodopsin absorbs the light that passes through the lens of your eye, initiating the chemical chain reaction we call vision. Eating foods rich in carotenoids won't cure your astigmatism or near-sightedness, but it will help protect your night vision.

Why pick carrots? Because they store well. Green leafy vegetables, the cheapest, most available source of carotenoids, cannot be stored unless they are dried, but drying reduces their vitamin A content by about 50%. The carotenoids in one 2-ounce fresh carrot provide 7,930 IU vitamin A activity, 159% of the RDA for vitamin A for a grown man; 198% of the RDA for a grown woman.

CATS

At night, a cat will crawl up to your face and suck the breath out of your body. Cats do like warm places and will crawl up next to you in bed each night, perhaps even perching on your chest. But the cat may be easily dislodged by your simply moving in your sleep. The idea that the cat is drawing in close to you as a preliminary to inhaling the breath from your body derives not from science but from the the old-fashioned notion that a cat is a witch's "familiar" (the instrument through which she accomplishes her magic).

Cats cause leukemia. Feline leukemia is a contagious disease among cats, but there is to date absolutely no evidence to suggest that it is also contagious to human beings.

See also CANCER.

CAUL

A baby born with a caul has 'special powers.' A caul is the inner membrane surrounding the baby in its mother's womb. The membrane is usually ruptured at birth, but occasionally a baby is born with the membrane intact around its head or, less commonly, around its entire body. Although the caul holds an important place in many folk cures and remedies, it clearly has no special powers nor does the infant on whose body or head it is found.

CAVITIES

See CHEWING GUM.

CHAMPAGNE

Champagne makes you high faster than still wine. Probably. The carbon dioxide bubbles in champagne move the alcohol faster along to your small intestine, the main site for the absorption of alcohol into the bloodstream. As a result, all other things being equal— the number of drinks, the amount of food you have eaten and the amount of time that has passed between drinks—you really are likely to feel the effects of a glass of champagne faster than you feel the effects of a glass of still wine.

CHEWING

Chew your food (35) (50) (100) times before swallowing. Though the magic number may vary, the idea behind this advice is always the same: You'll get more nourishment from food if you chew it to smithereens before you swallow it. Is it true? Not really.

Digestion does begin in the mouth, where enzymes in saliva begin to break down food, particularly high-fiber complex carbohydrate foods such as grains, nuts, and beans, but the major part of the digestive process occurs in the stomach and intestines. Does that mean you can gulp your food and forget about chewing? Definitely not. Taking small bites and chewing thoroughly is the best way to avoid accidentally choking on food (which is a more common occurrence than you might think).

See CHOKING, GAS, INTESTINAL.

CHEWING GUM

If you swallow chewing gum, it will stick to your stomach. Nope. The insoluble fiber (gum) used as a base for chewing gum is indigestible. Like the insoluble fibers in wheat bran or pop-corn, it moves intact straight through your digestive tract.

Caution: One instance in which swallowing gum may be hazardous is when the person who swallows the gum is a very young child whose throat is narrow enough to be obstructed by the gum. To be safe, keep chewing gum out of the hands (and mouths) of children too young to handle it.

Chew on gum to clear your ears in an airplane. A good idea. When a plane takes off, the air pressure inside the cabin is lower than the pressure inside your ears. As a result, your ear drum—the membrane that separates the external ear passage from the eustachian canal, the tube from your ear that opens into the back of your throat, bends outward. To correct this, you have to allow air to escape from the eustachian canal into the back of your throat. The physical movements of your mouth and throat as you chew gum makes this happen.

When the plane comes down, the situation is reversed. Now the air pressure inside the cabin is greater than the pressure inside your ears. The ear drum is pushed painfully inward. To push it out again, you have to force air up from your throat through the eustachian canals, against the back of the distorted ear drum. This is a lot trickier than letting air escape from the eustachian canals, but chewing and swallowing may just help.

When you have a cold, if you have a choice, don't fly. Because your air passages are already clogged, you are guaranteed to end up with pain in your ears on takeoff and/or landing. People with allergies are in the same situation. The constant swelling caused by their nasal tissues "weeping" in response to allergens can permanently narrow the eustachian canals and cause a pain in the ears on every flight in a plane with less-than-perfect pressurization.

Note: Blowing your nose is not a good way to clear your ears in a plane. It may even make things worse. The Valsalva maneuver—pinching your nostrils shut, closing your mouth and blowing gently—can actually force mucus into your eustachian canals, clogging them even further and, perhaps, triggering an infection.

Chewing gum gives you cavities. Not necessarily. It's true that sugary foods such as chewing gum increase your risk of cavities because the sugar provides nourishment for bacteria that cause decay. Sugar also makes your mouth more acid, and thus more hospitable to the bacteria. But any chewing gum, with or without sugar, increases the flow of saliva in your mouth. Saliva is basic (alkaline), so it makes your mouth less acid and more resistant to tooth decay bacteria. As long ago as 1955, researchers in Germany discovered that encouraging confectioners and bakers to chew gum during working hours, when presumably they were snacking on the products they were making, decreased their incidence of new cavities from an average of four a year to fewer than two.

An increased flow of saliva bathes the teeth in minerals that harden the tooth surface plus organic constituents such as phospholipids and phosphoproteins, bactericidal natural antacids that reduce the acidity in your mouth and may create a barrier that protects teeth from bacteria.

Finally, chewing gum may also be an easy way to increase the flow of saliva as we get older. With age, our gums recede naturally, exposing the roots of our teeth, which are less resistant than the upper tooth surfaces to decay. At the same time, our production of saliva may slow down, either as a natural consequence of age or because we are taking increased amounts of medications that promote "dry mouth." That may trigger an unexpected second wave of cavities among older people that chewing gum might help to stem. *Note:* The chewing gum remedy is ineffective for people whose salivary glands have been damaged, perhaps by radiation treatment for cancers of the head and neck.

CHICKEN SOUP

Chicken soup cures a cold. Several years ago, some unfeeling cur of a scientist announced that not only didn't chicken soup cure colds, it wasn't even very nutritious, because the chicken doesn't give up all that much to the soup.

Little did he know. In March 1976, when the Food and Drug Administration's advisory review panel on OTC Cold, Cough, Allergy, Bronchodilator and Anti-Asthmatic products submitted its report, the committee chairman said that chicken soup was "as good as anything else in relieving the symptoms of a cold." So there.

Of course nobody's saying that the stuff will cure a cold, but in 1978, a study at Mt. Sinai Hospital in Miami showed that drinking chicken soup really does help you to clear out your stuffed nasal passages. At first, the study's author, Dr. Marvin Sackler, thought that the active ingredient might be the soup's warm steamy vapor. But when he tried plain steamy water vs. steamy chicken soup, the soup worked better. Other studies have failed to confirm this, so the true reason for chicken soup's success remains elusive.

CHINESE FOOD

One hour after eating Chinese food you'll be hungry again. If you are, blame the veggies. Water chestnuts, Chinese cabbage, bamboo shoots and sprouts are very bulky and may fill up your stomach while you're eating. Then, an hour later, when your stomach has emptied out naturally, the contrast is so striking that you are apt to feel hungry even though you really don't need more food just yet. One solution is to eat more slowly so your stomach doesn't fill up as fast. A second is to balance the veggies with beans and rice or chunks of chicken, meat or fish, all of which are higher in fat and digested (moved out of your stomach) more slowly than the vegetables and keep you feeling fuller longer.

See also CALORIES.

CHOCOLATE

Chocolate causes acne. No, but if you are allergic to chocolate and already have acne, eating the candy might trigger the rash and may make your existing acne worse. Otherwise, there's no connection between the two.

Chocolate is fattening. It depends strictly on how much you eat. One ounce of plain bittersweet chocolate, about one-third of an ordinary chocolate bar, has approximately 135 calories; an ounce of milk chocolate has about 147. Plain, unsweetened, low-fat cocoa powder, such as Hershey's, has about 54 calories to the ounce, and you only use one-third to one-half of that to make a cup of cocoa. If you're nuts about chocolate, you can probably fit it into any diet, so long as you're careful about quantity.

Chocolate is high in cholesterol. It depends on the form of chocolate. No vegetable food contains cholesterol, so plain dark bittersweet chocolate and plain cocoa powder, both made from ground cocoa beans, are cholesterol-free. However, milk chocolate does contain cholesterol because it contains milk. Bonbons or bars covered with dark chocolate also contain cholesterol if their fillings are made with butter, milk or cream.

On the other hand, people who are watching their cholesterol intake may still wish to avoid chocolate because cocoa butter, the fat that gives chocolate its smooth, creamy texture, is relatively high in the saturated fats believed to raise the level of blood cholesterol. Cocoa butter is 60% saturated fat and 3% polyunsaturated fat. By comparison, corn oil is 13% saturated fat and 59% polyunsaturated fat.

Chocolate has empty calories. Far from it. Plain cocoa powder is a good source of copper and dietary fiber. Plain bittersweet chocolate and milk chocolate provide minerals, including calcium, phosphorus and iron (all of which are also present in milk chocolate). In fact, one ounce of milk chocolate provides 50 mg calcium, about 6% of the recommended dietary allowance (RDA) for a person older than 25. One ounce of semisweet chocolate has 1 mg iron, 7% of the RDA for a woman of childbearing age. One ounce of plain cocoa powder has 8.5 g dietary fiber, four times as much as an ounce of dried prunes or cooked lima beans.

Chocolate is energy food. True. Chocolate candy contains sugar, plus the naturally occurring stimulants caffeine (a central nervous system stimulant also found in coffee, tea and mate) and theobromine (a muscle stimulant peculiar to the cocoa bean). Together, the sugar and the stimulants can give you an emotional as well as a physical lift. Chocolate also contains fat, which is digested more slowly than sugar and continues to provide energy over a period of several hours. That's why chocolate is a better source of energy in emergency situations than plain sugar candies or coffee, with or without sugar.

Chocolate is addictive. Anyone who has ever tried to eat just one piece of chocolate knows how hard it can be to stop there. Some say that's just because the stuff tastes so good; others theorize that chocolate's caffeine and theobromine are mildly addictive, no surprise to any coffee freak. But it is only fair to point out that there has never been any indication that people who have been gorging themselves on chocolate and then stop experience the characteristic headache or muscle tremors that may affect coffee drinkers who precipitously give up their favorite brew. (To give up coffee without experiencing withdrawal symptoms, try to cut down slowly rather than stopping cold turkey.)

Adding chocolate to milk destroys the calcium in the milk. Cocoa powder contains oxalic acid, the naturally occurring chemical that contributes to the sharp flavor of spinach. The oxalic acid gives plain cocoa powder a bitter flavor. To counteract the slight bite, some cocoa makers "Dutch" their cocoa powder, that is, they add basic [alkaline] chemicals to neutralize the cocoa's acidity and make it more palatable for those who prefer their chocolate mild.

Because oxalic acid binds to calcium, some people once believed that the oxalic acid in cocoa would keep your body from absorbing and using the calcium in milk. Not to worry: Literally dozens of scientific studies, some dating as far back as the 1940s, show that this reaction never occurs. The calcium in chocolate milk is as available to your body as the calcium in plain milk.

Chocolate ruins your teeth. Anything that contains sugar is potentially cariogenic (cavity-causing), because it provides nourishment for the bacteria that cause cavities. It also makes the mouth more acid and thus more hospitable to the bacteria. But the less time a sugared food stays in your mouth, the less dangerous it is to your teeth. As a result, a cup of cocoa or a piece of chocolate candy you swallow *quickly* is potentially less troublesome than a hard candy you suck on for minutes at a time or a piece of dried fruit that stays stuck in your teeth.

CHOKING

When someone is choking on a piece of food, lift his arms over his head and slap him on the back. Bad advice. Lifting the arms over the head has no effect at all on a piece of food stuck in the throat. Smacking the choking person on the back may make things worse by dislodging the food so that it falls further back into the throat.

For detailed instructions on how to perform the Heimlich Maneuver, a series of abdominal thrusts designed to dislodge food stuck in the throat, see either *The American Medical Association Handbook of First Aid and Emergency Care* (New York; Random House) or *American Red Cross Standard First Aid* (The National American Red Cross).

When some food is stuck in your throat, swallow a small piece of soft white bread to clear it away. No again. Never give a person who is choking anything to swallow until the food that is blocking her throat has been dislodged. (See above.)

CHOLESTEROL

Low cholesterol prevents heart disease. Maybe. Cholesterol is a fatty substance, the most abundant natural steroid found in animal tissues, including foods such as meat, chicken, milk and eggs that come from animals. It is part of the wall of every living cell in your body and a constituent of bile, the natural solvent that helps digest fats.

Some of us process fats less efficiently than others. As a result, we have higher-than-normal amounts of cholesterol in our blood, a condition known as hyper-cholesteremia. Blood levels of cholesterol are measured in terms of milligrams (mg) cholesterol per deciliter (dL) blood serum. Some people with severely impaired ability to metabolize cholesterol may have serum readings as high as 600 mg/dL. This excess cholesterol is believed to contribute to the buildup of fatty deposits on the walls of the arteries, sometimes blocking the arteries so severely that blood cannot flow through unimpeded, and contributing to the risk of heart attack.

For some people, reducing or eliminating the cholesterol they get from food may lower serum cholesterol levels into "normal" range. Others need to use cholesterol-lowering drugs along with diet. But even if this works, lowering cholesterol level into the "safe" under-200 range is no guarantee of avoiding heart disease.

Cholesterol travels through the body on fat and protein particles called lipoproteins. Regardless of the total cholesterol count, people with a large amount of low-density lipoproteins (LDL), the particles that carry cholesterol into the arteries, may be at higher risk than people with a large amount of high-density lipoproteins (HDL), the particles that carry cholesterol into the liver, where it is metabolized and eliminated from the body. The ratio of LDLs to HDLs is largely genetically determined. While cutting back on cholesterol and saturated fats in your diet may lower your overall cholesterol levels, the only factor currently known to increase the percentage of HDLs in your blood serum is exercise.

CIRCUMCISION

Circumcision protects against cancer. Maybe. Cancer of the penis is most common in areas of the world where circumcision is uncommon and personal hygiene poor. It is least common in places like the United States, where circumcision of newborn baby boys has been routine and fewer than 1,000 new cases are diagnosed each year. Circumcision reduces the risk of transferring human papilloma virus (a microorganism linked to penile and uterine cancer) during sexual intercourse. Finally, it reduces the incidence of urinary tract infections. In 1989, the American Academy of Pediatrics changed an earlier position against routine circumcision of newborns on the grounds that circumcised men may be as much as 11 times less likely than uncircumcised men to develop urinary tract infections.

Circumcision increases (or decreases) sexual pleasure. Who knows? Lacking data compiled by men who have experienced sex before and after circumcision, the safest conclusion seems to be that the pleasure quotient of sexual activity depends on the person and not on his circumcised (or uncircumcised) parts.

CLAY

Eating clay while pregnant relieves nervous tension. Eating non-food items such as clay, earth or laundry starch—a phenomenon known as *pica*—is most common among people whose diets are nutritionally deficient, so scientists speculate that it may be a way for the body to get the minerals it is missing. Clay is rich in iron, but consuming it is an inefficient way to fill out your diet because the clay forms a filter in your stomach that can actually block absorption of the iron. In the southeastern United States, eating clay while pregnant is a routine pre-natal ritual, particularly among lower-income women of all races. White clay is preferred, but women will settle for red clay if the white is not available. Sometimes bags of clay are available in the supermarket; frequently, the women dig it from road and riverbeds by hand.

Eating clay while pregnant keeps the growing fetus free of 'marks.' False. This is another justification for consuming clay; it has no effect whatsoever on whether or not the baby will be born with birthmarks.

CLEANLINESS

Cleanliness is next to godliness. Good personal hygiene and good community sanitation have important benefits for reducing the spread of a number of diseases. But excessive washing can make sensitive skin itch and flake. Daily showers or baths may be excessively drying, especially in cold weather when low humidity and indoor heating increase the evaporation of moisture from the skin.

COBWEBS

Apply a cobweb to a bleeding wound to stop the blood from flowing. The assumption here is that the blood will adhere to the strands of the web, clot and form a scab more quickly. Well, maybe.

But there is no mysterious Clotting Compound X in cobwebs. Indeed, as Australian science writer Earle Hackett points out in *Blood*, his wonderful book on our life's fluid, laboratory tests in which blood was poured into two sets of test tubes, one with cobwebs inside and one without, showed no difference at all in clotting time. On the downside, though, there is the indisputable fact that cobwebs are always contaminated with microscopic dirt and debris that can infect an open wound. Stick to commercial bandages and leave the cobwebs to the spiders.

COFFEE

Drinking coffee makes you nervous. Maybe. The caffeine in coffee is a central nervous system stimulant that can make your heart beat faster, temporarily raise your blood pressure, make you breathe more quickly for a while, and change the rate at which your body produces hormones. But like many other drugs, caffeine has different effects on different bodies. You may feel your nerves jangling after just one cup of coffee, while the person sitting next to you may be able to tolerate as many as four or five before she feels any effects at all.

Drinking coffee keeps you up at night. Again, the answer is, maybe. One rule of thumb is to assume that the caffeine in a cup of regular coffee will exert its effects for about seven hours after you drink. If you are sensitive to caffeine, then, yes, even a cup of decaf after late afternoon may keep you up for hours.

But some people actually find a cup of coffee relaxing before bedtime. To complicate things even further, the effect varies not only from person to person, but from day to day. The same cup of coffee that has no overly stimulating effects on a reasonably calm day, may keep you jangling through the night on a day when things are truly hectic or upsetting.

Coffee can cure a headache. It depends what's causing your head to ache. Many headaches are triggered by the engorgement (stretching and filling with blood) of blood vessels in your head and neck. Caffeine is a vasoconstrictor, a substance that can reduce this engorgement. Caffeine is also a mood elevator that can lift your spirits and make you feel better, while the mild warmth from the steaming cup may help relax your facial muscles. If these are the things that are causing your headache, then a cup of coffee plus a mild analgesic such as aspirin or acetaminophen for the pain may chase your headache away.

Coffee sobers you up. Because caffeine is a stimulant, it may alleviate the mild depression some people feel when they drink. But coffee does not speed the elimination of alcohol from your body, a process totally dependent on your body's producing sufficient quantities of the enzymes needed to metabolize the alcohol. Until the alcohol is metabolized and excreted, the only effect coffee can exert is to turn you into what the scientists at the Rutgers Center of Alcohol Studies have called, ''a wide-awake drunk.''

Black coffee is a great diet drink. It doesn't have calories, and, as a mild diuretic, black coffee can help slightly to eliminate excess water and thus a small amount of excess weight. But coffee stimulates the production of stomach acids that trigger the sensation we call ''hunger pangs.'' This can make it even harder to avoid food between meals. In addition, these acids may irritate your stomach, sometimes badly enough to make you think you have an ulcer when you don't. For all these reasons, most experts advise you eat a little food with your coffee.

Coffee is bad for children. Obviously, a central nervous system stimulant such as caffeine is going to have an effect on a child's body and behavior, just as it does on an adult's. But parents who give their kids soda to avoid the caffeine in coffee are kidding themselves. A 12–ounce glass of a cola made with caffeine may contain 46 mg caffeine, about 42% of the caffeine in a cup of drip brewed coffee and as much as 21 times as much caffeine as you might get from 1 cup of decaf.

COFFEE, DECAFFEINATED

Drinking decaf won't keep you awake. It depends on how sensitive you are to caffeine. Decaffeinated coffee is made from beans that are treated to remove 97% to 98% of the caffeine, but what's left, little though it is, can be enough to keep some people hopping.

Decaffeinated coffee won't upset your stomach. False. What stimulates the production of the acids that can trigger hunger pangs and irritate the lining of your stomach isn't the caffeine, it's the natural oils from the coffee beans. These oils, which contribute to the wonderful flavor of coffee, are present in decaffeinated as well as regular brews.

COLDS

A cold lasts a week if you treat it, seven days if you don't. Close enough. According to the American Pharmaceutical Association, the incubation period for a viral infection such as the common cold (the time before you notice any symptoms) is from one to four days. You begin to shed viruses and can pass your cold along about a day or so before you show any symptoms. After symptoms appear, the cold will last a few days more. On average, the total time people are sick with colds is about nine days.

Experts at the National Jewish Center for Immunology and Respiratory Medicine in Denver suggest that, except in rare cases, a respiratory infection that sticks around longer than two weeks may be either an allergy, a complication such as a sinus infection, or the flu.

Children are more likely than adults to catch cold. True. According to statistics from the Federal Centers for Disease Control in Atlanta, children age one to five average six to 12 respiratory illnesses (primarily colds) each year, while people older than 20 average only three or four.

One explanation for the difference is a child's lack of immunity to cold viruses. To date, scientists have identified nearly 200 different viruses that can cause the common cold. Once you are exposed to one of them, your body manufactures antibodies that protect you next time you encounter the same virus. Because children have been exposed to fewer cold viruses, they are more likely than adults to be susceptible to infection. Interestingly enough, children who attend day-care centers are exposed to cold viruses early on; they are less likely than children who stay home to catch colds when they enter kindergarten.

Kissing spreads colds. Unlikely. Kissing spreads some viral infections such as herpes, mumps and infectious mononucleosis (sometimes known as "The Kissing Disease"). But it rarely transmits the common cold because rhinoviruses, the cold viruses scientists know most about, do not live comfortably in the mouth, where the temperature is lower than it is in the nasal passages.

To keep from spreading your cold, cover your nose or mouth when you sneeze or cough. Most cold researchers believe that this is polite, but probably ineffective unless you wash your hands afterward.

According to researchers at the University of Virginia School of Medicine, one way we spread colds is by direct contact—touching our nasal membranes or the virus-laden droplets we discharge when we sneeze or cough and then touching someone else who touches his nose.

On the other hand, cold researchers at the University of Wisconsin Medical School say that colds are more likely to be spread through the air by the virus-laden droplets we discharge when we sneeze or cough. Covering nose and mouth stops the spray but can spread the virus unless you wash your hands. Tissues alone don't do the job.

In 1979, cold researchers ran a cold study in Antarctica in which the 200 people stationed there were given tissues saturated with an iodine compound known to kill cold viruses. As soon as they handed out the medicated tissue, the number of people with respiratory diseases dropped precipitously, and it stayed down the rest of the season.

To confirm the effectiveness of the viricidal tissues, in 1981–1982, at the University of Wisconsin, Dr. Elliott Dick invited eight volunteers with bad colds to play poker with eight healthy but susceptible volunteers. Again, using tissues impregnated with viricidal chemicals to cover a sneeze and wipe hands stopped the transmission of colds.

In 1984, the Kimberly-Clark company test-marketed a tissue called Avert, a three-layer tissue impregnated with citric acid and malic acid, chemicals that occur naturally in fruits such as oranges and apples. The acids did not kill cold viruses, but did keep them from going through the tissue and stopped the transmission of colds so long as people did not touch the side into which they had coughed or sneezed. Avert was taken off the market after one year because of consumer resistance to its price, $1.00 to $1.30 for a package of 60 tissues.

Smokers are more likely than non-smokers to catch cold. True. According to *The Surgeon General's Report: Reducing the Health Consequences of Smoking, 25 Years of Progress* (1989), people who smoke have a significantly higher risk of respiratory diseases, including the common cold. The American Lung Association adds that a smoker's risk of dying from pneumonia or influenza is nearly twice that of a non-smoker.

Here's why: To infect you, a cold virus must penetrate through the nasal mucous membrane. People who smoke one pack of cigarettes a day, inhale tobacco smoke 70,000 times a year. The smoke contains chemicals that alter the consistency of the mucus, making it easier for the virus to get through. In addition, tobacco smoke contains toxins that slow down the cilia (tiny hairs) that continually beat back and forth to keep microbes and debris out of your nose. Finally, inhaling tobacco smoke reduces the activity of phagocytes, white blood cells that ordinarily attack invading disease organisms.

Sleeping in a cold room and taking cold showers will increase your resistance to colds. False. When you are exposed to very hot weather, your body adapts over a period of about a week with a series of physiological changes designed to keep you cool. You perspire more, producing moisture that cools as it evaporates on your skin. Your blood circulation slows, so that less blood flows up to the surface of the skin where it would be heated before returning to the center of your body and raising the temperature there. You conserve salt by excreting less in your urine. And your breathing and heartbeat speed up to cope with the stress of the heat.

There are no such documented changes in cold weather, say researchers at the Army Research Institute of Environmental Medicine in Natick, Massachusetts. The best you can do is lower your shivering threshold so that it takes a lower skin temperature to trigger shivering, which is your body's last-ditch effort to warm up. But you will still be cold and miserable; you never really adapt.

And you won't have reduced your risk of catching cold. In fact, you may increase it, because continued exposure to cold may dry out the nasal passages and make it easier for cold viruses to penetrate.

Steam relieves nasal congestion. The old wisdom is that breathing steamy air clears the nasal passages. The new wisdom is that it depends on how hot the steamy air is.

In 1990, a team of researchers at the Cleveland Clinic Foundation in Cleveland, Ohio, asked 66 volunteers with mild colds and stuffed noses to inhale air from nozzles held about an inch from the nose. Half the group inhaled dry, room-temperature air; the other half, hot humidified air.

One week later, the researchers were astounded to find that the people who inhaled the dry air were better off than those who had inhaled the hot, humidified air. Measuring nasal congestion with a rhinomanographer (a machine that gauges the resistance to air flow through the nose), they discovered that the people who inhaled dry, room temperature air were breathing 11% easier while the people who breathed the hot, moist air were 6% more stuffed up.

The researchers say that the experiment doesn't mean that it's wrong to use a room vaporizer when you have a cold, because a vaporizer moistens room air without heating it up, and the moist air seems to make breathing through a stuffed nose easier.

Caution: Never lean directly over the vaporizer or over a sink with steam rising from running hot water. Inhaling the hot steam may injure the nasal membranes.

Even in the dead of winter, bundling up and soaking in the sun will cure a cold. No, but, in theory, it might reduce your risk of passing your cold on to someone else.

Rhinoviruses, the viruses that cause most colds, live best at 33° C (91.4°F) to 34° C (93.2°F), the normal temperature inside your nasal passages. That is why they are linked to upper respiratory infections rather than to infections in your lungs, where the temperature is normally several degrees higher. Theoretically, sitting bundled up in the sun might raise the temperature of your nasal passages and reduce the rhinovirus population inside your nose, which would make you less likely to pass on your cold.

Because cold viruses are sensitive to direct exposure to ultraviolet radiation, including the UV rays in sunlight, sitting in the sun might also reduce the virus population on your hands and clothes. (It won't affect the viruses inside your nose because the skin blocks the rays from penetrating.) *Caution:* If you chose to sunbathe, wear a sunscreen. Even in winter, exposure to the sun's rays can damage skin.

Cover yourself with a piece of warm red flannel to 'draw out' a cold. A warm but ineffective remedy. Mary Chamberlain, author of *Old Wives' Tales: Their History, Remedies and Spells,* explains that the cloth's reputation as a cold-killer comes from its color, which is associated with blood, warmth and healing. In reality, although the flannel wrap may be warm and psychologically soothing, it has no effect at all on the course of your cold.

If all else fails, retreat to your bed with a hot rum toddy. Omit the rum, and you're on the right track, says Robert J. Pandina, Ph.D., scientific director of the Center of Alcohol Studies at Rutgers, the State University of New Jersey. "Drinking when you have a cold is not a good idea," he says. "Alcohol stresses your immune system and dilates your peripheral blood vessels, the ones near the surface of your skin and in the membrane lining of your nose. Taking a drink can make you feel warmer for a few minutes, which is nice, but it can also temporarily increase nasal congestion, which is not.''

In addition, alcohol may interact with some ingredients in over-the-counter cold remedies, increasing the sedative effects of antihistamines and the irritant effects of analgesics.

See also ASPIRIN, BALSAM, CHICKEN SOUP, DRAFTS, FEVER, HATS, MUSTARD, WET FEET.

COTTON SOCKS

Wearing white cotton socks prevents athlete's foot. Nothing's perfect, but *clean, dry* cotton socks are definitely a strong weapon in the fight against athlete's foot. The fungi that cause this infection flourish on warm humid surfaces such as damp feet, so, changing socks frequently protects by keeping your feet dry, especially important for people whose feet get very sweaty. What makes cotton such a good choice? It is cooler and more absorbent than either wool or nylon.

There is no evidence that the fungi prefer one color to another, but if you perspire heavily, some fabric dyes may run onto your skin which can be irritating if you are sensitive to the coloring agent.

See also ATHLETE'S FOOT.

CRANBERRY JUICE

Cranberry juice prevents bladder infections. It certainly may help. In 1985, a team of researchers led by Anthony E. Sobota, Ph.D., professor of biology at Youngstown (Ohio) State University reported the discovery of a still-unidentified substance in cranberry juice that makes it more difficult for the bacteria that cause urinary tract infections to cling to the walls of bladder cells. In the Youngstown studies, the "anti-cling" chemical was detected in the urine of both animal and human test subjects as early as one hour after they drank cranberry juice, and it retained its ability to keep bacteria off bladder cells for as long as 12 to 15 hours.

Caution: Untreated urinary infections can lead to serious kidney damage. Cranberry juice may be a useful folk medicine, but it is no substitute for your own doctor's diagnosis and treatment which may include antibiotics to control the infection.

D

DANDRUFF

To prevent (or cure) a case of dandruff, massage your scalp with olive oil. This is exactly the wrong treatment. Dandruff may look like dry scalp, but it is really a form of dermatitis that now appears to be caused by a yeast-like organism called *Pityrosporon ovale*. Oiling up your scalp will not affect the organism but it can irritate the skin and might even increase the flaking. The more effective course is to check with your dermatologist who may prescribe a shampoo that contains ketoconazole, a drug used to treat other fungal and yeast infections. Tar shampoos are also useful because they soothe the inflamed skin on the scalp.

A lemon rinse will cure your dandruff. No, again. But if you've tried the oil treatment, the acid lemon juice will help clean the oil out of your hair when you shampoo. And it can also make blonde hair shine.

See also LEMONS, HAIR.

DAYDREAMS

Daydreaming is a waste of time. Not necessarily. Although the daydreaming child or adult may seem to be the perfect picture of a time-wasting idler, daydreaming, like dreaming during sleep at night, can be an invaluable aid to problem solving. Although nobody knows exactly how it works, psychologists have recognized for a long time that people who go to sleep with problems on their minds often wake up with the solutions which they may or may not remember having come up with in a dream. The same applies to daydreaming. What looks like mooning about may actually be a way of setting the mind free to come up with imaginative solutions.

DIAPER RASH

Dust cornstarch on the baby's bottom to prevent diaper rash. Because cornstarch helps keep baby's bottom smooth and dry under ordinary circumstances, it's a nifty way to treat prickly heat, says the venerable Dr. Spock. But neither cornstarch nor any other dusting powder can prevent diaper rash caused by contact with wet diapers. A wet diaper simply contains too much liquid for the cornstarch to absorb, and once the baby's skin is irritated enough to become rashy, a powder/urine paste may only irritate it further.

Hang your baby's diapers out in the sun to dry. Sunlight sterilizes them and prevents diaper rash. It couldn't hurt. The ultraviolet light in the sun's rays is a natural germicide available all year long, even in the dead of winter. Hanging washed diapers out to dry in the sun can help eliminate bacteria lurking on the cloth and thus prevent or even cure a diaper rash.

DIARRHEA

Eating burnt toast cures diarrhea. There is a theoretical, but entirely unproved, rationale for this home remedy: Burnt toast, like activated charcoal, may absorb toxins in the gastrointestinal tract that are causing your upset stomach. If your diarrhea persists for more than 24 hours or is profuse or bloody or accompanied by other symptoms of gastric distress such as vomiting, forget the toast and call your doctor.

Rice water cures baby's diarrhea. Maybe, but it depends on how serious the problem is. Sweetened rice water (water in which rice has been boiled) is a South American home remedy used to treat very mild diarrhea. It's better than milk because a bout with diarrhea can temporarily inflame the lining of the stomach and gut, depleting its supply of lactase, the enzyme needed to digest lactose, the sugar in milk. Sweetened rice provides fluids without upsetting a temporarily milk-sensitive tummy.

There are two notes of caution. First, the rice water should be sweetened with sugar, not honey, because honey may be contaminated with a strain of bacteria known to cause infant botulism. Second, always check with your doctor before using this or any other home remedy for infant diarrhea. During a bout of profuse diarrhea, the body loses both fluids and electrolytes, chemicals that maintain fluid balance and enable muscles to send electrical signals from one cell to another. A simple sweetened rice water solution may be too low in electrolytes to replace what has been lost.

DIET

You need more food in winter than in summer. Not necessarily. Contrary to popular belief, it takes as much energy (food) to keep your body cool in summer as it does to keep it warm in winter.

The easiest way to eat well is just to pick a variety of foods. True, but the variety has to include choices from the boring but dependable four basic food groups: meat, fish and poultry, or a protein equivalent such as beans or eggs; milk and milk products, preferably low-fat; grains; and fruits. Eliminating any one of these basic groups entirely can make it harder to meet your normal nutritional requirements.

Left to their own devices, children will end up choosing a healthful diet. Probably true. In the late 1920s, Chicago pediatrician Dr. Clara Davis conducted an experiment in which infants who had just been weaned were allowed to pick anything they wanted from meal trays presented to them by a nurse. Some children stuck with one food for a while, but by and large, over the length of the experiment, the kids did pick a nutritious variety of foods.

Ever since, scientists have questioned whether the experiment was objective. For example, there were only limited kinds of food on the trays. There were no true sweets, such as candy, and the children did pick the sweetest foods offered, milk and fruit, more often than they chose other foods. And many experts have suggested that the adults who served the food may have affected the children's choices by subtly expressing approval or disapproval.

So, in 1991, a team of researchers at the University of Illinois at Champaign-Urbana repeated the experiment. Once again, although the children sometimes chose strange combinations such as liver and orange juice for breakfast and nothing but bananas for lunch, their overall daily calorie intake remained relatively constant and they chose a fair variety of different foods during the course of a day.

Conclusion? Don't force your kids to eat, the researchers said. On their own, most children who are offered a healthful variety of foods will eat enough food in sufficient variety to stay healthy and trim.

Athletes need more protein than the rest of us do. Not true, says the National Research Council (NRC), the group responsible for establishing the recommended dietary allowances (RDAs) for vitamins, minerals and other nutrients. According to the NRC, there is virtually no evidence to suggest that exercising your muscles increases your need for protein. What does make a difference is extreme physical stress, such as infection, fever or surgical trauma, which may lead to protein loss and thus raise your protein requirements. During periods of rapid growth, we also need more protein, which is why infants and adolescents need more protein, pound for pound, than adults do.

Protein Requirements for Healthy People

Sex	Age (yrs)	Grams/Kg*
Both	0–0.5	2.2
	0.5–1	1.6
	1–3	1.2
	4–6	1.1
	7–14	1.0
Females	15+	0.8
Males	15–18	0.9
	19+	0.8

*one kg = 2.2 lbs. To find the g/lb equivalent, divide the figure in this column by 2.2. For example, infants, age 0–6 mos. require 2.2 g protein for each kg weight, which equals 1 g for each pound.
Source: National Research Council, *Recommended Dietary Allowances* (Washington, D.C.: National Academy Press, 1989)

Never eat more than one kind of food at each meal. Different foods are digested at different rates, and if you eat more than one kind of food, something will remain undigested in your stomach. False. Your digestive enzymes plus your stomach acid are designed to handle anything edible you toss at them. Sometimes, combining two different foods at the same time is the more nutritious way to go.

The best example of this kind of effect is the phenomenon known as "protein complementarity." Proteins are composed of amino acids. The proteins in foods of animal origin, such as meat, fish, poultry, eggs and milk products, are considered "complete" because they contain all the essential amino acids (the amino acids we must get from food because we cannot manufacture them inside our bodies). The proteins in plant foods, on the other hand, are sometimes labeled "incomplete" because they contain sufficient amounts of some but not all the essential amino acids.

By combining plant foods in the same dish, it's possible to create a meal with all the essential amino acids. One good example is beans-and-grains (usually, beans-and-rice), a dish popular in various parts of the world where animal foods are in short supply. The proteins in grains such as rice are deficient in the essential amino acids lysine and isoleucine but contain sufficient amounts of the essential amino acids tryptophan, methionine and cysteine; the proteins in beans are exactly the opposite. Put them together in the same dish and your body recognizes the proteins they supply as being "complete."

DIETING

When you're trying to lose weight, cut down on starchy foods such as pasta and potatoes. An old-fashioned, false idea based on the fact that when you eliminate carbohydrates from your diet, you urinate more frequently, losing water and thus weight. But the weight is quickly regained. In fact, ounce for ounce, carbohydrates such as pasta and potatoes have about half as many calories as fats—four calories per ounce for the carbohydrates vs nine calories per ounce for the fats. Protein also has about four calories per ounce, but many high-protein foods, such as meat, eggs and whole milk products, have significant amounts of fat. "Starchy" carbohydrate foods such as pasta, potatoes and beans do not, so you can consume larger amounts of them while spending fewer calories.

See also CALORIES, OBESITY.

DIGESTION

Drinking wine with meals helps digestion. Like mustard and some other spices, beverages with a low concentration of alcohol stimulate the flow of saliva and gastric acids, both of which make digestion possible. Wine's special reputation as a digestive aid almost certainly arises from the fact that ounce for ounce it delivers less alcohol than distilled spirits do, which is why it is used as a beverage with meals.

But there's nothing magic in the wine. In fact, you can produce a beverage with an equally low concentration of alcohol by mixing your spirits (whiskey, rum, gin or vodka) with water or a soft drink. One ounce of spirits plus four ounces of water is generally considered to deliver the same amount of alcohol as five ounces of wine.

Caution: If you have gastritis, ulcers or any other medical condition or are taking any medication that requires you to avoid alcohol beverages, all liquor should be considered off limits unless specifically exempted by your own physician.

DOCTORS

Doctors cannot operate on members of their own families. There is no legal reason why doctors cannot treat people to whom they are related, but common sense suggests that the emotional complications of dealing with a relative's illness could make it hard to deal coolly with the medical issues involved. Of course, some doctors are cooler than others, so when it comes to treating relatives, some do, some don't. But it's always a matter of individual choice.

Doctors are less afraid of death than we are. Not true. In a 1965 study, psychiatrist Herman Feifel suggested that one reason people become physicians is precisely to control their own excessive fear of death by acquiring the power to cure. Doctors try to beat death, Feifel concluded, not only to save their patients but to reassure themselves, which is why they often react in ways we interpret as callous, either by pushing medical treatment past points layman consider cruel or by psychologically "abandoning" patients who are hopelessly ill.

The desire to be associated with the medical profession in order to beat death is not confined to people who become doctors and nurses. According to James A. Knight, M.D., author of *Doctor-To-Be: Coping with the Trials and Triumphs of Medical School,* some people marry medical students or doctors as a way of acquiring this kind of magical protection.

DOG BITES

A human bite isn't as dangerous as a dog bite. Wrong. Because so few people take human bites seriously, they may be even more dangerous. The human mouth is brimful of all manner of microorganisms that can invade your bloodstream if the bite breaks the skin. It can be just as dangerous to hit someone in the mouth and break the skin on your knuckles against his teeth. If you ignore this kind of wound, it may quickly progress to an infection. To avoid problems, see your doctor right away any time you are bitten, either by a human being or an animal.

Who's most likely to be bitten by another person? Dentists seem a reasonable guess, but in 1977 when a doctor at the University of Miami School of Medicine simply asked people who came to the emergency room with a bite what they did for a living, the most common answer was, police officers.

Let the dog who bit you lick the wound to speed healing. A bad idea, say the experts at the Animal Medical Center in New York. The dog's rough tongue can irritate the wound, and the bacteria from his mouth can infect the wound.

DOWN'S SYNDROME

The older a woman is when she becomes pregnant, the greater the chance that her baby will be born with Down's syndrome. True. The incidence of babies born with Down's syndrome rises from about one in 1,000 when the mother is 30 years old or younger, to about one in 250 when she is 35, one in 100 when she is 40, and one in 50 when she is older than 45.

Nobody knows exactly why this should be so, but there are several workable theories. The most popular is that the chromosomes in a woman's eggs, all of which are formed in her ovaries before she is born, age and become "overripe" by the time she reaches her thirties and forties.

Others suggest that because an older couple is likely to have intercourse less frequently, a sperm may fertilize an egg that has been out of the ovary several days and is degenerating when it meets the sperm. Research conducted at Fairleigh Dickenson University in New Jersey late in the 1970s suggested that a couple who have intercourse every two days during the fertile period at ovulation greatly increase the chances that a healthy viable sperm will meet a healthy viable egg, to produce a healthy child.

See also BIRTH DEFECTS.

DRAFTS

Sitting in a draft can give you a cold. Not unless the draft blows some cold viruses your way. People who are sensitive to changes in temperature may develop a condition called vasomotor rhinitis when they go from a warm environment to a cold one or even sit in a draft. The cold air may cause blood vessels in the mucous membrane lining of the nose to swell and leak a moist discharge. The result is a stuffy, runny nose, similar to that caused by the viral infection of a cold. But the trigger is a change in temperature, not a viral infection.

Sitting in a draft can cause muscle cramps or 'charley horse.' It's possible that a sudden chill may trigger the muscle spasm we call a cramp. If it does, the pain may be relieved fairly quickly by moving out of the draft, and warming and gently moving the muscle.

See also AIR-CONDITIONING, COLDS.

DREAMS

People don't dream in color. Sure they do. It's just that few are trained to remember dreams in their entirety, and what little they do remember usually centers on what's important, which is to say, the content not the color of the dream. If you train yourself to write down your dream the minute you wake up (or as soon as you can handle the pencil), you may be surprised to find that you recall colors along with the action of the dream.

Dreams foretell the future. Sometimes they seem to. But it usually turns out that a dream that "tells the future" is really just a self-fulfilling prophesy. That is, the dreamer, who's working with known facts, sets up a situation and proceeds (in his dream) to follow it through to a logical, hoped-for, or feared, conclusion. Once awake, he may consciously or unconsciously begin to follow the path the dream laid out in an effort to produce the same result. When it works, he may fleetingly think the dream foretold the future; when it doesn't, he forgets the dream.

See also DAYDREAMS, NIGHTMARES.

DROWNING

Drowning people come up for air twice before going down for the third time. This is a neat formula that owes a lot to the "magic" number three, but it isn't necessarily valid. Bodies will bob to the surface just as long as there is enough gas inside to make them buoyant in the water. The gas may be either the air in living lungs or, later on, the gases formed by decomposition after death, which is why it is virtually impossible to keep a corpse from rising out of the water unless you anchor it to something really heavy.

People drown more quickly in fresh water than in salt water. The most important cause of death by drowning is asphyxiation, the oxygen starvation caused by swallowing enough water to block air from reaching the lungs. In this regard, salt water and fresh water are equally lethal.

But a contributing cause of death by drowning may be heart failure triggered by chemical changes in the blood caused by absorbing water through the tissues of the lungs. In this case, the kind of water you inhale may make a slight difference.

It is a rule of physics that solutions flow through membranes (in this case, body tissue) from the side where the solution is less concentrated to the side where it is more concentrated. This phenomenon is known as osmosis.

Fresh water is a less concentrated solution than blood. If it flows into your lungs, fresh water will move quickly across membranes into your blood stream, creating a sudden increase in the amount of fluid flowing through your circulatory system. This leads to an imbalance in the chemicals (electrolytes) that enable the heart to send electrical signals from cell to cell. The result may be irregular heartbeat and/or heart failure.

Salt water, on the other hand, is more dense than blood. If it flows into your lungs, liquid (water) from your blood will flow across the walls of your blood vessels towards the salt water. This loss of liquid from the blood makes the blood more viscous. If the loss of fluid from the blood continues, the thickened blood will eventually cause your heart to stop. But a short-term loss of water from the blood does not significantly affect electrolyte balance. Swallowing salt water is less likely than swallowing fresh water to be immediately life-threatening as long as breathing can be restored.

E

EARS

· **To get rid of a bug in your ear, pour in a drop of mineral oil.** In 1986, doctors in the emergency room at Charity Hospital in New Orleans had a chance to perform the first scientifically controlled test of this bug-in-the-ear folk remedy.

Faced with a patient who had two live roaches, one stuck in each ear, the researchers poured a drop of mineral oil into one and squirted lidocaine, a local anesthetic, in the other. The result: The lidocaine did a better job because it caused the bug to have a seizure, let go of the ear, and pop right out. Mineral oil just suffocated the little bugger, which meant that the doctors had to go in and dig him out. Conclusion: If you get a bug in your ear, seek medical help. If you poke around inside your ear yourself, you might scrape the ear canal or damage the ear drum.

A drop of peroxide helps clean wax out of your ears. It's the effervescent bubbles that do the job, say experts at Manhattan Eye, Ear and Throat Hospital in New York. Flushing your ears afterward with a mildly acidic solution of one teaspoon white distilled vinegar in a cup of warm water helps fight bacteria that might cause infection.

Caution: Check with your doctor before attempting this home remedy. If you have an ear infection, a punctured eardrum or a tube inserted in your ear, any self-treatment may worsen the condition.

Rub your ear with red flannel to cure an earache. This folklore mixes magic with a dash of science. The magic lies in the color. In most cultures, red means warmth, so red materials are often used in a like-cures-like manner to draw heat out of a wound or ache. Today, we use antibiotics to cure infections, but we may still use warmth to help drain the wound or soothe the ache, and that's the scientific component of this myth. If your doctor prescribes a warm dressing for your earache, you can put the two together with a home-made red flannel "earmuff" that is psychologically comforting and physiologically valid.

See also CHEWING GUM.

ECZEMA

Eczema is contagious. No. Eczema is an itchy, blistery, some-times oozing or crusty rash, a form of contact dermatitis that occurs when a person is exposed to substances or materials to which he is sensitive. No matter how unpleasant it looks, eczema cannot be passed from one person to another. Of course, if the eczematous rash becomes infected, the infection can spread from one person to another through direct contact.

Only children get eczema. Sorry, no. Eczema can pop up at any time in your life. In fact, for some unknown reason, men older than 40 are particularly likely to develop eczematous patches on the back of the legs or around the waist.

EPILEPSY

Epilepsy is hereditary. Epilepsy is the name we use to describe neurological disorders characterized by the imbalances in the electrical impulses in the brain that produce the physical effect we call seizures. We cannot inherit epilepsy, but we may inherit a susceptibility to seizures. Epilepsy is most commonly caused by brain damage resulting from an injury. Because brain injury may occur in the womb or during birth, some babies are born with epilepsy. Their affliction is congenital (acquired before birth) but not hereditary (passed from parent to child in the genes).

Other causes of seizures are chemical dependency or withdrawal from drugs, fever or infectious diseases, and brain tumors.

People with epilepsy are mentally retarded. Mental retardation occurs with about the same frequency among people who have epilepsy as it does among people who do not have epilepsy. Epilepsy *per se* has absolutely no relationship with intelligence. People who have epilepsy may be intelligent, average or stupid—just like anyone else.

To end an epileptic seizure, dash cold water in the victim's face. No. Once a seizure has begun, nothing can stop it from running its natural course. Worse, dashing cold water in a person's face while he is in the throes of a seizure might cause him to inhale the water and choke on it.

A person who is having a seizure should be restrained, by force, if necessary. No, again. Some seizures *(petit mal)* are so mild that no one other than the person experiencing it will know that it is happening. On the other hand, a visible *(grand mal)* seizure may be frightening to bystanders who assume that the person having the seizure will hurt himself. But this is more likely to occur if the victim is restrained and struggles to free himself. The safest course, for both victim and onlooker, is simply to make sure that the victim is lying comfortably and then allow the seizure to run its course.

During a seizure, put something between the victim's teeth so he doesn't bite his tongue. If you can insert a soft object, like a folded handkerchief, between the victim's teeth without force, fine. But you should never attempt to insert something hard like a piece of wood and you should never attempt to force open the jaws of a person who is having a seizure, since doing so might trigger muscle contractions strong enough to break the person's teeth.

EXERCISE

Never drink liquids while exercising. The idea behind this outdated myth seems to have been that drinking liquids would bloat the body and make the athlete less efficient. In fact, as any serious athlete knows, boxers, dancers, football players, long-distance runners, tennis players and the like may drop as much as 5 pounds while performing. This weight loss represents a loss of fluids, not fat. If the fluid is not replaced, the athlete is at risk for heat stroke or dehydration.

For safety's sake, don't wait until you are thirsty to drink. According to the *Tufts University Diet & Nutrition Letter,* exercise can blunt your body's thirst signals. The *Letter's* better way: 2 cups of water about 15 minutes before you start exercising, and about a half cup of water every 10 to 15 minutes while you are playing, exercising or working out.

Never drink cold water while exercising. Actually, cold water (about 40°F, the temperature inside most refrigerators) is the most efficient cooler because it leaves your stomach more quickly and thus rehydrates your body faster than either luke-warm or hot beverages.

Exercise makes a woman's muscles bulge. Muscle development is determined by genetic programming, hormones and body type as well as how often and how vigorously you exercise. Both men and women have male hormones and female hormones, but men have more testosterone, the male hormone that encourages muscle growth, while women have more estrogen, which inhibits the growth of thick, ropy muscles. A woman who has a typical pear-shape feminine body with narrow shoulders and broad hips will never develop muscles as bulgy as a man's no matter how much she exercises. Even a well-muscled female body builder is always smoother and more compact than her male counterpart.

Women who overtrain their bodies have trouble delivering babies. As long as her pelvis is sufficiently wide to permit the baby to slip easily through the birth canal, a woman with a well-trained body may actually have an easier time during labor.

Strenuous exercise makes a woman less fertile. Until recently, it was taken as gospel that women who trained strenuously were likely to reduce their chances of becoming pregnant because exercise tends to reduce the fat content of the body. Ordinarily, a woman's body is approximately 18% to 25% fat (a man's is ordinarily 15% fat). A woman who reduces the amount of fat in her body below 15% may also reduce her production of hormones, and this was believed to affect her menstrual cycles and lower her chances of ovulating, which would, in turn, lower her chances of conceiving.

In 1990, however, researchers at the University of British Columbia in Vancouver, Canada, reported the results of a study of 67 female volunteers (21 marathon runners, 23 recreational runners and 23 who did less than an hour of aerobic exercise a week) that, for the first time, seem to show that exercise alone had no effect on menstrual cycles in women who otherwise had normal menstruation. Nor did the exercise regimes affect ovulation. While many of the women with normal cycles failed to ovulate (and thus could not become pregnant), the failure to ovulate occurred in women in all three groups. It was not tied to heavy exercise. There will certainly be more to come on this one.

The only exercise that helps you lose weight is exercise that works up a sweat. False. Walking, which leaves you feeling fine but not winded, can do the job as well as running. And it works without subjecting your muscles and joints to the stress of pounding the pavement.

How much can you lose when you walk? According to a recent study from the University of Massachusetts, a 150-pound person who begins an exercise program of walking at the rate of four miles per hour, 45 minutes every other day while holding his calorie intake steady will burn enough energy to take off about 18 pounds in one year. If you weigh less, you will lose proportionally less; if you weigh more, you will lose more.

Exercise lowers the risk of heart disease. It may. Not only does it increase your oxygen intake, it also seems to increase the ratio of high-density lipoproteins (HDL), the fat and protein particles that help carry artery-clogging cholesterol out of our bodies. *Note:* Before beginning an exercise program, check with your doctor. During exercise, seek medical attention immediately if you experience chest pain or pain in the upper arm, nausea, weakness, or difficulty in breathing.

No pain, no gain. This modern myth of the '80s fitness craze is not only silly, it's dangerous. Pain is your body's signal that it's been injured, not stimulated.

Exercising a specific part of your body, like your upper thighs, can help you "spot reduce." Sort of. When you exercise, you lose fat all over your body because you increase the number of calories you burn. In the early 1980s, when researchers at the University of Massachusetts put a group of college men on an exercise program consisting of sit-ups, they found that the men lost as much weight in buttocks and at the base of the shoulder blades as they did from the abdomen. That's the bad news. The good news is that exercising a specific set of muscles tightens and tones them so that the spot looks better even though weight loss is even all over the body. That's what gives leg lifts and sit-ups their undeserved reputation as spot reducers.

"Setting-up" exercises get you going in the morning. A logical assumption. The sleep cycle is tied to body temperature, which rises and falls naturally in the course of the 24-hour day. We fall asleep at night when our body temperature is going down and wake

up in the morning as body temperature starts to rise. People who are alert as soon as they wake up probably warm up faster than those of us who stumble around a while in the morning before everything coordinates. "Setting-up" exercises that warm up the body may speed up the waking process.

EYEBROWS, EYELASHES

Once you shave or cut your eyebrows or eyelashes, they will never grow back. It may seem like forever, but eyebrows and lashes do grow back. Eventually. The problem is that the tiny hairs are not replaced on a schedule as regular as that for the hairs on your head or other parts of your body that are constantly being shed and replaced. Eyebrows and eyelashes grow for about 10 weeks at a time and then stop growing for months at a time, so it can take as long as nine months to replace a plucked or shaven brow.

EYE COLOR

All babies are born with blue eyes. The eyes of most fair-skinned newborns look blue even though they may eventually turn green, hazel or dark brown, but the eyes of dark-skinned infants, including Asians, are brown right from the start.

Blue-eyed blondes are delicate people. Although artists and writers from Western countries often draw or describe their tender romantic heroines as light-eyed people with flaxen hair, there are absolutely no studies linking physical strength or emotional stability to hair or eye color.

EYES

Reading in bed or in a moving car can ruin your eyes. Neither will do you any lasting harm, but both can cause eyestrain or give you a headache. A person who reads in bed may twist her body into a position that demands an almost impossible adjustment of the muscles that govern the movement of the eyeball. That strains the muscles and makes them ache. Sitting straight up in bed to read may prevent this kind of strain.

Reading in a moving car can also cause eye muscle strain as you try to concentrate on a moving target—the book in your hands. The letters you are trying to read are in constant motion. Watching them requires an equally constant readjustment of the eye muscles that can lead to eyestrain, headache or nausea. (People who are susceptible to motion sickness sometimes find that concentrating on an immovable object, such as the horizon, may help avoid a jumpy stomach.)

Overuse will wear out your eyes. When we say "overuse," most of us mean the kind of activity that causes muscle strain (see above). This muscle strain can make you uncomfortable but it won't "wear out your eyes," says the American Optometric Association. To relieve the strain and make things more comfortable, check with your ophthalmologist who may prescribe new glasses or a stronger reading light.

Splashing cold water in your eyes makes them bright. The clean, cold water or a compress soaked in cold water may constrict the blood vessels on the surface of the eye so that the white looks clearer and, perhaps, brighter.

Press ice cubes against your closed eyelid to relieve fatigue. Cold compresses, yes (see above); ice cubes, no. Ice cubes are potentially hazardous since they can freeze the eye if left on too long.

When your eyes are puffy, soothe them with wet teabags. Tea leaves contain tannin, a natural astringent that can make skin swell slightly so that it feels a little bit tighter for a while. But the tea may also stain your skin and if it gets into your eyes, it can cause redness and inflammation. All in all, a cool water compress works as well without side effects.

See also CARROTS.

EYES, CROSSED

Children will outgrow crossed eyes. It takes a newborn baby a few months to learn how to focus his eyes. During this time, the eyes may "cross." This kind of crossed eyes usually goes away by the time an infant reaches six months. But if one eye continues to "wander," a condition known as amblyopia, the child may need glasses with the lens over the stronger eye blacked and a corrective lens for the weaker eye, or exercises to strengthen the muscle of the weaker eye, or surgery to correct the muscles of one or both eyes.

Ignoring crossed eyes or waiting for a child to "outgrow" the problem can lead to the loss of sight in the weaker eye as the brain, which cannot cope with the double vision presented by the two differently focused eyes, adapts to the signal sent from the stronger eye and ceases to decode signals from the weaker one. If this continues until age five to seven, binocular vision (seeing with two eyes) and depth perception (the ability to see how far away things are) may be lost forever.

F

FACE/FACIAL EXPRESSION

Be careful or your face will freeze like that. This is usually something a parent says to a kid who's got his face screwed up into some impossibly horrendous expression, but it's actually good advice for adults, too. Our faces really do "freeze" (or wrinkle) into the pattern of creases we create whenever we smile, frown, talk and so on. While there is no way to avoid wrinkles entirely as we get older, it is trite but true to point out that smiling—which uses fewer muscles than frowning—really does make fewer wrinkle lines.

People who live together eventually begin to look like each other. Over the years, people who live together may begin, however unconsciously, to mimic each other's facial and speech patterns and even to move their bodies in similar ways. As a result, after a while even people with no objectively similar features may begin to resemble each other.

FAINTING

If you feel faint, sit down and lean forward, with your head between your knees. Fainting—also known as syncope (sin-co-pay)—is a sudden loss of consciousness caused by a diminished flow of blood to the brain. This may be the result of an irregular heartbeat or low blood pressure or a spasm in a blood vessel in the brain caused by a drug reaction or simply hyperventilating during an exercise session. Although sitting down and bending over so that your head is level with your knees should relieve the dizziness, when you feel faint there is always the possibility that when you lean forward your body may follow your head down so that you tumble right off the chair. A better idea, therefore, is simply to lie down flat on a bed, a couch or even the floor until the faint feeling goes away. *Caution:* If a fainting spell doesn't end within seconds, get medical help immediately. It's also a good idea to seek medical evaluation for any recurring dizzy spells, no matter how brief.

To revive a person who has fainted, splash water on her face. A splash of cold water on the face will stimulate nerve endings on the skin and send a temporary alert signal to the brain. But if you splash water on the face of a person who is unconscious, she may breathe in the water and choke on it.

The American Medical Association Handbook of First Aid and Emergency Care recommends this course instead:

[ ] Keep the unconscious victim lying down and comfortable. So long as the loss of consciousness was not caused by a head injury, elevate her feet a few inches above the floor.

[ ] Loosen any tight clothing and keep her airway open.

[ ] Turn the victim's head sideways to prevent her choking if she vomits.

[ ] Bathe her face gently with cool water, but do not give her anything to drink until she is fully conscious.

[ ] If she does not recovery completely within a few minutes, seek emergency medical help.

A sip of whiskey will revive someone who has fainted. Another bad idea. An unconscious person cannot control his throat muscles and might choke on any liquid forced into his mouth. In addition, alcohol beverages lower blood pressure, a problem for people who have just fainted.

FASTING

Fasting clears the head and cleans out the body. There's nothing surprising about the fact that when you stop eating, your body will eventually stop manufacturing solid waste, which is what most people mean when they talk about getting rid of "toxins in the body." Nor is there anything surprising about the fact that when you don't eat, you feel light-headed. Deprived of food, your body begins to reduce the flow of oxygen to your brain. Less oxygen means light-headedness, a condition some people confuse with a sense of religious or spiritual enlightenment.

They are wrong. Continued fasting is called starvation, not enlightenment. The body cannot differentiate between voluntary starvation (as in fasting) or involuntary starvation (as during a famine). All it knows is that it isn't getting any food.

With no source of energy coming in, the body will start to produce ketones, an energy source made from body fat. As the amount of ketones in the blood increases, the body begins to eliminate them through excess urination. That can lead to dehydration and an imbalance in electrolytes, chemicals that make it possible to maintain fluid balance and transmit electrical impulses between cells. At the same time, the body will also begin to digest its own tissues, particularly its protein muscle tissues, including the muscle of the heart. That may lead to heart failure. Eventually, a starving person loses the ability to digest food at all.

Fasting shrinks the stomach. When it is empty, the stomach contracts, but only temporarily. As soon as a person begins to eat again, the stomach will stretch to accommodate the food.

FAT PEOPLE

Fat people are jolly. Fat people may assume a mask of jollity because society expects them to, but in reality they are ordinary people, no more or less likely than anyone else to be jolly.

See also OBESITY.

FEAR

You can 'go white with fear'. Absolutely. Faced with an imminent physical or emotional challenge, your body responds with a classic series of instinctive reactions designed to batten down the hatches, so to speak, and get you ready for fight-or-flight.

First, your adrenal glands secrete extra amounts of adrenalin. Your bladder and rectal muscles may contract to cause involuntary urination or defecation that makes your body lighter so that you can move more quickly. And your surface blood vessels may constrict so that blood flows away from the skin to the center of your body, and you will lose less blood if your skin is injured. It is this last event that accounts for the observation that people look pale when frightened. Someone whose light skin is normally rosy with the blood flowing through those tiny surface blood vessels really may temporarily turn "white with fear."

Fear can make your hair stand on end. Sort of. When you are frightened, your muscles tense up. All of them. Including the muscles in your scalp. Tight muscles in the scalp can make the hair shafts stand up a little. You'd have to have a real crew-cut to get a total porcupine effect, but even long hair will ripple a bit if you are scared enough to make your muscles tighten.

Fear can 'scare a person to death.' Maybe. Severe emotional stress produces strong physical reactions, including an increased production of the fight-or-flight hormone, adrenalin, and a constriction of the surface blood vessels so that blood flow is diverted from the skin to the deeper muscles. If the stress continues and blood vessels remain constricted, the surrounding tissues may become starved for oxygen, causing a decrease in blood pressure that, if not relieved, may (rarely) be fatal.

In primitive societies, the witch doctor has always drawn his strength and reputation from his ability to use suggestion to provoke this kind of reaction; the "black magic" or voodoo that can destroy people who really believe that they are under a curse. In so-called civilized societies, it is rare (or maybe just rarely admitted) that people are this susceptible to suggestion.

Animals can smell fear. It's clear that animals respond to olfactory clues, the natural emission of chemicals called pheromones. Both animals and human beings release chemicals to signal sexual readiness or, as a dog marks a trail with urine, to warn others away. Because frightened or excited people tend to perspire excessively, it is possible that the perspiration carries olfactory clues that animals can recognize to "smell fear."

What is even more interesting is the fact that people also react to these clues. For example, a newborn baby can recognize the scent of her own mother, and there is a growing body of evidence, dating back several decades, to suggest that adults also react to olfactory signals, sometimes in surprising ways.

In 1971, for example, a now-classic study of a group of women students at a Boston college showed that after a few months in a dormitory, the women began to experience synchronized menstrual cycles. Six years later, researchers at San Francisco State University were able to synchronize menstrual cycles among young women volunteers by dabbing a small sample of perspiration in alcohol to the volunteers' upper lips. The perspiration came from a woman with a history of "driving" someone else's menstrual cycle; when she shared a room with a female friend, the friend's menstrual cycle slowly came into synchrony with hers.

Among the women exposed to the perspiration, menstrual cycles began to synchronize, ultimately grouping within three days of the driver's. Among a control group who were dabbed with alcohol alone, there was no deviation from their ordinary cycles.

FENNEL

Fennel tea relieves a baby's colic. It may. Colic is a condition characterized by painful intestinal spasms that may be caused by a baby's having swallowed air, been upset or simply eaten too much. Fennel tea's usefulness is generally attributed to the oil in fennel seeds. The oil is a carminative, an agent that helps expel gas from the intestines, perhaps relieving the baby's colic.

FEVER

Feed a cold and starve a fever. Or is it the other way around? Either way, it's impractical advice.

When you have a fever (a normal defense mechanism that inhibits the growth of some disease organism), your body is burning energy more quickly. Theoretically, you need more calories than normal. But it's hard to eat when you have a cold because your sense of taste, which is linked to your ability to smell the food you eat, is out of whack. In addition, people who are running a fever may also have an upset stomach.

The usual compromise, therefore, is to pass up the food and take enough liquids to prevent dehydration. The liquids will also keep mucous membranes in your nose moist, making it easier for you to clear your nose and cough up mucus from your throat. How much is enough? The most common recommendation is eight glasses a day. Which liquid you choose is irrelevant. Chicken soup, though pleasantly warm and tasty, is no more or less effective than plain water or juice.

FINGERNAILS

Your fingernails keep growing after you're dead. No. Alas for all the mystery writers who made a cracking good thing out of the coffin opened to show a corpse with fingernails two or three inches long, the truth is that your nails stop growing when you draw your last breath. But the tissue (cuticle) around the nail shrinks after death, and that may make the nails look longer.

Fingernails grow faster in the summer than in the winter. True. The average healthy fingernail grows at the rate of 0.5 to 1.2 millimeters a week. (Toenails grow about one-third as fast.) The rate does speed up a bit in the summer, as well as during pregnancy or when the nail is injured, but nobody is sure why.

Biting your nails will make them grow more slowly. No, but biting your nails down to the quick can reduce the length of the nail from the cuticle to the tip so that if you do stop biting and let the nail grow free, it may not be as strong or flexible as it would have been had you never bitten it.

Drinking gelatin makes your nails strong. Like claws, hooves and horns, nails are made of keratin, a protein. Because gelatin is pure protein, extracted from animal bones, skin and hides, it's logical to think that eating it would strengthen your nails. Logical, but wrong. The proteins in gelatin are incomplete. They lack the essential amino acid tryptophan (destroyed when the hides, bones and skin are processed) and are deficient in several other essential amino acids, including lysine. As a result, drinking gelatin dissolved in liquid has no effect whatsoever on your nails.

Rub olive oil into your nails to strengthen them. It couldn't hurt. Strong healthy nails contain enough moisture (water) to keep them from cracking or splitting. But when nails lose moisture as a natural result of aging (brittle nails are common after menopause) or from exposure to harsh cleansers and other chemicals, they may begin to split or break easily. How to replace the moisture? This way: Soak your (unvarnished) nails in warm water for a few minutes, then coat them with the olive oil. Petroleum jelly (Vaseline) or a lanolin- or oil-based nail cream will do as well, serving as a temporary sealant that keeps the water from evaporating from the surface of the nail. If brittleness and splitting persist, check it out with your dermatologist. Brittle nails may also be an early symptom of such medical conditions as anemia, poor circulation, thyroid disease or psychological stress.

Nail polish keeps your nails from breathing. Like your hair, your nails are made of non-living material (except at the root/cuticle), so polishing can't suffocate them. On the contrary, so long as you are not allergic to the polish, the coating may actually offer your nails some protection against the buffeting they take in everyday life. But polish remover is very drying. Use it as infrequently as possible, touching up chips rather than removing all the polish, whenever you can.

If the skin under your nails is pale, you're anemic. Maybe. The pinkish color under your nail is created by the circulation of blood through the tiny surface blood vessels there. If the skin under the nail is very pale, that may suggest either anemia or poor circulation. The same goes for the skin inside the eyelid or in the creases of the palm of your hand. In fact, the color of the skin in these three places is considered such a reliable clue to the status of your circulatory system, that if you are scheduled for an operation requiring general anesthesia you will be required to remove all nail polish before you head for the operating room so that the surgeon can have a clear view of the nail.

Dark 'moons' at the base of the nails indicates that a person who seems to be white actually has some 'black blood' in his background. The lunula ("moon") at the base of your nail is the visible portion of the matrix, the living part of the nail behind the cuticle. Once upon a time, when people cared about such things, a dark lunula was believed to be a foolproof way to figure out whether an apparently white person had black ancestors.

In reality, the color of the skin under your nails or on the palms of your hands or the soles of your feet simply mirrors the color of the skin on the rest of your body. Light-skinned people have lighter lunulae, palms and soles than dark-skinned people. Period.

See also SKIN COLOR, TOENAILS.

FISH

Fish is brain food. A reasonable assumption. Great-grandma's faith in fish was based on the fact that saltwater fish (and vegetables grown near the sea) are rich in iodine. The thyroid gland needs iodine to make hormones vital to quick movement and thought. People who do not get enough iodine may move and think more slowly than normal, in rare cases, appearing retarded even though they are not. Today, the use of iodized salt has virtually eliminated iodine deficiency in the United States, but when it was a problem, in landlocked areas, such as the Mid-West, salt-water fish remedied the deficiency and eliminated the mental fog.

Modern nutritionists have another reason to call fish "brain food." According to Judith J. Wurtman, Ph.D., research scientist at Massachusetts Institute of Technology, eating high protein, low fat, no carbohydrate foods may increase alertness by providing to your brain the amino acids it needs to create chemicals that make you more alert.

Brain cells transmit signals through chemicals called neurotransmitters. Two neurotransmitters, dopamine and norepinephrine, are "alertness" chemicals that can make you feel energized. The most important amino acid in these neurotransmitters is tyrosine which is found in high protein, low fat, no carbohydrate foods such as lean meat, skinless chicken, egg whites, and, of course, fish.

See also PSORIASIS.

FLEAS

Feed your dog brewer's yeast to chase his fleas away. A high-yeast diet might work for you, say veterinarians in the dermatology department at the Animal Medical Center in New York, but it won't work for Fido. Human beings give off a flea-repelling odor when they excrete yeast by-products in sweat. But a dog's sweat glands are limited to his nose and paws, where fleas never light, so yeast is of very little benefit to him. Stick with flea powder, spray or shampoo.

FLUORIDATION

Fluoridated water causes cancer. Since 1945, when Grand Rapids, Minnesota, became the first city in the United States to fluoridate its water supply, a vocal minority of Americans have resisted fluoridation on the grounds that drinking fluoridated water causes cancer. Extensive research over the years by the National Cancer Institute and others has failed to turn up any evidence to support this claim. But early in 1990, the National Toxicology Program, a branch of the National Institute of Environmental Health Sciences, released the result of a study in which four male rats out of 1,360 rats and mice developed osteosarcomas (bone cancers) after being given long-term doses of fluorides 50 to 100 times higher than those consumed by human beings who drink fluoridated water. Because there was no increase in the risk of bone cancers for female rats or mice of either sex, and no increase in the incidence of other cancers in mice, the study is not regarded as conclusive by either side in this debate.

FOOD POISONING

You can tell when food is spoiled by the way it smells. Not necessarily. Although many of the organisms that spoil food and make it dangerous to eat do make the food smell bad, some do not. For example, *Clostridium botulinum*, whose toxin causes the deadly form of food poisoning called botulism, spoils food without making it smell bad.

C. botulinum, an anaerobic microbe that flourishes in the absence of air, is most likely to be found in canned or vacuum-sealed foods. As it grows, it releases gases that may actually cause a can of food to bulge outward. If you find a can bulging at the end, throw it out without opening the can; the botulinum toxin can contaminate your can opener.

Heating food protects you against food poisoning. Sometimes, yes; sometimes, no. Thorough cooking at high temperatures can kill many of the potentially dangerous bacteria and/or parasites in raw fish, poultry, pork, beef and milk. But you should never rely on reheating to make questionable leftovers or canned food safe. And no amount of cooking, regardless of the heat, will neutralize the toxins in such hazardous plants as the poisonous varieties of Amanita mushrooms, or in shellfish contaminated with the microorganisms known as "red tide," or in foods contaminated with environmental poisons such as pesticides or toxic metals.

The mold on cheese is safe to eat. It depends. Molds that are indigenous to the cheese, such as the one that grows inside blue cheese, are safe to eat. But mold that springs up uninvited on cheese should be considered potentially hazardous. The safest course: Toss out the cheese.

FOOT ODOR

To prevent foot odor, line your socks with bran or oatmeal. This British folk remedy is ineffective. Plain bran or oatmeal will sop up wetness just as talcum powder does, but it isn't a deodorant and it won't prevent foot odor.

FRECKLES

Lemon juice, buttermilk or yogurt can bleach away freckles.
Each of these alleged freckle removers is an acid with a mild bleaching effect, but none is strong enough to make your freckles disappear. In addition, lemon juice is an irritant that can damage sensitive skin.

Note: You dermatologist should examine any "freckle" that gets bigger or darker to rule out an early skin cancer.

FRIED FOODS

Eating fried foods gives you acne. No such link has ever been proven.

FROSTBITE

Rub a frostbitten area with snow. Definitely not. Frostbitten skin is cold; you want to warm it up, not chill it more. Moreover, the cells in frostbitten skin are frozen and brittle. Rubbing will damage them further and may even lead to gangrene. As first aid to bring frostbitten skin back to normal temperature, the American Red Cross recommends immersing the affected area in warm (100°F-105°F) water. Never use hot water. Frostbitten skin cannot feel pain, and very hot water might scald without warning.

Frostbitten skin is pale because the cold has constricted small blood vessels on the surface. When the skin begins to turn pink, which means the blood vessels have relaxed and blood is flowing through, the temperature of the skin is returning to normal. As soon as this occurs, it is time to seek medical assistance to make sure there is no permanent damage.

When caught in the cold, stamp your feet to stay warm and ward off frostbite. When you're active, you burn calories. Burning calories creates warmth. So if your problem is staying warm while waiting for a bus, stamping your feet and moving around really will help. But there are limits to how much energy you can generate and to the cold your body can take without harm. It's all well and good to stamp your feet at that bus stop, but it's no way to stay warm in an Arctic blizzard.

Tuck your hands into your armpits to prevent frostbite. It's good common sense, says Stanley M. Zydlo, Jr., M.D., director of the Department of Emergency Medicine at Northwest Community Hospital in Arlington Heights, Illinois and co-editor of *The American Medical Association Handbook of First Aid and Emergency Care*. The skin under your arms and in your groin is the warmest surface on your body because both areas are junctions through which the major arteries run to carry warm blood from your heart out to your arms and legs.

Will keeping your hands under your arms prevent frostbitten fingers no matter how long you stay out in the cold? No. The body produces heat by metabolizing food and loses heat as warm blood circulates up to the skin where it is chilled before it comes back into the heart. Warm clothes keep you safe for a while, but if you stay outside for excessive periods of time in very cold weather, your body will eventually lose more heat than it can generate, and parts of your body, starting with your fingers, toes, ears and nose, will begin to freeze.

See also BRANDY.

G

GARLIC

Garlic protects you against germs. Probably not. Generations of Eastern and Southern European grandmothers believed that eating the smelly plant or hanging a clove around your neck would keep colds away. Alas, garlic's only known virtue as a cold preventive is the power of its aroma to keep other people, including those with colds, away from you, thus reducing your exposure to the cold virus.

Garlic prevents (or cures) cancer. An intriguing but unproven possibility. Like onions, scallions, leeks, shallots and the other members of the *Allium* family, garlic contains chemicals called allyl disulfides that give these plants their distinctive smell. Allyl disulfides appear to slow down tumor formation in laboratory animals exposed to carcinogens. Researchers at the National Cancer Institute believe that it is too early to make any definite recommendations about changing our diet, but note that there is suggestive evidence that eating allium vegetables does lower the risk of stomach cancers among human beings. Among animals, there is evidence that these vegetables also lower the risk of other kinds of cancers, too.

Garlic is good for the heart. There is growing evidence in both animals and human beings to suggest that this is true. In a 1990 address to the First Annual Congress on the Health Significance of Garlic and Garlic Constituents co-sponsored in Washington by Penn State University and the U.S. Department of Agriculture, Dr. David Kritchevsky of the Wistar Institute in Philadelphia sketched the history of research into the effect of raw garlic, garlic juice and oil of garlic on serum cholesterol levels.

In 1973 and 1975, researchers at Tagore Medical College in Udaipur, India (a country where garlic is a long-time folk remedy for heart disease), fed male volunteers a diet that included 3.5 ounces of butter a day. The men who got the butter alone had an average 16 point rise in serum cholesterol; those who were given garlic oil or garlic along with the butter had an average drop of 15 to 16 points in their cholesterol levels.

Two years later, in 1977, Dr. Kritchevsky fed laboratory rabbits with atherosclerosis (blocked blood vessels) corn oil plus garlic oil and found that the oils reduced the blockage by as much as 31%.

In 1987, researchers at Loma Linda University in Loma Linda California, reported the results of a study in which 15 volunteers (including eight vegetarians) followed their regular diet plus 1,000 mg of deodorized garlic a day for six months, while a control group of 12 volunteers (six vegetarians) who also followed their regular diet got no garlic. At the end of six months, cholesterol levels for the people who got the garlic dropped 36 to 78 points; while the controls lost at most three points. No one knows exactly how the garlic works, or exactly how much garlic is an effective dose. For now, experts caution that large amounts of garlic may cause digestive upset, skin irritation, and, occasionally, allergic reactions.

Garlic stimulates digestion. The oils in the garlic bulb are carminatives, agents that break up and expel gas from the intestines. Some people think of this as an aid to digestion; others call it an embarrassment.

See also ONIONS.

GAS, INTESTINAL

Eating dried beans makes you gassy. True. Dried beans are wonderful food: cheap, high in protein and carbohydrates, with very little fat. Unfortunately, they also contain raffinose, stachyose and other complex carbohydrates (sugars) that are unaffected by the digestive enzymes in the human mouth and stomach. As a result, these sugars move undigested to the lower part of the gastro-intestinal tract (the colon), where resident bacteria begin to digest them. As by-products of this digestive process, the bacteria produce hydrogen, carbon dioxide and methane. In a word, gas.

One way to reduce the gas production associated with eating beans is to remove some of the complex carbohydrates by soaking the beans before you cook them. Because the troublesome sugars leech out into hot water, experts at the U.S. Department of Agriculture say you can reduce the sugars in the beans by as much as 80% by covering the beans with water, bringing the water to a boil for a few minutes, then turning off the heat and letting the beans soak for four hours. Drain the beans before using in your recipe, and the sugars will float off down the kitchen sink. Remember, it's vital to bring the water to a boil. Soaking in cold water for as long as eight hours would only remove about 2% of the sugars, about 40 times less what you take out with the hot-water soak.

Other foods known to promote the formation of intestinal gas are the cruciferous vegetables (brussels sprouts, broccoli, cabbage, cauliflower, radishes); apples, apricots, citrus fruits, prunes; bran and whole wheat products; milk; and the sugar substitutes sorbitol and mannitol.

The older you get, the more likely to are to have gas. Maybe. The digestion of carbohydrate foods starts in the mouth, where specialized digestive enzymes in saliva begin to break down the carbohydrates. As we get older, saliva production slows, the supply of enzymes drops and more carbohydrate foods go untouched to the intestines, where they are digested by bacteria that produce gas as a by-product. The greater the amount of undigested carbohydrates the bacteria have to work on, the more gas they make.

See also CHEWING.

GERMAN MEASLES (RUBELLA)

If a pregnant woman catches German measles, her baby will be born with birth defects. Whether or not a baby born to a woman who has rubella while pregnant will be damaged by the virus seems to depend on when the woman gets sick.

According to *The Merck Manual,* as many as half of the children born to women who have rubella during the first eight weeks of pregnancy will develop the disease, and an infected fetus' risk of being damaged by the rubella virus is about 85% in the first two months of pregnancy. Only 10% of the children born to women who get rubella in the fourth month of pregnancy will develop the disease. By the fifth month of pregnancy, the fetus' risk of being damaged by its mother's rubella has dropped virtually to zero.

GIN

Gin spiked with pepper is an aphrodisiac. Pepper contains irritating oils that are eliminated from the body through the urinary tract. As they pass through, they may create an uncomfortable burning sensation. Some people, masochistic people to be sure, might mistake the urinary irritation caused by the pepper for sexual arousal. Boy, are they wrong.

See also MARTINIS.

GINSENG

Ginseng increases sexual potency and slows down the aging process. Like the mandrake root, the ginseng root sometimes looks faintly humanoid, with a long "trunk" and "legs" branching off at the bottom. For centuries, this resemblance to the human body gave Chinese ginseng *(Panax ginseng)* a totally unproven reputation as a nerve tonic, heart stimulant, aphrodisiac and general all-around health and anti-aging potion.

Virtually all information about the supposed healing properties of ginseng comes from anecdotal evidence rather than from well-controlled scientific studies. Just about the only thing science knows for sure about the beneficial effects of ginseng is that it makes a nice tea, a use for which it has been approved by the Food and Drug Administration.

However, some side effects of ginseng have been identified. For example, the herb liberates histamine, which can make tissues swell, so it may be hazardous for people with asthma or emphysema. Because ginseng contains chemicals similar to estrogen, some researchers attribute estrogen-like effects to the plant. A few studies have suggested that consuming large amounts of ginseng may cause painful breast enlargement, lumps in the breast or vaginal bleeding.

GLAUCOMA

Seeing halos around a light at night means you have glaucoma. It may. Glaucoma is characterized by increased pressure inside the eyeball that causes a slow, progressive loss of vision. One symptom of this increasing pressure is seeing halos around bright electric lights. Others include frequent changes in eyeglass prescriptions, continuing mild headaches and a newly developed difficulty in seeing when you walk from a bright room into a darkened one.

Glaucoma is a condition of old age. In most cases, yes. But increased pressure inside the eyeball may (rarely) appear in newborns as the result of a congenital defect in the eye. Prompt surgical treatment to remedy the defect may preserve the baby's vision.

GOUT

Gout is a man's disease. True, by a margin of nine-to-one. Gout is a form of arthritis that often runs in families. People with gout seem to inherit a reduced ability to excrete uric acid, a by-product of the metabolism of purines, a substance in proteins. As a result, uric acid crystals begin to collect in joints, particularly the joint of the big toe. There, they break down into an inflammatory substance called sodium urate. It is sodium urate that precipitates the painful inflammation characteristic of an acute attack of gout.

No one has yet identified a "gout gene," but the tendency to high blood levels of uric acid appears to be either gender- or hormone-related. As a general rule, men have higher blood levels of uric acid than women do, and post-menopausal women (the women most likely to develop gout) have higher blood levels of uric acid than do women who have not yet gone through menopause.

Gout is a rich man's disease. Only in the sense that foods such as anchovies and pates which are high in purines once graced the tables only of the rich. The hole in the argument is the fact that modern medicine has come to downgrade the importance of a link between what you eat and whether or not you get gout. Increasing the consumption of purine-rich foods doesn't seem to raise the risk of an acute attack; reducing consumption doesn't seem to lower it.

Only intelligent people get gout. True, there have been some spectacularly intelligent people on the list of gout sufferers: Alexander the Great, Charlemagne, Michelangelo, Luther, Calvin and Charles Darwin, to name a few. But linking your risk of gout to your I.Q. is as unscientific as linking your risk of gout to your bank account. Neither is a reliable risk predictor.

Saffron cures gout. Definitely not. Saffron (*Crocus sativum*), the yellow spice used in many Middle Eastern dishes, is totally un-related to meadow saffron (*Colchicum autumnale*), a poisonous plant also known as autumn crocus. Although the seeds of the meadow saffron are the source of colchicine, an alkaloid (nitrogen-containing compound) used as a drug to treat gout, every part of the meadow saffron plant is potentially lethal in the natural state. Consuming meadow saffron may cause nausea and vomiting, intense diarrhea and abdominal pain, kidney and respiratory failure, convulsions, delirium, coma and heart failure. Amateur herbalists should be exceedingly careful not to confuse it with true saffron.

H

HAIR

Shock can turn your hair white overnight. Well, not exactly white, and maybe not overnight, but shock may create a turn of events that can lead to the hair looking distinctly lighter.

We all shed some hair every day. This lost hair is gradually replaced by new growth, so that we almost never notice what's happening. However, severe emotional or physical trauma may interrupt the normal schedule of loss and replacement, accelerating the loss and slowing the replacement. If that happens, although the hair does not change color, it may look lighter for a while because the scalp is more visible through the thinner hair.

Eating organ meats, beans, shellfish, nuts, cocoa and other foods high in copper keeps your hair from turning gray. Not likely. Although gray hair is one symptom of copper deficiency in laboratory rabbits, a severe lack of copper is virtually unknown among human beings. The single exception is a baby born with Minkes syndrome, a rare hereditary metabolic disorder that impairs the body's ability to absorb copper.

See also REDHEADS.

HAIR CARE

Brush your hair a hundred times a night to make it shine. An old-fashioned idea that stems from the days when bathing and shampooing were once-a-week events. Brushing does remove dust and make your hair shinier by stimulating the oil glands in your scalp, but it also strips away the layer of scales that surround the fibrous core of the hair shaft and may split the ends so that the hair looks frizzy and unmanageable. Brushing hair while it is still wet after shampooing can be even more destructive; it can pull the hair right out of your head. The safer course is to wash your hair frequently to get rid of the dirt and massage your scalp to get those oil glands working without damaging your hair.

A natural bristle hairbrush is safer than a brush with nylon bristles. It depends on the toughness of the bristles. Some nylon bristles are so sharply edged that they can cut the hair shaft, but nylon bristles with rounded ends are considered as safe as natural bristles made from boar's hair.

Brushing your hair with nylon bristles makes it unmanageable. Maybe. Brushing with nylon bristles can create static electricity that makes the hair stand up in a halo around your head. You can reduce the effect by spraying the bristles with hair spray before you brush your hair.

An egg shampoo makes hair shine. True. In the normal course of events, the naturally smooth surface of the hair shaft can be cracked by brushing, combing and the simple fact of its drying out. The tiny cracks or damages on the surface of the hair shaft cause the shaft to reflect light unevenly so that the hair looks dull. (The damaged hair may also be dry and frizzy or "fly-away"). Eggs contains proteins that can cling to the surface of damaged hair, filling in the cracks and making the hair look smooth. At the same time, natural oils in the egg yolk make the hair shine.

Modern cosmetic shampoos use a variety of protein compounds to produce the same result, but you can make your own old-fashioned, fresh egg shampoo if you prefer by whipping a fresh egg into a few tablespoons of plain shampoo—no hair coloring tints, no conditioners, please. *Caution #1:* Make just enough for one shampoo, and be sure to discard the leftovers because the concentration of preservatives in the shampoo are not strong enough to protect the solution from bacterial contamination once you add an egg. *Caution #2:* Never use an egg shampoo if your hair is bleached or tinted blonde. Natural sulfur compounds in eggs can react with the bleach or tint to give your hair a greenish cast.

Hair grows faster in warm weather. True. So do your nails. But dandruff production slows down during the summer, and the rate of natural hair loss and replacement is highest in late fall. These phenomena, though well known, are little understood.

Hair continues to grow after death. No, but after death the soft body tissues around the hair shaft shrink and pull back so that the hair may look a little longer.

Washing your hair every day makes it fall out faster. No. Like your skin, your hair gets dirty every day, probably more so in the city (or anywhere there is ambient dirt in the air) than in the country. Frequent washing simply keeps it clean.

Frequent cutting makes your hair grow thicker. Alas, no. Every hair on your body grows out of its own individual tiny hair follicle. To make your hair look thicker you would have to increase the number of hair follicles on your scalp. That you cannot do. But frequent trimming gets rid of the split ends that can make hair look "thin" and frizzy, and a well-shaped haircut can make your hair look thicker and fuller.

Singe your hair to 'seal in the nutrients.' Every single hair on your head is a hollow tube of dead cells; there are no nutrients to seal inside. Worse yet, hitting the end of the hair with a hot iron to singe it splits the ends and makes the hair look frizzed.

See also LEMONS, VINEGAR.

HANDS

Cold hands, warm heart. This piece of folk wisdom says less about any individual woman's romantic nature than it does about the fact that women of childbearing age may be mildly anemic because they lose blood while menstruating and do not consume sufficient amounts of iron-rich foods. People who are mildly anemic often feel chilly, and their hands and feet may feel "tingly" or intermittently numb; thus the maxim.

HANGOVER

Drinking whiskey gives you a worse hangover than drinking vodka. Some alcoholic beverages, such as bourbon, blended whiskeys, rum and brandy, contain relatively high concentrations of flavoring agents called congeners that seem to play a role in causing some of the discomfort associated with a hangover. Vodka has significantly smaller amounts of congeners, but the difference is not the significant factor in whether the vodka you drink gives you a hangover.

What matters is how much you drink. The body metabolizes alcohol through the action of a specific enzyme, alcohol dehydrogenase (ADH). An average-size adult can produce enough ADH to metabolize the amount of alcohol in one drink in about one to two hours. When more alcohol is consumed than the body can metabolize, the unmetabolized alcohol begins to build up in the bloodstream. This excess, unmetabolized alcohol interferes with your liver's ability to metabolize fats; decreases your absorption of water from your kidneys and increases urination; raises the level of lactic acid in your muscles, which makes you irritable; causes the blood vessels in your head to swell and throb; and irritates the lining of your stomach. In short, a hangover.

Taking two aspirin before you drink can prevent a hangover later. False. Worse yet, the results of a study released in 1990 by researchers at the Bronx Veterans Affairs Medical Center and the Mount Sinai School of Medicine in New York suggest that aspirin consumed with food before drinking alcoholic beverages may actually increase the effects of the alcohol. In laboratory studies with both animals and human beings, the aspirin appears to reduce the action of gastric alcohol dehydrogenase, an enzyme that helps to oxydize alcohol and prevent it from entering the bloodstream. With enzyme activity lowered, more alcohol flows into the bloodstream, raising the blood alcohol level and increasing the effects of the alcohol.

Vitamins cure a hangover. Alas, no. Vitamins are no more effective than any other home remedy against a hangover. The only true cure is time, which allows your body to produce sufficient quantities of ADH to metabolize the alcohol and excrete it from your bloodstream.

Raw eggs, tomato juice, milk, salty foods, spicy foods (you name it) cures a hangover. No dice. See above.

The 'hair of the dog that bit you' cures a hangover. True, but only temporarily. Alcohol is a sedative that really can calm the jumpy nerves that are one symptom of a hangover. But it also puts alcohol back into your system, starting anew the cycle that led to your hangover.

HATS

To keep colds at bay, put on a hat. Wearing a hat won't necessarily protect you from colds, but it will definitely make you more
comfortable in cold weather.

When you are exposed to the cold weather, your body attempts to
conserve warmth by constricting the small blood vessels in your arms,
hands, legs and feet so that less blood flows up from the warm center
of your body, where it will be chilled on the surface of the skin and
then chill your body as it circulates back.

The blood vessels in your head (face and scalp) do not constrict as
efficiently as other surface blood vessels. As a result, you may lose
between 7% and 55% of your total body heat from your head. How
much heat you lose depends on how hard you are working or exercising. The harder you work, the more blood circulates to your head
and the more heat is lost.

Wearing a hat cuts this heat loss. A face mask will reduce the loss
of heat from your face. It will also reduce the stress cold weather
imposes on your heart. Here's why: When you inhale cold air, nerve
endings in your nose, throat and upper respiratory tract signal the
blood vessels in your heart to contract in an effort to slow blood
circulation to the skin surface and preserve body warmth. A face
mask that warms the air you breathe will reduce this effect.

See also COLDS.

HEADACHE

*A vinegar-soaked compress on your forehead cures a head-
ache.* Maybe. In medicine, irritating substances (called "counter-ir-
ritants") are sometimes applied to the skin in an effort to divert the
patient's attention from his pain. That's the principle behind some
over-the-counter arthritis remedies that make the skin feel warm. If
yours is a tension headache caused by tightened muscles on the side
of your face, the irritant fumes from the vinegar compress may be
enough to take your mind off the pain and allow the muscle spasm
to subside.

*Press the white side of a lemon peel against your head to
cure a headache.* Another counter-irritant. But this one should be
used with caution because the oils in the lemon peel are potential

allergens. If your skin reddens or itches under the peel, take it off immediately.

See also MIGRAINE.

HEART, BROKEN

She died of a 'broken heart.' This romantic cliché is one way to explain what happens when a person dies soon after the death or estrangement of a loved one—a spouse, a sweetheart, a child or a close friend. While it's true that the heart never actually "breaks," it's also true that the psychological effects of loss can impact on body systems, causing stress and/or a loss of immune function that really does hasten a person's demise. Some studies do show an increased death rate among widows and widowers in the year after the spouse's death; others show no such effect.

HEART DISEASE

Women have a natural protection against heart disease. It certainly seems that young women do. First, women have a life-long advantage in that they are more likely than men to have high levels of high-density lipoproteins (HDL), the protective fat and protein particles that carry cholesterol out of the body. Second, during their childbearing years, women produce large amounts of the female hormone, estrogen, which appears to offer added protection against heart disease. As a result, figures compiled by the National Center for Health Statistics show that among Americans age 20 to 34, four times as many men as women die of coronary heart disease; from age 35 to 64, the ratio is slightly less than two-to-one. After age 65, however, the numbers begin to level off. By age 75, deaths from heart disease are nearly equally divided between men and women.

See also BRANDY, CHOLESTEROL, GARLIC, ONIONS, SEXUAL INTERCOURSE.

HEIGHT

Every generation of Americans is taller than the one before. Not anymore. This delightful fact of American history was much beloved by the makers of motion pictures who created a virtual visual cliché out of the (short) immigrant father and his (tall) "American" son. What lay behind the cliche was the simple fact that until the middle of the 1950s, every succeeding generation of American children got a better, more balanced, more nutritious diet than the generation before it. The natural result was bigger, taller, stronger people. When our diet more or less stabilized after World War II, so did the growth rate. American children born to American parents are no longer noticeably taller than their mothers and fathers. Of course, new immigrant parents may, once again, find themselves looking up in awe at their bigger, taller children. The same thing has happened in other countries, such as Israel, where continued waves of immigration are still the rule.

HEMOPHILIA

Only men get hemophilia. Hemophilia is a genetic defect transmitted through a gene carried on the X chromosome, one of the two chromosomes (X and Y) that determine our gender. Men have one X and one Y chromosome; women have two X chromosomes. Therefore, if a man inherits an X chromosome with the hemophilia gene from his mother, he will be an hemophiliac. A woman who inherits an X chromosome with the hemophilia gene from one parent can still be protected by the normal X chromosome she gets from the other. (All women who inherit an X chromosome with the hemophilia gene are carriers who can pass the chromosome to their children.)

Only a woman who inherits an X chromosome with the hemophilia gene from both parents will develop hemophilia; the number of women who get two such X chromosomes is very small.

People with hemophilia can bleed to death from a pinprick. Not likely. People with hemophilia lack or are deficient in one or more "clotting factors," natural substances that enable blood to clot. It is true that people with hemophilia will continue to bleed from a pinprick longer than a person without hemophilia, but this kind of bleeding is not truly dangerous. The real problem hemophiliacs face is bleeding from a massive wound or during surgery or uncontrolled bleeding under the skin or into a joint that might eventually destroy the joint and cripple the patient.

Hemophilia is a 'royal' disease. Hemophilia's reputation as a disease of kings and queens derives from its higher-than-normal occurrence among Queen Victoria's children and grandchildren. Because none of her ancestors had suffered from hemophilia, it is believed that Victoria had a mutated gene, which she passed to her son, Prince Leopold, who developed hemophilia, and her daughters, Princesses Alice and Beatrice, who were carriers.

Alice's daughter Alix (later Alexandra) married Nicholas, the last tsar of Russia, and gave birth to the most famous of the royal hemophiliacs, the tsarevich Alexis. Alexis's illness is often considered a contributing factor to the Russian Revolution because his suffering made his mother a willing disciple of Rasputin, whose presence is said to have calmed the child and eased his bleeding episodes but also to have inflamed the revolutionary climate by urging the Czar to avoid compromise with his critics. Royals and revolutions aside, however, hemophilia is a distressingly democratic condition that strikes wherever the gene occurs.

HEMORRHOIDS

Being pregnant causes hemorrhoids. No, but being pregnant may accelerate the development of varicosities in women who are predisposed to develop them.

During the first few months of pregnancy, a woman's body releases hormones that make the walls of her blood vessels dilate more easily, the better to accommodate the increased blood supply for mother and fetus. This can create swelling in the veins of the legs (varicose veins) or around the anus (hemorrhoids). Once the pregnancy ends, many of these swollen veins return to normal; some do not.

HERBAL TEAS

Herbal teas are safer and more nutritious than ordinary tea. Not necessarily. Many people prefer herbal teas because they are caffeine-free. But it is important to remember that what makes so many herbal remedies useful is the fact that the herbs contain pharmacologically active ingredients that may be harmful if misused.

For example, the foxglove plant is the source of digitalis, a potent cardiac medicine, but tea brewed from foxglove is poisonous and can be lethal. Even ordinarily harmless herbs may cause problems for some people. Chamomille tea can make blonde hair shine, but it is also a potential allergen for people sensitive to ragweed.

A Representative List of Hazardous Herbs Once Used as Food or Medicine but Now Considered Unsafe as Food or Home Remedy

---

Arnica (once known as bane or mountain tobacco)
belladonnna (deadly nightshade)
bittersweet (bitter nightshade, felonwood)
black cohosh (black snakeroot)
bloodroot (Indian paint)
blue flag (liver lily, water flag)
broom (broom tops, Irish broom, Scotch broom)
caper spurge
castor bean
cherry laurel
comfrey
foxglove
henbane (poison tobacco)
horsechestnut
jalap
jimson weed (mad apple)
lobelia (Indian tobacco, wild tobacco)
mandrake (love apple)
mayapple (American mandrake)
mistletoe
mountain laurel
pennyroyal
poison hemlock (fool's parsley)
rue
sassafras
senna
shave grass
sweet flag (calamus, flagroot)
tansy (bitter buttons)
tonka bean
Virginia snakeroot (snakeweed) .
wahoo (burning bush)
white snakeroot (snakeroot)
wintergreen (teaberry)

HICCUPS

To cure the hiccups, take a deep breath or breathe into a paper bag or take a drink of water from 'the wrong side' of the glass or have somebody scare you or swallow a teaspoon of sugar. True. The audible sign of the hiccup is the sudden expulsion of air from the mouth caused by involuntary spasms of the diaphragm accompanied by the involuntary closing of the glottis, the opening at the back of the mouth that leads into the throat.

To end the hiccups, you have to end the spasms. One way to do that is to take a really deep breath that interrupts the contractions of glottis and diaphragm. Trying to drink from the "wrong side of the glass" may distract you for a moment, so that you hold your breath, which stops the spasms. Ditto for the effects of having someone sneak up and scare you.

Breathing into a paper bag (*never* a plastic bag which is dangerous because it can cling suffocatingly to your nostrils) is a more complicated cure. It works by increasing the level of carbon dioxide in your blood. This tells your brain to signal your diaphragm to deepen its contractions so as to bring more oxygen into your body. The deepened movement of the diaphragm, once again, ends its spasm and stops the hiccups.

Swallowing a teaspoon of sugar, another classic "remedy," may work because the granules of sugar irritate the throat, interrupting the impulses from the phrenic nerve that stimulate the diaphragm, thus (hopefully) ending its spasms.

Press a cold knife or coin against the back of your neck to stop the hiccups. Ditto.

To stop the hiccups, yank (but not too hard, please) on the tongue. Okay, if chilling doesn't interrupt the impulses from the vagus nerve to the glottis, maybe a sudden (minor) physical stimulus will.

Sneeze to cure the hiccups. When you sneeze, the muscles around the glottis contract. Theoretically, the sudden contraction may interrupt the rhythmic hiccup spasms, breaking the cycle and ending the hiccups.

To stop your hiccups, sniff a very small amount of black pepper. An attempt to trigger a sneeze (above).

Hiccups are a minor problem. In most cases, yes. But hiccups that go on hour after hour, day after day, can make it hard to eat and sleep and even breathe normally. The first medical treatment for intractable hiccups is usually a stepped-up version of one of the home remedies listed above—inhalation of a mixture of carbon dioxide and oxygen instead of breathing from a paper bag or stomach washing instead of drinking a glass of cold water.

If the hiccups persist, sedatives may be used in an attempt to slow and stop the glottal and diaphragmic contractions. If these measures fail, doctors may try to block the impulses from the phrenic nerve with injections of procaine, a local anesthetic, or by cutting the phrenic nerve, but there have been cases in which not even these measures were able to stop the spasms.

HOMOSEXUALS

Homosexuals can't have children. Of course they can. So long as a woman's ovaries are releasing one mature egg each month or a man's body is producing sufficient quantities of viable sperm, sexual preference has no effect on fertility.

HONEY

Honey is a 'safe' sweetener for people with diabetes. Every time you eat, your pancreas secretes insulin, a hormone your body needs in order to use glucose, the ultimate fuel derived by metabolizing food. What makes people with diabetes different is that they either produce no insulin at all or cannot effectively use the insulin they do make. As a result, their bodies cannot use or store glucose, so it continues to circulate in their blood until it is filtered out by the kidneys. That's why people with diabetes have high levels of sugar in their urine.

Because both table sugar (refined white sugar) and honey contain sucrose, a disaccharide ("double sugar") made of one molecule of fructose and one molecule of glucose, the body sees them as equals. Both are restricted on a diet for people with diabetes.

Honey has more nutrients than plain white sugar. Honey does have small amounts of some minerals such as calcium, phosphorus and potassium (table sugar has none), but the quantities are so small as to have no nutritional significance in a normal, balanced diet.

HOT WEATHER

Cool your wrists to cool your body. The idea is that if you cool the blood at a pulse point, the cooled blood will circulate from there through your body, cooling down everything as it goes. It's an attractive concept, but it won't work. Running cool water or an ice cube over the pulse point in your wrist will cool your wrist, but to cool down the rest of you, you need to immerse your entire body in a cool bath or shower.

To keep cool in warm weather, wear white. The theory behind this one has always been that white clothes reflect the sun's heat away from your body while black draws it in. However, a study conducted by Harvard scientists in 1986 showed that wearing black clothes may be more effective if the black clothes are as loose and swirling as a Bedouin's robes.

It's not that the white doesn't reflect the heat away. It does. Nor is it that the black doesn't draw the heat in. It does.

But the extra heat drawn in by the black clothes appears to create a chimney effect inside the garments, pulling air up and out from the bottom of the garment so that perspiration evaporates more quickly, and there is, believe it or not, a higher net heat loss than there would be if you were wearing the same loose clothes in white. Presumably, the same effect would hold for swirly skirts and pajama-like pants; there are no rulings on tee-shirts and shorts.

Everyone should take salt tablets in hot weather. In a word, no. Salt tablets, which usually contain ordinary table salt (sodium chloride) plus potassium, were once routinely prescribed in hot weather to protect against the loss of large amounts of sodium in perspiration or through urination. They are no longer widely used because they can make you sick to your stomach (if you vomit, you'll lose even more salt) and because excess salt may be hazardous to anyone with heart disease or high blood pressure. To prevent serious salt loss, have some pretzels or salty crackers with each glass of water or drink iced bouillon.

As first aid in cases of heat cramps (muscle spasms caused by the loss of salts and water) or heat exhaustion (pale moist skin, headache, nausea, dizziness and vomiting caused by a loss of salt *and* water), the American Red Cross recommends cold packs or cool wet towels to cool the victim down, and then if he or she is fully conscious, half a glass of water every 15 minutes for an hour. Victims of heat stroke, a medical emergency during which the body loses its ability to control its internal temperature, require immediate medical treatment to cool the body.

I

ICE CREAM

Eating ice cream makes your head ache. It may. If you are
sensitive to cold, the "ice cream headache" usually begins when you
bite into an ice cream cone or when a spoonful of ice cream comes
in contact with the roof of your mouth. The pain is caused by the
sudden stimulation of the ninth cranial nerve (which carries sensations from the back of the mouth) and the fifth cranial nerve (which
carries sensations from the front of the mouth). To ease the pain, curl
your warm tongue back against the top of your mouth. Or you may
be able to avoid the headache entirely by letting the ice cream melt a
bit before you put it in your mouth.

Eating ice cream makes you cough. True again. A cough begins with a deep breath, followed by the constriction of the glottis
(the opening from the back of your mouth into your throat), the re-
laxation of the diaphragm and then muscle contractions that push air
back up the throat against the glottis. The result is an explosive expulsion of air, creating the sound and movement we call a cough.
Eating very cold foods or drinking very cold beverages or breathing in very cold air may all trigger this sequence of events through
stimulation of nerves in the roof and back of your mouth.

Ice cream is junk food. Aw, c'mon. Ice cream is made from
milk, so it contains all the nutrients found in milk, including protein,
calcium and vitamin A. In fact, ounce for ounce, ice cream has more
vitamin A than whole milk. Unfortunately, ice cream is also high in
fat, but people who want to reduce the amount of fat and cholesterol
they get from frozen desserts can switch from ice cream to ice milk.
(Lowfat frozen yogurts may be similar in content to ice milk but they
are quite variable.)

| Comparing the Nutrients in One Serving (4 fluid oz)* | | | |
	Whole Milk	Skim Milk	Ice Cream**	Ice Milk***
Calories	75	43	135	92
Protein (g)	4	4	3	3
Fat (g)	4	0.2	7	3
Cholesterol (mg)	17	2	30	9
Carbohydrates (g)	6	6	16	15
Calcium (mg)	150	151	88	88
Vitamin C (mg)	1	1	0.4	0.4
Vitamin A (IU)	154	250	272	107

*Ordinarily rounded to the nearest whole number
**Vanilla, (11% fat) ***Vanilla, (hardened, 4%)
Source: *Composition of Food*, Dairy and Egg Products, Agriculture Handbook No. 8-1 (Washington D.C.: Agricultural Research Service, USDA, November 1976)

INFECTION

Cover a cut with wet bread to prevent an infection. This old-fashioned home remedy, now outdated by antibiotics, is a dandy example of medical folklore zipping ahead of medical fact.

Several hundred years before Sir Alexander Fleming discovered the antibacterial properties of the mold steadily chewing a path through the clumps of bacteria growing in his laboratory Petri dishes in 1928, European housewives had become accustomed to stashing a loaf of bread out of sight up in the rafters or down in the cellar to let it mold away until somebody needed first aid for a cut or scrape.

Then the loaf was brought out, a slice was cut, mashed to a paste with water and smeared over the injury. When the folk remedy worked, it was almost certainly because the mold on the bread was, by happy accident, producing penicillin. Today, of course, it's best to leave the bread in the bread box, discard any that molds (many molds produce carcinogenic substances), and rely on common antibiotics to protect against infections.

INFERTILITY

Adopt a child to combat infertility. A myth. Some previously infertile couples do conceive after adopting a child, but that's coincidence, not magic. In fact, approximately 5% of all previously infertile couples eventually conceive on their own whether or not they adopt a child or seek medical treatment for their reproductive problems.

Mistletoe is a remedy for infertility. The ancient Druids considered mistletoe a sacred plant, and British folklore held that beverages made from the plant would cure infertility. Little wonder, then, that we still consider it lucky to kiss under a sprig of bright red berries at Christmas. But modern science says that kissing underneath the sprig is as close as we should get to using the plant to boost fertility. Mistletoe's leaves as well as its berries are poisonous. Be sure to hang the branch high, well of out reach of children and pets.

Infertile men do not produce any sperm. Except in very unusual cases, all adult men produce some sperm. The question is, how many?

Ordinarily, a fertile man ejaculates 60 million to 120 million sperm per milliliter of seminal fluid. However, men with sperm counts are as low as 20 million sperm per milliliter of seminal fluid have been able to impregnate their partners if their sperm are healthy and able to move quickly through the vaginal canal and up past the cervix into the uterus to meet the waiting egg.

Wearing boxer shorts rather than athletic briefs improves a man's fertility. Not necessarily, but it is true that warmth, even the warmth produced by wearing very tight underwear, can temporarily impede sperm production and may temporarily reduce fertility.

INSECTICIDES

Insecticides cause cancer. There is no general rule to this one. Some chemicals used to kill insects are carcinogenic, but others, such as 1,1'-(2,2,2–Trichloroethylidene)bis[4–chlorobenzene], the pesticide better known by the initials DDT, are not.

INSOMNIA

Exercise wards off insomnia. True, but timing is all. Exercise in the afternoon or early evening can make us feel better and seems to increase deep sleep later at night, but exercise right before bedtime can work the opposite way, making us too bouncy to fall asleep.

See also ALCOHOLIC BEVERAGES.

IODINE

Painting a cut with iodine makes it sterile. Hardly. A swipe with the iodine applicator may eliminate the bacteria in the immediate area, but the bacteria that live naturally on everyone's skin will move right back in again.

To tan safely, rub iodine and baby oil on your skin before going out in the sun. A bad idea. The iodine will stain your skin temporarily, but it won't protect you against the sun's burning rays. Neither will the baby oil, which is nothing more than mineral oil. For a golden look without spending time in the sun, choose a cosmetic "bronzer." For protection in the sun, choose an adequate sunblock.

I.Q.

Your I.Q. tells you how smart you are. Not necessarily. The I.Q. (intelligence quotient) is a score that shows how your performance on a standard test compares with the performance of other people your own age. A score of 100 is average, so a score higher than 100 says that you do better than the average person; a score lower than 100 says that you do worse.

But an I.Q. test does not measure either creativity or adaptive behavior. Nor, as the eminent geneticist Theodore Dobzhansky is reported to have said, does it measure "cleverness, aptitude or wit. Still less does the I.Q. give an estimate of the value or worth of the person." Finally, some people think I.Q. tests are culturally biased. As science reporter Anthony Smith writes in *The Body,* "a chimpanzee will only start scoring well on intelligence tests when another chimpanzee has set them."

A child's I.Q. is a good indicator of how well he or she will do later in life. Although your I.Q. as a child may be a fair predictor of what your I.Q. will be when you grow up, it is a poor predictor of whether or not you will be successful in your life and career. In fact, according to a 1976 study at Fels Research Institute in Yellow Springs, Ohio, there is only a 60% chance that a child's I.Q. at age seven will accurately predict his or her performance later in life.

Nevertheless, many educators still base their evaluation of children on an I.Q. test at age seven or even younger, which means large numbers of children are invariably short-changed as regards expectations about their abilities to succeed as adults.

I.Q. stays the same throughout life. Probably not. A wealth of external conditions, including your home life, your health, your diet and, above all, your experience, may affect your performance on an I.Q. test.

IRON DEFICIENCY

Unless she eats some red meat, a woman of child-bearing age can't get sufficient quantities of iron from food alone. That may turn out to be true. Non-heme iron (the form of iron found in plants) is harder for us to absorb than heme iron, the form of iron found in meat, fish and poultry. Even with fortified cereals and bread, it's difficult for a woman of childbearing age to get the iron she needs from food if she gives up red meat.

Vegetarians have always disputed that, citing a plethora of scientific studies showing no significant difference in the incidence of iron deficiency anemia between meat eaters and vegetarians like the Seventh Day Adventists. It now seems possible, however, that these older studies did not show a true picture because they were derived from tests less sensitive than those currently available.

According to researchers at the U.S. Department of Agriculture (USDA) Human Nutrition Research Center in Grand Forks, North Dakota, when you test for iron deficiency simply by measuring hemoglobin (the red pigment in blood cells where iron is used to carry oxygen), vegetarians seem no more likely than meat eaters to be iron deficient. But a more sensitive indicator of mild iron depletion is to measure the amount of iron-protein complexes called ferritin in her blood. The level of blood ferritin indicates the amount of iron stored in the body. A vegetarian's ferritin level is usually lower than a meat-eater's. As a result, her body will absorb the iron from plant foods more efficiently in an attempt to build up body stores, a common reaction among people who have low iron reserves but are not overtly iron deficient.

See also POTS AND PANS.

ITCH

Scratching soothes an itch. Clearly, the answer is yes. This is the scientific explanation: We detect an itch with the same nerve endings in the skin that detect pain. When we scratch, the pain we provoke sends a message to the brain that fleetingly overrides the sensation of the itch. Engaged by the "pain" of the scratch, the brain ignores the lesser sensation of the itch.

Hot (or cold) compresses relieve an itch. They are certainly worth a try. Like scratching, icy cold or hot compresses overload the sensors in our skin, fooling the brain into "forgetting" a localized itch.

When you're itchy, bathe in oatmeal. Exactly how it works remains a medical mystery, but an oatmeal bath is an effective remedy for some kinds of itches, particularly those caused by weepy wet rashes. Before stepping into the bath, be sure to check with your doctor to make certain that your itch will not be exacerbated by the drying oatmeal. If you get the go-ahead, be sure to use a commercial product that contains "colloidal oatmeal," a form of oatmeal that will be evenly suspended through the liquid when you add water (regular oatmeals may clump in the tub). Finally, rinse very thoroughly after soaking. Oatmeal left to dry on your skin will only make you more itchy.

J

JADE

Close the openings of the body with jade to keep a dead body from decaying. In Chinese tradition, jade is credited with conferring immortality on those who wear it, and during the era of the Han dynasty (206 B.C.–A.D. 221), wealthy Chinese families put pieces of jade jewelry at the mouth, nose, eyes, ears and other body orifices of their dead in the belief that this would keep the bodies from putrefying. Alas, the jade had no effect at all on the bodies, which turned to dust as corpses must. But the decomposing bodies did change the appearance of the jade, turning it chalky white in the tombs. What happened? Simple. As body tissues liquefy, they produce ammonia solutions. In the confines of the tomb, these solutions ate away at the jade, producing the discoloration.

JELLYFISH

Bathe jellyfish stings in sea water to relieve the pain. Sea water neutralizes the irritant in stingers left in your body when a jellyfish or man-of-war attacks. So does rubbing alcohol. Please note that fresh water, i.e., water from the tap, will not soothe the sting. Instead it may make things worse by setting off stingers that are embedded in your skin but haven't yet released their irritating chemicals. Stubborn stingers may have to be scraped off, perhaps with a stiff object such as a credit card.

Caution: Forget the home remedies and head straight for the emergency room if you know you are allergic to insect venom or if you develop ANY warning sign of allergic (anaphylactic) shock such as headache, shortness of breath, or gastric upset after being stung by a jellyfish or any other denizen of the sea.

K

KISSING

Kissing an injury can make the hurt go away. What, you have doubts about this? Are you also against motherhood and apple pie? Shame on you for not knowing that tender loving care can soothe most minor (and some major) aches and pains. The scientist might say it works by signaling the brain to release natural painkillers called endorphins; the sentimentalist knows it works by magic.

Kissing spreads germs. It depends on the germ. An exchange of saliva through kissing is an efficient way to spread some germs such as the ones that cause herpes, mumps and infectious hepatitis, but it is a poor way to spread the virus that causes the common cold because the cold virus does not thrive in the relatively cool environment in your mouth.

See also COLDS.

L

LARD

To heal a sprain, wrap it in chilled lard. This quintessential country remedy is messy but sound. Cold compresses such as an ice pack or even cold lard make small blood vessels under the skin and torn tissue cells around a sprain (an injury to a ligament) or a strain (an injury to a muscle) constrict. This may help to slow the bleeding into the skin that causes black-and-blue marks and reduce the loss of fluid from torn cells that creates swelling at the site of the injury.

LEMONS

Watching someone suck a lemon will make your mouth pucker. True. For some people, just thinking about sucking on a lemon can have the same effect. The sudden inability to produce enough saliva is a conditioned reflex, similar to that experienced by Russian physiologist/psychologist Ivan Pavlov's famous dogs, who were conditioned to salivate involuntarily at the sound of a bell they had learned to associate with dinner.

LEMON JUICE

After a shampoo, rinse your hair with lemon juice to make it shine. A good idea. Lemon juice is an acid that can dissolve the dulling alkaline residues left on the hair by soaps or an alkaline shampoo or hard water loaded with alkaline minerals. Acids such as lemon juice also help smooth down the tiny scale-like structures on the outer surface of the hair shaft that are ruffled up when you wash your hair.

As your hair dries, these tiny scales are left standing up every which way, so that when light hits your hair, it reflects off in dozens of different directions. The practical result is that your hair looks dull instead of shiny. The lemon juice smooths down the scales and makes the surface of the hair shaft smooth so that it reflects light evenly, which makes it shiny. To make an after-shampoo lemon rinse, stir the strained juice of one lemon into an 8–ounce glass of warm water. Pour it on your hair, work it through, then rinse it off thoroughly with more warm water.

After shampooing, a lemon juice rinse makes oily hair more manageable. True. Shampoo and plain water may not dissolve the oily coating left on your hair by secretions from glands in the scalp. After shampooing, an acid lemon juice rinse helps loosen the coating so that it rinses off with clear warm water.

A lemon juice rinse lightens the hair. True, but only very mildly. For serious bleaching, turn to a commercial hair lightener.

A drop of lemon juice makes your eyes shine. Only with tears. This old-fashioned European cosmetic tip is an out-dated example of the adage that women had to suffer for beauty. Forget it.

LEMON RIND

Rub the skin with the inside of a lemon rind to get rid of freckles. It won't. While the inside of the rind is irritating and may make your skin peel, the small marks will still be there when the skin heals. *Caution:* Consult your doctor about any freckle that darkens, crusts, bleeds or enlarges to rule out the possibility of early skin cancers.

Rub the hands with the inside of a lemon rind to make them smooth. Well, there is a chance that it may produce a temporary change in skin texture. Rubbing the skin gently with a wash cloth or a loofa sponge or even the inside of a lemon rind removes the dead cells that collect naturally on the the top layer of the epidermis. As a result, the skin feels smoother for a while, or at least until a new layer of rough dead cells gathers.

LICORICE

Eating licorice soothes an upset stomach. True, but only if you are talking about candy or tea made from the root of the licorice plant, an herb generally available in health food stores. Glycyrrhizic acid, the chemical that makes the licorice root sweet, can soothe irritated skin and mucous membranes, including the membranes lining your digestive tract.

Because there is no glycyrrhizic acid in the artificial licorice flavoring used in most of the candy sold as "licorice," the imitation stuff won't work. *Caution:* If you have high blood pressure, the licorice home remedy is not for you because glycyrrhizic acid can increase your body's retention of sodium and water, thus worsening your hypertension. It may also interfere with the effectiveness of drugs used to treat heart disease.

Eating licorice cures an ulcer. No, but licorice root does contain mucilage, so it is a demulcent (an agent that soothes mucous membranes). It is also the source of carbenoxolone sodium, an experimental drug that seems to promote the healing of active ulcers.

Eating lots of licorice helps you lose weight. Not unless you consider an upset stomach a diet aid. Consuming large amounts of natural licorice may cause gastrointestinal problems such as constipation, diarrhea, and ulceration of the intestinal tract. It may also cause high blood pressure and an irregular heart beat. How much is too much? In one study, these effects occurred when volunteers were given portions of licorice equivalent to slightly more than one-half ounce per day for a 150 pound person for four weeks.

LIGHTNING

If you're outside during a lightning storm, avoid the highest place or the tallest object in the area. Good advice. Lightning is likely to hit the highest thing around, including hill tops and tall trees. For safety's sake, seek the low ground: a cave, a ditch, or just plain flat ground.

When a lightning storm strikes, avoid metal fences, metal sheds and metal sports gear, such as fishing rods and golf clubs. True. All metal objects can conduct an electrical charge.

During an electrical storm, if you feel tingly or your hair stands on end, lightning may be about to strike. True. According to the National Oceanic and Atmospheric Administration, these are warnings that lightning is about to strike in your immediate vicinity. If they occur, NOAA advises you to drop immediately to the ground.

Don't use the telephone during a lightning storm. This advice is most sensible in the country where above-ground, unprotected telephone lines can conduct the electricity right into the hand   ˥lding the telephone. In cities, where the wires are underground, the theoretical danger remains but the likelihood of its occurring is less.

You can be electrocuted if you touch a person who has been struck by lightning. No. People who have been struck by lightning may be burned, but their bodies do not harbor a stored-up electrical charge. This myth probably arises from fact that if you touch a person who is in direct contact with a live source of electricity, the current can be transmitted through his body to yours.

People who have been killed by a lightning strike can be brought back to life. Many basic body functions including heartbeat, respiration and brain activity are triggered by electrical impulses transmitted between cells. Being struck by lightning can interrupt the rhythm of these transmissions, stopping the heart and lungs. Prompt cardio-pulmonary resuscitation (CPR), the mouth-to-mouth resuscitation and heart massage routinely used to treat people whose hearts have been stopped by a heart attack, may restart the regular transmission of impulses between cells and restore heartbeat, breathing and consciousness, bringing the victim "back to life."

See also THUNDERSTORMS.

LIMES

Limes protect you against scurvy. True. So do cantaloupe, lemons, oranges, sweet and hot peppers, broccoli, potatoes, strawberries and all other foods high in vitamin C.

In 1753, Scottish naval surgeon James Lind published a groundbreaking report of an experiment on British ships that showed that feeding sailors oranges and lemons on long voyages prevented scurvy, a condition then endemic among sailors deprived of fresh fruits and vegetables for months at sea. By 1795, the link between citrus fruits and scurvy was so well established that all ships in the British Navy were henceforth required to carry a supply of limes, the citrus fruits that kept best on long voyages. And that, naturally, gave rise to the use of the word "limey" as a nickname first for British sailors and later for Englishmen in general.

M

MANDRAKE ROOT

Mandrake is an aphrodisiac. Because it has a faintly human form, with branched "legs" descending from a straight "trunk," the mandrake root (*Mandragora officinarum*) has often been credited with human qualities. The plant was once thought to scream when pulled from the earth, and eating it was believed to increase sexual desire, fertility and the chances of conception.

None of these beliefs is true. More to the point, the mandrake root is toxic. It contains the Belladonna alkaloids atropine and scopolamine, powerful drugs that can reduce the flow of saliva, nasal mucus, gastric and intestinal fluids, sweat and tears; slow down the natural movement of the intestinal tract; make your heart beat faster; cause your pupils to dilate; and increase the pressure inside your eye.

Because they block the action of acetylcholine, a chemical that transmits impulses to nerves that stimulate contractions of certain muscles, including those of the gastrointestinal tract, Belladonna alkaloids are used in medicine as effective antispasmodics to treat spastic disorders of the stomach and intestines. They may also be used in combination with anti-anxiety drugs.

MARIJUANA

Smoking marijuana is safer than smoking tobacco. Or to get right down to basics: "Smoking marijuana doesn't give you lung cancer."

Right now, nobody knows for sure whether this is true. It may take as long as 30 or 40 years of smoking cigarettes before lung cancer appears. While there is currently no hard evidence to link the use of marijuana cigarettes to lung cancer, many researchers believe that the history of heavy marijuana use in America may simply be too short to show any such effects.

Smoking marijuana makes you sexy. Although smoking marijuana can make you feel relaxed and happy, it may also interfere with a man's ability to achieve and sustain an erection. In addition, habitual use of marijuana has been shown to decrease sperm production in male laboratory monkeys and suppress the production of sex hormones in females; as yet, there are no studies to show that this happens in human beings.

MARRIAGE

Love and marriage, as it says in the song, 'go together like a horse and carriage.' Yes, but not necessarily forever. In fact, a 1975 study at Rosary College in Buffalo, New York, seemed to show that people fall more deeply in love after becoming engaged and that the intensity of their emotion continues to increase during the first three years of marriage. But after that, it's downhill all the way to year seven, when most couples seem to reach a plateau.

The love-leading-to-marriage link also seems to run in cycles. According to the 1990 edition of *The World Almanac*, there were 9.3 marriages for every 1,000 persons in the United States in 1900. In 1910, the figure was 10.3. In 1920, with the end of the First World War and the advent of an era of general prosperity, it rose to 12 marriages for every 1,000 Americans. In 1930, the beginning of the Depression sent the number down to 9.2. In 1940, with young men about to go off to war, it went up to 12.1. In 1950, during the Togetherness Era, it was to 11.1. In 1960, it went down to 8.5; in 1970 and 1980, it went up to 10.6; in 1988, down to 9.7.

The median age at which we marry has followed a similarly circular pattern. In 1890, it was 26.1 years for men and 22 years for women. By 1940, that had dropped to 22.8 for men, 20.3 for women. In 1990, census figures show that it was pretty much back to where it was about 100 years ago: just under 26 years for men and just under 24 years for women.

Married people live longer than single people. Yes. In 1990, two researchers at Princeton University released the results of a comprehensive study of death rates dating back to 1940 in 16 industrial countries that validated this long-lived bit of folk wisdom.

Comparing the death rates of single, widowed and divorced men and women with the death rates of married men and women, the researchers found that the average death rate for unmarried men was twice as high as that for married men; for unmarried women, the death rate was 1.5 times as high as that for married women. In general, the results of this study were confirmed by a second one in 1990 at the University of California, San Francisco, where a survey of 7,651 American adults showed that unmarried men age 45 to 65 who live alone or with someone other than a spouse are two times as likely to die within 10 years as men who live with their wives.

Whether the marriage advantage is due to the fact that healthy people marry or because marriage provides an opportunity to solve health problems that would otherwise lead to death remains a mystery. The researchers didn't even hazard an answer, so your guess is as good as theirs.

MARTINIS

Martinis are more potent than other alcoholic beverages. True, but it's the quantity of the alcohol not the type of the drink that makes the difference. In scientific terms, a "drink" is the amount of alcohol contained in 1.25 ounces distilled spirits or 5 ounces of wine or 12 ounces of beer. A mixed drink made with spirits usually contains 1 ounce of the spirits (gin, rum, vodka, whiskey) plus a mixer. A martini, however, may be as much as two or three ounces of plain gin or vodka flavored with a hint of vermouth.

Clearly, that packs more of a punch than a mixed drink. Dilute the martini by serving it on the rocks, and you dilute its impact a bit, but there is no way to alibi away the difference in the amount of alcohol you get from 3 ounces of gin vs. 1 ounce of some other spirits.

MASTURBATION

Masturbation makes you crazy or blind. To put it bluntly, No. But—and it's a big "but"—if you really believe that these things are true, it is always possible that your own sense of guilt about masturbating can cause any and all of the imaginative punishments men and women inflict upon themselves. Which might include skin problems and even hysterical blindness.

Masturbation makes hair grow on your palms. Not a chance. No matter how guilty you feel, you will *never* grow hair on your palms. Or on the soles of your feet, either. The skin there is totally devoid of hair follicles. No hair follicles, no hair. Period.

Masturbation 'saps a man's vital juices.' Frequent ejaculations, whether through masturbation or sexual intercourse, can temporarily reduce the number of sperm in a man's seminal fluid, but it will not interfere with potency (the ability to achieve and sustain an erection). In healthy, fertile men, simply refraining from masturbation or intercourse for a few days will restore sperm counts to normal.

Masturbation makes a man impotent. Not unless he thinks it does, in which case his own guilt feelings may interrupt the delicate sequence of events that allows him to attain and sustain an erection, which is the definition of male sexual potency.

MATURATION

Each new generation of American women matures earlier. Not according to a 1976 study of female puberty conducted by the National Institutes of Health, Massachusetts Institute of Technology and Massachusetts General Hospital. The study concluded that on the average, middle-class girls in the United States reach menarche (the first menstrual period) at exactly the same age their mothers did.

The age at which individual women reach menarche can vary wildly, from as early as nine years of age to as late as 17; the average age at menarche in the United States was exactly the same in 1943, 1954, and 1973: 12.8 years. Girls whose diet and health conditions were notably better than their mothers' did begin to menstruate earlier, but their experience was atypical.

MEAT

Eating meat makes people warlike. No, but it may make them more alert.

Brain cells transmit messages via electrical impulses and chemicals known as neurotransmitters. Three neurotransmitters, dopamine, norepinephrine and serotonin, are synthesized by the brain from the food we eat. Dopamine and norepinephrine are "alertness" chemicals: They make you feel energized and turned-on. Serotonin is a "calming" chemical; it can make you feel smooth and mellow.

Dopamine, norepinephrine and serotonin are synthesized from amino acids in protein foods, specifically tyrosine and tryptophan. Tyrosine is the most important constituent in dopamine and norepinephrine; tryptophan predominates in serotonin.

Tyrosine, tryptophan and several other amino acids are all absorbed into the brain through the same chemical pathway (receptor), but tyrosine is taken up first; tryptophan, which is the least plentiful, comes last. Thus, if you eat a meal high in protein, you will get plenty of tyrosine and your brain can produce plenty of the alertness chemicals dopamine and norepinephrine.

But eating protein won't get that tryptophan into your brain. According to research conducted by Dr. Judith Wurtman at the Massachusetts Institute of Technology in the early 1980s, the way to get tryptophan into your brain is to eat carbohydrates.

When you eat a meal that is high in carbohydrates, with very little protein, your pancreas releases insulin to help you metabolize the carbohydrates. The insulin keeps tyrosine and other amino acids circulating through your body so that your brain has open pathways through which tryptophan can enter. When it does, the brain uses it to make the calming chemical serotonin and you feel pleasantly calm and focused.

In short, while every body is slightly different in its reactions to food, the odds are that downing a steak can make you feel more energetic while dining on pasta can help you mellow out.

Eating raw meat makes you strong. Meat is a good source of heme iron, the form of iron most easily absorbed by our bodies, but there's no benefit to getting the iron from raw meat rather than cooked meat. In fact, there are definite drawbacks. Raw or undercooked meat may be contaminated with a whole slew of unfriendly organisms, including tapeworms, salmonella bacteria and the parasites that cause toxoplasmosis. All these can be killed by thorough cooking, which makes the meat safer without reducing its iron content.

It's not natural for people to eat meat. Wrong. There is a lot of evidence to suggest that early man ate more vegetables than meat, but he definitely did eat meat. In fact, the human intestinal tract is equipped to digest both plants and animals. Unlike the grasseaters (cows, horses, sheep, and so forth) whose multiple stomachs allow them to get nutrients out of foods such as hay which the human body rejects as ''insoluble fiber'' or the meat-eaters (lions, tigers, sharks) whose gut is so short that they can only get nutrients out of flesh foods, human beings can get the nutrients they need from a variety of foods, including meat. The design of our teeth reflects our ability to eat everything: Tearing tools in the front for meat, grinders in the back for plants.

Our closest animal relatives, the apes, don't eat meat. Actually, they do. According to anthropologist Marvin Harris, Ph.D., author of *The Sacred Cow and the Abominable Pig,* monkeys pick at their food not because they are picky eaters but because they are looking for scrumptious bugs (meat) among the leaves. Baboons not only eat other animals, they may pick on game as large as antelopes. Chimpanzees eat small animals, sometimes, in cannibalistic fashion, small monkeys. In fact, the only truly vegetarian primate seems to be the gentle gorilla whose proportionally longer colon allows him to ferment and digest complex plant foods.

MEAT TENDERIZERS

Meat treated with tenderizer will eat away your stomach walls. It may seem sensible to think that anything strong enough to soften up the protein fibers in raw meat is probably strong enough to do serious damage to the mucous membrane lining of your stomach. Not to worry. Papain, the papaya enzyme that is the active ingredient in meat tenderizers, is inactivated by heating. It can dissolve the proteins in raw meat—and on your skin—but it stops working when you cook the meat.

See also MOSQUITO BITES.

MEDICINE

The newest medicine is the most effective one. Not necessarily. The newer the drug, the less time there has been to evaluate the side effects that are likely to pop up uninvited when the drug is used by large groups of people, rather than the relatively small groups used in the tests required by the Food and Drug Administration to certify the drug safe and effective for sale in this country.

The history of unexpected results, ranging all the way from hair growth due to anti-hypertensives to birth defects due to a pregnant woman's use of the anti-acne medication isotretinoin (Accutane) to potentially fatal allergic reactions to penicillin, suggests that these things are more likely to surface once the new drug is introduced into the marketplace.

MENOPAUSE

Women who have gone through menopause can still get pregnant. In early 1990, researchers at the University of Southern California announced the results of a study in which four of seven post-menopausal women implanted with donated eggs fertilized with sperm from the women's husbands were able to carry and deliver healthy babies. (One of the other three women had a stillborn baby. One miscarried. The third, whose husband's sperm were defective, did not become pregnant.)

But this experiment does not change the original fact: Women who have gone through menopause no longer ovulate and thus cannot become pregnant on their own. However, menopause is a gradual event that may stretch out over several years. A woman may miss one menstrual period, then begin to menstruate again, then miss another period or two, and menstruate again, and so on until she finally ceases to menstruate.

For this reason, it is imperative that women who do not wish to become pregnant continue to use contraception until they have missed a full two years' worth of menstrual periods. After two years without ovulating and menstruating, pregnancy is highly unlikely, but, given the variability of the human body, it is still safest never to say never.

Once past menopause, a woman is no longer interested in sex. Not true. In fact, many women find that no longer having to worry about becoming pregnant makes sex after menopause more spontaneous and more enjoyable. A natural shrinkage and drying of the vaginal tissues after menopause may make intercourse less comfortable, but the problem can be solved with either estrogen supplementation or simple vaginal lubricants.

Menopause makes you fat. All human beings, male and female, tend naturally to gain weight as they get older. That includes post-menopausal women who, when they gain weight, are likely to gain it in the abdomen not on the hips or thighs, a "typical" male fat-distribution pattern that may be caused by a loss of estrogen. But it is also a fact that women who exercise and watch what they eat can avoid getting fat.

Menopause cures migraines. Curiously, for reasons which are not yet understood, it is often true that women who have suffered from migraine headaches are less likely to experience them after age 50, which fits in neatly with menopause (the average age for menopause in this country is now 52). Whether this is due to a physical or a psychological alteration is unknown.

MENSTRUATION

Women become fertile as soon as they reach menarche (the first menstrual period). Not necessarily. In some instances, there may be a gap as long as two years between menarche and the ability to conceive. However, women who do not wish to become pregnant should begin using birth control as soon as they become sexually active.

A woman can't get pregnant while she has her period. It depends on how long her period lasts. Ovulation (the release of a mature egg from the ovary) occurs at mid-cycle, approximately 14 days before menstrual bleeding begins. The egg remains available for fertilization for as long as 48 hours.

Because sperm entering the vaginal canal can live for as long as two or three days, a woman is presumed to be fertile from two days before ovulation to two days after. If the menstrual cycles are 24 or more days long, it is presumed that conception cannot occur during the first five or six days of menstrual bleeding because there is no egg available. But if the cycles are very short or so irregular that some menstrual periods are only 15 to 19 days apart, a woman might already be ovulating during the last days of her menstrual period. That means she is at risk of pregnancy if she has unprotected intercourse on these days.

Note: The length of the menstrual cycle is measured by counting from the first day of bleeding, however slight, not from the last day of the period.

Menstrual bleeding 'cleans out the bad blood.' This piece of folklore is based on the mistaken belief that the uterus stays closed tight most of the month while it fills up with "bad blood" that flows out when the cervix opens at the start of the menstrual period.

Not true. While the cervix may expand slightly during menstruation, the uterus is never "closed tight." In addition, the menstrual flow is composed of ordinary blood from vessels in the endometrium, the uterine lining that grows lush each month in preparation for the implantation of a fertilized egg. After ovulation, if no egg implants in the uterine wall, the endometrium begins to shrink back and eventually slough off, to flow out of the uterus through the vaginal canal.

The only time a woman can get pregnant is during her period. This misconception arises from the mistaken belief that the only time sperm can get into the uterus is when the cervix opens to permit the menstrual flow to escape. This is untrue; the entrance to the cervix is wide enough to permit sperm to enter at any time during the menstrual cycle.

It's unhealthy to have intercourse while menstruating. Messy, maybe; unhealthy, no. In fact, some women believe that the muscular release during an orgasm can actually relieve some menstrual cramps.

Menstrual cramps are 'all in your head.' More likely, they are in your cervix. Women who produce large clots of blood while they are menstruating are more likely than others to experience cramps as the clots move through the cervix, the opening from the uterus into the vagina. Endometriosis (the implantation and growth of uterine tissue in places outside the uterus) can make menstruation more painful. So can pelvic inflammatory disease (PID).

During her period, a woman will score poorly on any kind of physical or intellectual test. Not true. Although some women may feel that premenstrual tension or menstrual discomfort affects their ability to perform, most objective measurements show that there is no real difference in performance related to the phases of the menstrual cycle. In Olympic competitions, for example, women have won gold, silver and bronze medals regardless of where they were in their menstrual cycles at the time of the competition.

Catching a chill while menstruating causes tuberculosis. Tuberculosis is a contagious disease caused by exposure to the tuberculosis bacilli. Neither being chilled nor having your period affects your risk of acquiring this disease.

Menstruating women should not go out in the rain. A myth, based on the mistaken belief that getting chilled will stop the flow of blood.

Never eat citrus fruits or other 'acid foods' when you have your period. A myth based on the belief shared by many Latin

American women as well as women in the American south, that eating "cold" foods, such as citrus fruits, will stop the menstrual flow.

It's not safe to swim or take a bath during the menstrual period. A myth based on not one, but two misunderstandings, first that water will flow into the uterus through the supposedly "open" cervix, and second, that becoming chilled while swimming or after bathing will stop the flow of the blood.

The touch of a menstruating woman can turn milk sour. This is the quintessential old wives' tale, with more than a little anti-female prejudice thrown in besides. The fact is that anyone who touches milk with dirty hands can transfer to the liquid microorganisms, including bacteria and mold, whose uncontrolled growth turns the milk sour. Whether the dirty hands were male or female is totally irrelevant.

If a menstruating women picks up a newborn baby, the baby will develop stomach cramps. This is another version of the sour-milk story. The obvious solution is to wash your hands before picking up the baby in order to reduce the chance of passing bacteria along to the infant.

MIGRAINE HEADACHES

Women are more likely than men to suffer from migraine headaches. True, by about 10-to-1. On the other hand, men are more likely to suffer from cluster headaches, the severe and sometimes devastating headaches that comes in bunches, sometimes four or five a day, and then disappear for weeks or months or even years at a time. There is, as yet, no scientific explanation for the difference.

The more intelligent you are, the more likely you are to get migraine headaches. There is absolutely no scientific evidence to suggest a connection between intelligence and the risk of migraines, but there is plenty of circumstantial evidence to suggest that migraine headaches are more common among people with perfectionist personalities who want to be in total control of their lives as well as their surroundings.

When the barometer goes down, the incidence of migraines goes up. True. And the same thing happens when the barometer rises. Up or down, it is the change in air pressure that's the culprit.

Rainy weather triggers migraines. Not necessarily. In fact, according to researchers at the Royal Infirmary in Edinburgh, Scotland, fewer people get migraines when it's rainy or cloudy than when the weather is clear. How come? Nobody knows for sure, but scientists speculate that clouds block out the sun and eliminate visual glare, a known migraine trigger.

Drinking red wine causes migraines. It certainly seems to, say headache specialists at Queen Charlotte's Hospital in London, who also think they know why. Chemicals found in alcohol block an enzyme that normally protects us from headache. These chemicals are especially plentiful in red wine, which is why is it one of the worst offenders. White wine and brandy contain fewer of these chemical blockers; gin and vodka contain virtually none.

Migraine headaches are allergic reactions. Maybe, but there is no conclusive proof one way or the other.

Sugared coffee relieves a migraine. It may. Dr. Seymour Diamond, director of the Inpatient Headache Clinic at Louis Weiss Hospital in Chicago and founder of Chicago's Diamond Headache Clinic, says that the caffeine in coffee is a vasoconstrictor, a substance that can shrink painfully engorged cranial blood vessels. As yet, there's no science to the sugar, but headache specialists do know that low blood sugar can precipitate a migraine, which may be why these headaches often occur on the weekend when we sleep later than normal and are likely to wake up hungry.

See also MENOPAUSE.

MILK

Milk is the perfect food. Milk is an excellent source of protein and calcium, and it's enriched with vitamin D. Many babies thrive on it, and adults with digestive problems often feel better when they drink milk.

But that doesn't make milk a perfect food. It is not a good source of vitamin C and iron, and whole milk is high in saturated fat and cholesterol (skim milk is not). More important, millions of people, primarily Asians and American blacks, lack sufficient amounts of lactase, the intestinal enzyme required to digest lactose, the sugar in milk. As a result, they cannot digest the lactose, which ferments in their stomach, causing gas, cramps and diarrhea. That's probably why dairy products almost never show up in Asian cuisine. It may also be why yogurt is so popular in the Middle East. Yogurt is, in effect, predigested milk whose lactose has been broken down by the bacteria that thicken and sour the milk.

In short, milk's a good food, but far from perfect.

Adults don't need milk. False. The human body needs calcium as long as it lives. Although it was once thought that adults do not absorb calcium into their bones, it now appears that they do and that consuming a diet with adequate amounts of calcium can help protect bones well into old age. Adults who can digest milk will find it their most economical source of this important mineral. Three 8-ounce glasses of low-fat or skim milk provides 948 mg calcium, 129% of the 800-mg recommended dietary allowance (RDA) for a healthy adult. Two 8-ounce containers of low-fat yogurt provide 830 mg calcium.

'Line your stomach' with a glass of milk before an evening out and you won't become inebriated no matter how much alcohol you consume. It is an exaggeration to say that if you consume some milk before you go out you can drink as much alcohol as you want and still stay sober, but it is true that eating high-protein and/or fatty foods such as milk or cheese, which are digested more slowly than high carbohydrate foods such as alcohol, will slow your body's absorption of the alcohol.

A glass of warm milk at bedtime can help you get to sleep. Only if you have it with cookies. High carbohydrate foods are relaxing because they facilitate the body's uptake of tryptophan, a soothing amino acid. Milk has lots of tryptophan, but you need the cookies to make it possible for your body to use the amino acid from the milk. For a more detailed explanation of this phenomenon, see the entry for MEAT.

See also MOTHER'S MILK, STOMACH, UPSET.

MISCARRIAGE

Jumping up and down or falling can bring on a miscarriage. This is unlikely as long as the developing fetus is healthy. Inside the uterus, the developing fetus is cushioned by amniotic fluid much like an egg inside a jar of water. Even if you shake the jar up and down, the egg won't break because the liquid protects it from shock. Barring a truly traumatic injury, the same principle is believed to apply to a healthy fetus nestled inside the womb.

MOON

A full moon drives men mad. Human beings have always seemed to associate certain kinds of behavior with specific phases of the moon. The legend of the werewolf (a human being who temporarily turns into a wolf when the moon is full) is a dramatic example of this kind of folklore. There are gentler reminders in our use of the word lunatic (which comes from *luna,* the Latin word for moon) to describe people whose behavior is a tad strange.

Every now and then, some social scientists or even an enterprising reporter will look through local police records and discover a blip in the records of violent crimes that coincides with the full moon. In 1972, for example, a researcher at the University of Miami put together a chart detailing all the homicides in Miami over a 15–year period. When the crimes were grouped according to the phases of the moon, the chart clearly showed an uptick in the murder rate about a day before the new moon, a peak period when the moon was full, and then a decline, with the cycle repeating itself with each new rising of the moon, but this pattern has never really been proven.

See also THUNDERSTORMS, WEATHER.

MOSQUITO BITES

Take vitamin B1 to keep the mosquitoes from biting. Vitamin B1 (better known as thiamine) is vital for your nervous system, your digestion and your heart, but it won't protect you from mosquitoes.

In a rigorously controlled California study in the late 1960s, volunteers were given thiamine three times a day, first in 50-milligram doses, then in doses of 200 mg, 45 to 180 times the RDA for adults (1.5 mg for men; 1.1 mg for women). A control group got no thiamine at all.

Next, a mesh cage of mosquitoes was held just above the volunteers' forearms, to see if the mosquitoes would cluster at the bottom of the cage, heading for the tasty flesh below. Next, cylinders containing mosquitoes were placed directly on the volunteers' skin. Finally, the troops were sent shirtless into a room containing 100 females—the ones most likely to bite.

The result? Everyone got bitten. Taking thiamine had no effect, and even when thiamine was spread directly on the volunteers' skin, the mosquitoes refused to buzz off.

Dot on a paste of meat tenderizer and water to take the itch out of a mosquito bite. Yes, but with caution. When a mosquito bites, it injects a protein-based salivary secretion that keeps blood from clotting until the insect has finished its feast. The proteins in the secretion cause the allergic reaction that makes a mosquito bite swell and itch.

In theory, says Steve Tim, Ph.D., vice-president for science and publications at the Brooklyn Botanic Garden, meat tenderizer should stop the itch because it contains papain, a proteolytic (*proteo*-protein; *lysis*-break) enzyme from papayas that destroys the itchy proteins in the mosquito's saliva. But in practice, papain is irritating because it also breaks down proteins in the skin. It is also a strong allergen that may blister the skin.

Roll-on antiperspirant stops the itching from an insect bite. True. The aluminum compounds commonly used in anti-perspirants are astringents. They slightly irritate the skin and make it pucker slightly. Like the slight pain of a scratch, the slight irritation of the anti-perspirant fools your brain into forgetting the itch, at least for a while.

Caution: Use sparingly; the aluminum compounds that stop the itch may also irritate the skin.

See also ITCH.

MOTHER'S MILK

A drop of mother's milk protects a newborn baby's eyes. Human milk, like human tears, does contain antibodies and natural compounds that inhibit the growth of bacteria, at least in laboratory test-tubes. If this folk remedy appears to work, it is almost certainly because the condition it is used to treat is a self-limiting one such as conjunctivitis, the inflammation of the lining of the eyelid commonly called "pink eye."

Breast milk definitely will not cure any serious eye infections, such as those caused by an infant's acquiring gonorrhea, herpes or chlamydia during delivery when it passes through an infected birth canal.

See also BREAST-FEEDING.

MOTION SICKNESS

To avoid motion sickness in a car, sit in the front seat. When you were a kid, did you use the threat of getting carsick to wangle a front seat on long trips? If so, your siblings may have loathed you, but medical science is on your side.

Although emotions may play some role in developing motion sickness, what's much more important is the physical necessity to keep your eyes on a non-moving target like the sky about 45 degrees above the horizon. That's practically impossible to do if you are a small child sitting in the back seat of the car where your view is essentially the inside of a three-sided closed box bounded in front by the back of the front seat and on the sides by the doors.

Letting a child sit in front or, alternatively, in a car seat high enough to let him see out the window can change the view and maybe prevent the misery. No guarantees.

Chewing green olives prevents sickness. Maybe. When you are queasy, salivation increases. The extra liquid slides down into the stomach at the same time that the stomach lining itself is producing extra secretions and the stomach muscles are clenching. The combination of excess fluids and clenched muscles can make a person sick to his stomach.

Why would olives help? Theoretically, because they are high in astringent chemicals called tannins that may dry the mouth and decrease saliva production. The theory makes sense, but there are no controlled studies to show that it works.

MUD

Put mud (or manure) on a bee sting to take the sting out. The old wives who invented this one knew that a damp, cool dressing can relieve pain or itch. What they didn't know was that either one of these remedies carries the risk of tetanus. Bee stings and insect bites are puncture wounds. Mud and manure from open ground is almost certain to contain tetanus spores. Putting the two together spells trouble.

Mud makes a super facial. As it dries on your skin, mud hardens and tightens, pulling impurities up to the surface of the skin. Then, when you wash off this masque, you will also wash off the top layer of dead cells on the skin so that your face looks softer and smoother. A masque made from garden-variety dirt is unlikely to work this way, but mud made from earth that is rich in clay, the base used in some commercial "mud-pack" facial masques, might perform adequately well. The problem is that dirt you dig up on your own is likely to be, well, *dirty*. Which means loaded with insects and other debris. For safe, clean results, stick to a commercial product.

MUSHROOMS

A poisonous mushroom will blacken a silver spoon. Not necessarily. Silver blackens (tarnishes) when exposed to hydrogen sulfide, a chemical that occurs naturally in fresh air, onions and eggs, and some poisonous mushrooms. But many varieties of toxic mushrooms, including the notorious amanita, do not contain hydrogen sulfide and won't affect the silver.

If a mushroom is going to kill you, it will do so right away. Not true. His belief in this myth is said to have done in the Roman emperor Claudius. Like any good ruler of the day, he had his food tasted in advance. If the taster keeled over at the dinner table, Claudius turned down the dish. But the mushrooms whipped up for him by his wife Agrippina II and his stepson Nero were the slow-acting variety. Both Claudius and the taster did end up dead as the proverbial doornail, though later than expected.

There are some lessons here, of course. One is that unless you are an expert, it's best to avoid the wild stuff and stick to the mushrooms on sale at the supermarket. A second is that even if you are an expert, it's a good idea to keep repeating the familiar old refrain—"There are old mushroom hunters and bold mushrooms hunters, but there are no old, bold mushroom hunters."

MUSTARD

A teaspoon of mustard before dinner stimulates the appetite. Maybe. Mustard is an irritant that stimulates the secretion of stomach acid and triggers the contractions we call hunger pangs, thus stimulating appetite.

A mustard plaster cures a chest cold. In folk parlance, a "mustard plaster" is a cloth coated with a paste made of dry mustard powder and water and then applied to the skin. No mustard plaster can cure a cold, but carefully used, it may make the victim feel a little bit better for a while.

Why? Mustard irritates the skin and makes tiny blood vessels on the surface expand. As a result, more blood flows into the immediate area. That makes the skin look pinker and feel warmer, which can distract a person's attention from his cold. The same principle applies to other irritating substances such as wintergreen (methyl salicylate) and pepper (capsicum oleoresin), which were once used as dressings to relieve the aches and pains of arthritis or muscle strain.

Caution: All irritants must be used sparingly and with great care. Each is capable of severely irritating or even, in extreme circumstances, blistering the skin.

N

NATURAL FOOD

Food grown with 'organic' fertilizer is more healthful than food grown with 'chemical' fertilizer. As far as a plant is concerned, it doesn't matter a bit whether the fertilizer is "organic" (made from living matter) or "chemical" (made from synthetic materials).

The fact is that plants make use of a fertilizer until the ingredients in the fertilizer are broken down into their inorganic chemical constituents. In other words, while plants need specific nutrients such as nitrogen for healthy growth, whether the nutrients come from organic matter or synthetic chemicals is irrelevant.

Food grown in rich soil has more vitamins than food grown in poor soil. When you talk about soil being "rich," what you mean is that it has a high mineral content. High-mineral soil can support more healthy plants per acre and it can influence the mineral content of the fruits and vegetables grown there, but the mineral content of the soil has absolutely no effect on the vitamin content of the plants grown there. Minerals come from the soil, but vitamins are manufactured inside the plant itself.

Foods grown with 'natural' pest control are safer to eat than foods grown with synthetic pesticides. Synthetic pesticides have given us abundant harvests of good-looking fruits and vegetables. They have also given us lingering doubts about whether or not the foods they protect are safe to eat. It is an indisputable fact that using natural pest control—say, "good" (protective) insects to get rid of the "bad" (destructive) bugs that chew up our crops—does eliminate the possibility of our getting pesticide residues on or in our fruits and vegetables. But that doesn't answer the basic question: Are synthetic pesticides invariably hazardous to our health?

The truth is distinctly uncomfortable for people who want absolute answers. No, not all synthetic pesticides are hazardous. To find the dangerous ones, you have to evaluate these products one by one, and right now, we are not very far along in doing that.

See also VITAMINS.

NEWBORN BABIES

You have to slap a newborn on the rump to get him to take his first breath. A healthy newborn will begin to breathe spontaneously as soon as his airway is cleared of mucus and debris. Holding him upside down and slapping him on the bottom was a old-fashioned way of doing this. Some people now think it might even have been injurious to the infant.

In 1977, Yale University surgery professor Edmund S. Crelin, M.D., suggested that holding a baby by the ankles and slapping him on the rump could dislocate the infant's hips and might even cripple him for life. Today, the practice is increasingly rare as doctors prefer to use suction (via a bulb syringe) to clear the airway and help a baby take his first breath.

A baby born with bumps in his head is 'a child of the Devil.' Every once in a while, a baby injured during the passage down the birth canal will be born with a cephalohematoma (a small pool of blood between the skull and the membrane that covers it). As the injury heals, the spot may be filled with calcium, and the calcium hardens into a small hard bump. The bump, which disappears naturally as the calcium is absorbed into the skull, was once known as a "Devil's horn" and the infant as a "child of the Devil." Clearly, neither is true.

Never bathe a newborn until the cord falls off; the water might run into his body and drown him. Obviously, you're not going to let your baby go without a bath until the cord stump falls off, but you may want to wash around it for a while. The stump is not an open hole through which water can pour into the body, but it is a site of potential infection.

According the *The Merck Manual,* daubing the stump each day with 70% alcohol hastens drying and healing and reduces the risk of infection.

Don't take a flash picture of your newborn. It can damage his eyes. The flash is gone so quickly that it's unlikely to cause any damage. The real risk to a baby's eyes comes when a premature newborn is exposed for long periods of time to intense light in a hospital nursery.

In 1985, researchers at George Washington University released the results of a study of 60 premature infants in the nurseries at Georgetown University Medical Center and Children's Hospital National Medical Center in Washington suggesting that this prolonged exposure may increase the baby's risk of blindness due to retinal damage.

In the study, 19 (86%) of 21 infants kept in ordinary incubators and exposed to the ordinary bright lighting in a hospital nursery for premature infants developed retrolental fibroplasia (also known as retinopathy of prematurity), a condition that blinds approximately 500 to 600 American newborns each year. Only 21 (54%) of the 39 premature infants kept in shielded incubators that reduced the lighting level by more than 50% developed retinal damage.

Note: All the infants in this study were born weighing less than 2.2 pounds; babies born weighing more than that appeared to be less sensitive to the effects of light.

See also CAUL, EYE COLOR.

NIGHTMARES

Late night snacking triggers nightmares. When Ebenezer Scrooge tried to pin the appearance of Marley's ghost to an undigested bit of cheese, you can bet that lots of Dickens's readers nodded in agreement, but they were only partially right.

Every time you eat, your stomach releases gastric acids you need to digest the food. According to a 1990 report in the *Tufts University Diet & Nutrition Letter,* your stomach may continue to release acids for as long as seven hours after you eat. That means that late-night snackers who are susceptible to gastric upset or "heartburn" or who have an ulcer may be wakened in the middle of the night by indigestion. If they wake up while dreaming and the dream is a nightmare, they may think that's what woke them, and blame the dream on whatever they ate. That is a mistake: The only thing attributable to the food is indigestion. The nightmare was coincidental. The easiest solution, of course, is to eat earlier in the evening.

NOSEBLEED

To stop a nosebleed, tilt your head back. This sure seems reasonable because tilting your head back does keep blood from running out of your nose and down the front of your shirt. But that means the blood is dripping down the back of your throat (which can make you choke) and running into your stomach (which can cause nausea and vomiting).

It is better to overcome your instinct and follow the American Red Cross's advice: So long as the victim does not have a head, neck or back injury, she should sit up, lean slightly forward with her chin towards her chest, and gently pinch the bleeding nostril closed. Do not blow to clear the nose; this may start the bleeding off again.

Caution: Most nosebleeds are minor incidents caused by picking at the nose (the number-one cause) or blowing repeatedly to clear away the mucous of a cold or allergy. But if the bleeding does not stop immediately or if nosebleeds recur or if the bleeding is the result of an injury or if it is caused by a medical condition such as high blood pressure, do not rely on first-aid home remedies. Seek medical assistance immediately.

Press a cold metal key against the nape of your neck to stop a nosebleed. The large blood vessels that bring blood into your head run up the side and back of the neck. In theory, chilling the skin here should make these vessels constrict so that the flow of blood diminishes temporarily. In practice, though, it's not likely to work. Not only are these large blood vessels far from the site of the bleeding, they are also so large that to shut them down or even to slow the blood flow sufficiently to stop your nosebleed, you would have to chill your whole body virtually to the point where your heart stops pumping. This precise technique is used to reduce blood flow during open heart surgery, but it's hardly what you'd consider a handy home remedy.

Cold compresses applied gently to the side of your nose may constrict the tiny blood vessels there, but the American Red Cross says that direct pressure—pinching the affected nostril in towards the center of the nose—is more effective. See Caution note above.

Press a cold steel knife against your neck to stop a nosebleed. Another cold compress, much more dramatic but no more effective than a cold key. Besides, if the knife slips, you could end up bleeding from two places, rather than one. Pass on this one. See Caution note above.

To stop a nosebleed, wrap a knotted red ribbon around your neck. This traditional British folk remedy is entirely symbolic: Red for blood, knots for clots. It has no effect whatsoever on a nosebleed.

People with a tendency to nosebleeds should avoid heights. Probably. The question is, how high is high? As altitude rises, air pressure drops. The higher you are, the lower the pressure of the air against your body. But the pressure inside your veins and arteries (your blood pressure) remains essentially the same regardless of the altitude, so when you get to an altitude where the pressure inside your blood vessels is significantly higher than the pressure of the air against your body, it is possible that the blood in your veins and arteries may begin to seep out through the vessel walls, pushed by the higher pressure inside.

Some people with fragile blood-vessel walls and very high blood pressure can begin to experience this effect at surprisingly low heights. Others may never experience the problem in normal life, but run into trouble if they decide to go mountain climbing. Only your own experience and your doctor's careful evaluation can tell you what your particular high is likely to be.

People with a tendency to nosebleeds shouldn't fly in airplanes. Because the air pressure inside an airplane cabin can vary dramatically, this is really a variation on the how-high-is-high problem described above. If you are a person who suffers from recurring nosebleeds, check with your doctor before you take off.

Note: Variations in air pressure inside an airplane can also be troublesome for people with ear problems.

See also CHEWING GUM, EARS.

O

OBESITY

Obesity is inherited. The most persuasive evidence that heredity is destiny as far as body weight is concerned comes from studies of twins such as the one released in 1990 by a team of obesity researchers at the University of Pennsylvania.

The scientists observed 673 pairs of identical and fraternal twins whose average age was 58. The fraternal twins sometimes varied in weight, but the identical twins had nearly identical body mass indices (weight correlated to height), regardless of whether or not they grew up in the same household. That suggests that within the same culture it is heredity, not environment, that is most important in determining adult weight.

Which doesn't mean a person cannot stay trim regardless of his heredity. The further up the economic and educational scale you are, the less likely you are to be obese. This may be the result of a social prejudice against obese people that forces those who inherit a tendency towards obesity to control their weight, sometimes at great emotional and physical cost.

Some people can eat anything and never gain weight. This may turn out to be a corollary to the fact that heredity is a major determinant in body size. In 1990, researchers at Laval University in Quebec, Canada, published the results of study in which 12 pairs of identical male twins were put on a six-month diet that gave them 84,000 calories more than they had been eating before they entered the study. There are approximately 3,500 calories in a pound of fat, so everyone who consumes 84,000 extra calories should add 24 pounds of body fat.

But it didn't work that way. Although the twins in each pair gained the same amount of weight (more proof that heredity is destiny as far as body weight is concerned), the different twin pairs gained different amounts of weight. The average weight gain for the group was 18 pounds. The pair that gained the most put on nearly 30 pounds; the pair that gained the least picked up only nine pounds. This seems to substantiate what we all know instinctively: Some people really can eat what they want and not gain as much weight as others do.

Extra body fat protects you against the cold. It certainly seems logical to assume that extra body fat would insulate you against a winter's chill, but in this case what looks logical is at war with basic physiology.

Because the nerve endings that allow us to feel heat or cold are right next to the surface of the skin, fat people feel the cold as quickly as thin people do. And they may stay colder longer. Heat from the warm center of the body can radiate quickly to the outer surface of a thin person's skin. It takes longer for the warmth to radiate through the fatty layers covering a fat person's body, so her skin may stay cool longer than the thin person's.

Fat babies are healthier than thin babies. It depends on the situation. In a society where food is scarce, a well-fed, bouncy baby is obviously healthier than a skinny, starving one. But there is a world of difference between a baby who's thin because of starvation and one who is lean because of proper diet. A healthy lean child looks like a miniature athlete with bright eyes, good muscle tone and quick, energetic movements. When a child is skinny because he is starving, it's just the opposite: His eyes are dull; his muscles are slack; and he rarely moves about spontaneously.

Children outgrow their 'baby fat.' Not always. We store our body fat in specialized body cells called "fat cells" that get bigger or smaller depending on how much we eat. A child who is fat from babyhood has more fat cells than a lean baby. These cells are his for life, and they demand to be fed. A child who remains overfed and overweight into adolescence can almost always expect to have weight problems as long as he lives. His extra fat cells will make it impossible for him to slim down on a diet that contains a normal number of calories.

See also FAT PEOPLE.

ONIONS

Eating onions is good for your heart. Like garlic, onions are sharp and pungent. You have to be "strong" to eat them, so sympathetic medicine (a belief that like causes or cures like) says they are good for your heart. In fact, they may be.

A number of laboratory studies, starting with the pioneering report back in 1977 from the Department of Cardiology at the R.N.T Medical College in Udaipur, India, have suggested that the essential oils of both onions and garlic help to reduce the level of cholesterol in blood in test tubes. If the same thing were to happen in your body, the onions would "strengthen your heart." Whether they do remains to be proven.

See also GARLIC.

OPERATIONS, SURGICAL

'It's just a minor operation.' Although some surgical procedures are clearly less complicated than others, there is no such thing as a minor operation when general anesthesia is involved. Anesthesia always carries the possibility of complications up to and including cardiac arrest and brain damage.

Need convincing? Then consider this: Statistics compiled by the Commission on Professional and Hospital Activities of the American College of Surgeons show that in 1986, the last year for which these figures were available, 543 people died after appendectomy, and 119 after tonsillectomy.

OYSTERS

Never eat oysters in months without an 'r.' There are at least three reasons for the longevity of this old wives' tale. Two of the reasons are easily discounted; the third is a bit more troublesome.

The first explanation for the admonition is that it's hard to keep shellfish fresh in hot weather, but the advent of refrigeration (including refrigerated shipping containers) has gone a long way towards making this moot.

The second explanation concerns aesthetics. Oysters spawn in the summer months, so the ones you catch are likely to be small and stringy rather than plump and tasty. But that doesn't make them less nutritious.

The third reason for avoiding oysters from May through August—or, to be more precise and less folkloric, from July to October—is ecological. These months without an "r" are the ones in which the flotilla of reddish plankton known as "red tide" is most likely to cover the surface of coastal waters along the United States' northern Pacific and New England shorelines. These plankton produce a toxin that can cause serious gastric upset including nausea, vomiting and cramps, plus muscle weakness and/or paralysis. Shellfish that eat the plankton can pass the toxin along to you because even thorough cooking does not eliminate or inactivate the poison.

Eating oysters makes you sexy. Oysters are a good source of zinc, a mineral known to increase sperm counts and testosterone levels in infertile males. (It has no effect on fertile males). But beef, cocoa powder and wheat germ, among others, are also good sources of zinc. Oysters, though yummy to those of us who savor their briny goodness, are no magic aphrodisiac.

P

PARSLEY

Drink tea brewed from fresh parsley to cure a urinary infection. According to Walter F. Lewis and Memory P. F. Elvin-Lewis, co-authors of *Medical Botany,* parsley is a mild diuretic that can make you urinate more frequently. But it is not an antiseptic, so it will not clear up a urinary infection. To be safe, save parsley for your salads. See your doctor for urinary problems.

See also CRANBERRY JUICE.

PEPPER, HOT

Drink cold milk to douse the fire of a peppery chili or curry dinner. True. Capsaicin, nordihydrocapsaicin, and dihydrocapsaicin, the chemicals that make hot peppers hot, dissolve in fat and alcohol, but not in water. That's why milk—especially whole milk, which has more butterfat than low-fat or skim milk—is a more efficient way to cool your peppered palate than soda pop or plain cold water.

Cold beer works, too. True, again. The hot chemicals in hot pepper dissolve as well in alcohol as in milkfat.

See also GIN.

PERSPIRATION

Perspiration 'cleans out the pores.' When your internal temperature rises, your body begins to perspire, secreting moisture through the pores that acts as a natural air conditioner as it evaporates on your skin. But it does not clean out your pores. In fact, if your skin is oily, excessive perspiration can contribute to the development of whiteheads and blackheads, pores blocked by dirt and debris.

See also ACNE, COLDS, EXERCISE, FEVER, HOT WEATHER.

PICKLES

Eating pickles and milk together will make you sick to your stomach. The idea is that the acid pickles will curdle the milk in your stomach. It will, but it doesn't matter because as soon as any food you eat reaches your stomach, it is attacked by acid gastric juices that turn it into a kind of mush from which your body can extract (digest) the nutrients it needs and then expel the residue as waste. In other words, if pickles and milk are your cup of tea, enjoy.

PILLS

Leave the cotton plug in the pill bottle to keep the pills fresh. That's what most of us do when we open a new bottle of aspirin or vitamin pills, but we're wrong. The cotton is in there not to keep the pills fresh but to keep them from rattling around and breaking up before you open the bottle.

Once you open the bottle and pull out the cotton, it is contaminated with the bacteria that live naturally on your skin. So it is better to toss the cotton out than to stuff it back into the bottle.

PIMPLES

Never squeeze a pimple between your lip and your nose. When you pick at an infected pimple, you run the risk of spreading the infection by forcing bacteria out into the surrounding tissues. This is particularly hazardous around your nose and upper lip because there are so many blood vessels in the area that lead directly to the brain.

Theoretically, squeezing a pimple here could send bacteria up these pathways to your brain. The chance of this happening is small, but it is real, and the old wives' prohibition against fooling around with blemishes in the middle of your face makes good sense.

To heal a pimple fast, plaster it with a paste of soap or detergent and water. According to the National Institutes of Health, this home remedy is definitely on the "not recommended" list. Although soaps and detergents do dry and tighten your skin, and may force out the central "plug" in a blackhead or pimple, they are irritating and may damage the sensitive skin around the blemish. Soapy pastes, once a common folk treatment for pimples, have yielded to safer, more effective over-the-counter products.

PLANTS

Don't sleep in a room with plants. At night, they will use up the oxygen and asphyxiate you. The myth of the smothering plant is based on the undeniable fact that at night, when there's no light around to trigger photosynthesis (the light-energized formation of carbohydrates in the plant's chlorophyll-containing cells), plants continue to take in oxygen and give off carbon-dioxide as a by-product.

But the amount of oxygen they use up and the amount of carbon dioxide they release are so insignificant that you could, if you chose, spend all your nights sleeping in a greenhouse without its causing you any harm.

So how come nurses often take plants and flowers out of hospital rooms at night? There are several possibilities.

First, nurses hear the same medical folklore the rest of us do and may believe the myth. A second, more sensible, explanation is that having flowers and plants around increases the bug population in a hospital room. Cut flowers sit in water, a perfect breeding ground for bacteria; potted plants sit in dirt, which can be a natural host for all kinds of tiny crawling things, hardly welcome guests for someone who's already sick.

POISONING, ANTIDOTES FOR

Taken together, burnt toast, milk of magnesia and strong tea are a 'universal antidote.' No. Alone, each of these once seemed a sensible antidote for a specific kind of poison. Burnt toast contains carbon that might sop up various toxins in the stomach. Milk of magnesia is a basic (alkaline) solution once thought to neutralize acid poisons or coat the stomach walls and prevent the absorption of poison. Strong tea, an acid, was thought to neutralize basic (alkaline) poisons. A liquid, it was assumed to dilute the poison and make it less toxic.

None of these old-fashioned, generalized antidotes is considered safe and effective today, when modern toxicology tailors its antidotes carefully to the poison.

Caution: For specific information and help in an emergency poisoning, dial 911, your local Poison Control Center or your physician.

Make someone who has swallowed a poison vomit it up.
This is a dangerous prescription for anyone who has swallowed a
caustic poison such as drain cleaner, a poison containing a petroleum
distillate, or a poison that has induced drowsiness. Vomiting a caustic
poison will increase damage to the esophagus as the corrosive chemical comes back up. Vomiting petroleum distillates can force particles
into the lungs that cause chemical pneumonia (a lung infection due
to the presence of foreign material). Forcing a drowsy person to vomit
may make him choke or inhale particles of vomit, again raising the
possibility of pneumonia.

Caution: As a general rule, never induce vomiting in someone who
has swallowed poison without checking first with your doctor, a tox-
icologist or the Poison Control Center.

POISON IVY

'Leaves of three, let them be.' This is excellent advice, an
example of medical folklore at its scientific best.

Poison ivy plants can look like low bushes or sturdy vines. They
can grow in damp forests or dry, rocky places. Their leaves can be
long or short, shiny or hairy, oval or elongated, with smooth edges
or saw-tooth ones. Their color can change with the season—green in
spring and summer; pink, red or yellow in the fall. But one thing
never changes: The leaves on a poison ivy plant are *always* grouped
in threes.

If it has three leaves, please don't pick the pretty plant.

*Eating the leaves of the poison ivy plant will immunize you
against a reaction.* This is a false and potentially dangerous piece of
folklore. Eating poison ivy leaves confers no immunity against the
plant. Worse yet, it may cause an internal case of poison ivy allergy.

The offending chemical in poison ivy (and poison oak) is urushiol,
an oily substance found in every part of the plant, from the berries
right down to the roots. If you swallow poison ivy leaves, the urushiol in the leaves may cause the same burning, itching, blisters and
swelling inside your mouth and your gastrointestinal tract as it does
on your skin.

*If the poison ivy plant is dry and dead, it's no longer haz-
ardous.* Wrong. Even plants that look like they have long since given
up the ghost can contain active urushiol.

Your first exposure to poison ivy will cause the worst reaction. Not necessarily. Like all other allergic reactions, the poison ivy rash is caused by your sensitivity to a specific allergenic substance (urushiol) in the plant. Your first exposure to urushiol is the one that sensitizes you. The reaction to this first exposure is likely to be mild; each subsequent contact with urushiol is more likely to provoke an increasingly severe reaction.

Scratching spreads poison ivy. No. You can only develop the the allergic rash on the parts of your skin that have been exposed to urushiol. The liquid in the blistery rash is not itself an allergen. Rather, it is fluid that has spilled from cells damaged by the allergic reaction to urushiol. A poison ivy rash may appear to be spreading outward over a period of several days, but what is really happening is that the reaction is developing at different times in different places. Nevertheless, scratching is to be avoided if possible because it can cause an infection in an existing rash.

Poison ivy is contagious. No. Poison ivy is a form of contact dermatitis. It can be acquired only by coming in contact with urushiol. The poison ivy rash cannot be spread from one person to another. However, if the rash is infected, the infection may spread to anyone who touches it.

You can catch poison ivy by touching the clothes worn by someone who has it. This may sound far-fetched, but it is not only possible—it happens all the time. Urushiol is oily and can cling to clothes, as well as the handle of a tennis racquet, or the tires of a bicycle that's been pedaled through a patch of the allergenic plant. If you put on a pair of slacks that was worn by somebody who walked through a patch of poison ivy and has not been laundered since, you may come in contact with the urushiol on the fabric and end up with poison ivy yourself.

You can catch poison ivy by playing with the dog of a person who has the rash. Yes, but only if the pooch himself was romping through a patch of poison ivy plants and has urushiol on his collar or his body.

You can catch poison ivy out of the air. It sounds like fiction, but it is a definite possibility. When poison ivy plants are burned, droplets of urushiol become airborne, traveling on floating ash or soot. Should this droplets fall on your skin, a poison ivy rash may follow.

Scrubbing with strong soap and water cures a case of poison ivy. If you have just been exposed to poison ivy, washing thoroughly with lots of soap and water may help flush the urushiol off your skin and prevent your developing a rash. But once a rash has bloomed, repeated washing will only further irritate your sore and itchy skin.

Put wet tea bags on your skin to stop the itching from a poison ivy rash. Tea bags contain tannic acid, which may help dry the itchy oozing rash. But this home remedy only relieves symptoms. It doesn't "cure" poison ivy, which—like the common cold—is a self-limiting condition that lasts a week or two if you treat it and seven to 14 days if you don't.

POTATOES

Rubbing the cut surface of a sliced potato on your hands will soften the skin. Only temporarily. When you rub the potato against your skin, you leave behind a light layer of starch that makes your skin feel smooth and soft. But this only works as long as the starch is moist. If left to dry on your skin, it will harden, making your skin itch.

To soothe an itch, rub your skin with a sliced potato. The cut potato is a cool, wet dressing, an effective home remedy for temporary relief from itching. Naturally, it comes with a caveat, which is to rinse thoroughly after rubbing, or your skin will end up more itchy than it was when you started. (See above.)

Caution: If the itch is widespread, severe or persistent, check with your doctor before using any home remedy.

To darken your hair, boil potato peelings, strain them out and use the water as a rinse after shampooing. If this works, some say it is because the dirt left in the water from the potato skin coats your hair and makes it look darker. Others speculate that minerals leeching out of the skins might be the darkening agents. Owing to a lack of scientific observation and study, nobody knows for sure.

Green potatoes are poisonous. True. The green parts of potatoes (leaves, stems, spots on the skin, and sprouts in the "eyes") contain solanine, a natural neurotoxin (nerve poison) that interferes with the activity of acetylcholinase, a chemical that makes it possible for your cells to send messages to each other. Solanine poisoning caused by green potatoes is rare, but it does occur. Because neither soaking the potatoes in cold water nor cooking them will reduce the solanine content, it is safer to discard all potatoes with sprouting eyes or green spots on the skin. *Note:* Solanine is also found in the green parts (stems and leaves) of the tomato plant.

To get rid of a wart, rub it with the cut side of a sliced potato. Warts are viral infections that sometimes respond to the power of suggestion. There is no magic anti-viral compound in a potato, but if you really, truly believe that it will cure your wart, it just might. And then again, it might not.

See WARTS.

POTS AND PANS

Cooking or storing foods in aluminum pots darkens the pot and makes the food poisonous. Yes, to the first. No, to the second.

If you cook or store an acidic food or beverage such as apples, cabbage, tomatoes, vinegar, water or wine in an aluminum pot, the acids in the food will interact with the aluminum on the surface of the pot and blacken it. The same thing happens when you wrap these foods in aluminum foil. At the same time, the acid pulls aluminum ions off the surface of the pot or foil. These ions may darken the food and give it a metallic flavor, but there is absolutely no evidence to suggest that these color and flavor changes make the food unsafe or less nutritious.

Food cooked in aluminum pots can cause Alzheimer's disease. All food cooked or stored in an aluminum pot or in aluminum foil will pull some aluminum ions off the surface of the vessel or wrap. The more acidic the food, the more aluminum it will attract. For example, in 1985, researchers at the University of Wisconsin found that while green beans (a non-acid food) cooked in an aluminum pot appeared to have no more aluminum than raw green beans, tomato sauce (an acid food) cooked in an aluminum pot had about 550 times as much aluminum as uncooked tomato sauce or tomato sauce cooked in a stainless steel pot.

Because research over the past two decades has suggested that people with Alzheimer's tend to have larger-than-normal amounts of aluminum in the brain, many people worry that the aluminum we get in our food, including the aluminum that leeches off the surface of aluminum cookware, may increase our risk of developing Alzheimer's.

As of this writing, there are no scientific studies showing this to be true. In fact, there is at least one incident that suggests it is false.

Early in the 1970s, several kidney dialysis patients in Great Britain and the United States were inadvertently dialysed with water containing toxic amounts of aluminum. Some of the people dialyzed with the high-aluminum water died of aluminum poisoning. When autopsies were performed, pathologists found higher levels of aluminum in their brain tissue than has ever been found in the brain tissue of people with Alzheimer's. In spite of that, none of the patients who died of aluminum poisoning had shown any symptoms of Alzheimer's, nor did their brain tissue show the changes characteristic of the condition.

Cooking foods in iron pots makes the food iron-rich. Like aluminum pots (see above) and copper pots (see below), iron pots release metal ions into food. You can see the results when you cook white potatoes and cauliflower in iron pots: The iron leeching off the surface of the pot will turn the creamy pigments in the vegetables yellow.

Unlike aluminum ions, which seem to be nutritionally neutral, and copper ions, which can be poisonous, the iron that leeches into your food from the surface of an unlined iron stewpot or griddle are positively beneficial, as useful to your body as the iron you get naturally in food. In fact, some nutritional experts speculate that our having abandoned iron pots may be one reason for the prevalence of iron deficiency among American women who cannot get the amount of iron they need from the normal American diet of fewer than 3,000 calories a day.

How good a source of iron are iron pots? Very. In 1985, nutritional researchers at Texas Tech University in Lubbock measuring the amount of iron in foods cooked in iron pots vs. foods cooked in non-iron pots found that cooking in iron could increase the iron content of the food anywhere from two to 20 times.

For example, when raw, the ingredients in beef stew have about 0.7 mg for each 3.5-ounce (100-mg) serving. After the stew has been cooked in an iron pot for an about an hour and a quarter, though, its iron content goes up to 3.4 mg per 3.5 ounces vs. 0.3 in a non-iron pot. A 3.5-ounce portion of raw eggs has 1.9 mg iron. Fried in an iron pan for six minutes, the eggs have 3.5 mg iron vs. 1.8 mg if fried in a non-iron pan. A 3.5-ounce portion of raw pancake batter has 0.6 mg iron. When baked on an iron griddle, the pancakes have 1.3 mg iron per 3.5 ounce serving vs. 0.8 mg if baked on a non-iron griddle. Uncooked meatless spaghetti sauce has 0.6 mg iron per 3.5-ounce serving. Cooked for 23 minutes in an iron pot, the sauce will have 5.8 mg iron per 3.5-ounce serving vs. 0.7 mg iron if cooked for the same length of time in a non-iron pot.

Note: The recommended dietary allowance (RDA) for iron for a healthy, adult woman is 15 mg; for a healthy adult man, 10 mg.

Food cooked in copper pots is poisonous. Tin- or enamel-lined copper pots and pans are safe for cooking, but unlined copper pots or pots whose lining has been damaged may indeed be hazardous to your health.

Without the protective lining, the pot can release copper ions into your food. Minuscule amounts of copper are essential to life. They enable our bodies to use iron and to manufacture hemoglobin, the pigment in red blood cells that carries oxygen throughout the body. The recommended dietary allowance (RDA) for healthy adults is estimated to be 2–4 mg, but most Americans seem to get by on about 1.2–1.5 mg a day. Larger amounts, such as you might get if you cook or store food in an unlined copper pot, are potentially poisonous. A century ago, when unlined copper pots and pans were widely used, the symptoms of copper poisoning (nausea, vomiting, diarrhea and muscle pains) were fairly common.

The simplest way to avoid the problem is to discard or re-line any copper vessel whose lining is damaged. The Food and Drug Administration makes an exception for the small pans used for making sauces or the bowls used to whip egg whites. (Copper ions flaking off the bowl stabilize the proteins in egg whites.) Because they are used so infrequently, these pots and bowls are considered safe even if unlined.

Cooking in glass pots makes food less nutritious. It's true that glass lets in light, which can destroy riboflavin (vitamin B2), but the loss is so slight that it is of no nutritional importance.

PREGNANCY

A missed period is a sure sign of pregnancy. Make that "probable" instead of "sure," and you are more certain to be right.

Because a woman's menstrual cycle may be disrupted by any number of emotional and physical traumas, it usually requires at least two missed periods to confirm that conception has occurred. Even then it's a good idea to do a pregnancy test to confirm the pregnancy and to rule out other possible causes of amenorrhea (lack of menstruation), such as a disorder of the pituitary, thyroid or adrenal glands, polycystic ovarian diseases, under- or overweight, or the beginning of menopause.

Strange food cravings are normal during pregnancy. Common, yes. Normal? Maybe. The obvious explanation for food cravings is that they represent the body's need to satisfy some nutritional deficiency. For example, some nutritionists believe that an iron deficiency may be to blame for pica, the consumption of non-nutritive substances such as clay, dirt or laundry starch.

Fair enough. But does that mean that a craving for ice cream is caused by a calcium deficiency? Right now, although this is a question crying for an answer, especially for those expectant fathers sent out on the legendary trip through a midnight snowstorm in search of, say, peanut brittle and pickles, there is no scientific study to say one way or the other.

Pregnant women are 'eating for two.' Yes, if what you mean by "eating for two" is that a pregnant woman must consider the fetus when she chooses the foods she eats.

The recommended dietary allowances (RDA) for vitamins, minerals and other nutrients are significantly higher for pregnant women than for healthy adult women who are not pregnant. So are the energy (calorie) requirements. The National Research Council (NRC), which sets the RDAs, now estimates that a healthy, well-nourished woman should add at least 80,000 calories to her normal diet over the nine months of pregnancy, about 300 extra calories a day.

You lose a tooth for every child. Not if you floss every day and see your dentist on schedule. There is some evidence to suggest that hormonal changes during pregnancy can alter the chemistry of the mouth so as to make cavities more common, but proper dental care and scrupulous home cleaning every day can go a long way towards helping a pregnant woman avoid decay, periodontal disease and tooth loss.

After you've been pregnant, you can never be as slim as you were before. It's hard. Around the world, the average weight gain during a healthy pregnancy is just under 28 pounds: about 7.5 pounds for the baby, 6.5 pounds for the fluid surrounding it in the womb and 14 pounds of extra flesh for the pregnant woman herself.

Getting rid of the extra pounds can be a daunting task. According to a 1990 study of weight gain during pregnancy conducted by nutritional epidemiologists at the University of California, Berkeley, and the University of California, San Francisco, most mothers end up retaining about 2.2 pounds for each pregnancy. The more pregnancies a woman experiences, the more weight she is likely to retain.

Pregnant women are not interested in sex. Some are; some aren't. Either way, it can swing back and forth from day to day. In other words, just like the rest of us.

PRENATAL INFLUENCES

A pregnant woman's cravings and/or fears can show up as physical marks on her baby's body. For example, if she craves strawberries, or eats a lot of them, her baby will born born with a 'strawberry birthmark,' while a woman who is afraid of cats will have a baby who carries a cat-shaped mark. No. Period.

A pregnant woman can influence the intellectual development of her child by engaging in cultural activities while pregnant. Maybe. Take music, for example. Although the research is still, if you will pardon the expression, in the embryonic stages, studies have shown that the fetus in the womb can hear and respond to sounds from the outside world.

In 1982, Drs. Jason Birnholz of Chicago's Rush Medical Center and Beryl Benacerraf of Boston's Diagnostic Ultrasound Association used ultrasound pictures to show a fetus blinking its eyes in response to the sounds of a buzzer on its mother's stomach. Nobody has yet done tests to find out whether fetuses exposed *in utero* to Puccini are born loving opera, but it's certainly an intriguing possibility and there is definitely more to come on this one.

PSORIASIS

Psoriasis is contagious. No. Psoriasis is a condition caused by a disturbance of the immune system. If you have it, you can't pass it on to someone else. If you don't have it, you can't catch it.

Eating fish relieves the symptoms of psoriasis. Maybe. The National Psoriasis Foundation reports receiving many letters in which people with psoriasis claim that eating red meat and sugar seems to trigger psoriatic episodes, while eating fish and vegetables seems to alleviate symptoms.

The "bad" foods, which also include eggs and dairy products, all contain arachidonic acid (AA), a natural inflammatory substance that makes psoriatic lesions swell and redden. According to a 1986 study at the University of California, Davis, and the University of Michigan, the "good" foods, such as fish oil and raw veggies, interfere with the production of AA. Eating them may lengthen the time between flare-ups of psoriasis.

Q

QUICKLIME

Bury a body in quicklime to 'destroy the evidence.' Although enshrined in mystery novels as the perfect "murderer's helper," quicklime (also known as lime or calcium oxide) does only a so-so job. Because it is strongly basic (alkaline), quicklime will dissolve soft tissue such as skin, muscle, fat and organs. But it will not dissolve hard tissues: bones and teeth. Cover a body with quicklime and what you end up with is a perfectly preserved skeleton.

QUINCE

A dressing made of boiled quince seeds will heal burned or irritated skin. When you simmer the seeds of a quince, they yield a gummy substance sometimes used in drugs and cosmetics as a stabilizer (a chemical that keeps mixtures from separating) or a suspending agent (a chemical that keeps solid particles evenly dispersed in a liquid).

People who like to make their own cosmetics from "natural" ingredients sometimes use the gum from simmered quince seeds as a hair conditioner, but there is absolutely no scientific proof that quince gum has any healing properties. In fact, spreading this or any other sticky stuff on a burn is a bad idea because your doctor may have to scrape it off later to check out the injury.

R

RAINWATER

To get your hair super-clean, wash it in rainwater. Water drawn from ground wells is called "hard" or basic (alkaline) because it contains minerals such as calcium and magnesium. Because it is difficult to rinse these minerals off the hair, when you shampoo with hard water you are likely to end up with a residue that makes your hair sticky, dull or limp.

Water from surface reservoirs, on the other hand, is "soft" or acid because it does not contain these minerals. Soft water leaves your hair cleaner, but it may change hair color. The acid water sometimes corrodes pipes through which it travels, picking up copper or lead particles that discolor bleached or tinted hair.

What makes rainwater special is its supposed purity. In theory, rainwater should be free of the minerals found in groundwater and slightly less acid than water from a reservoir, which means, closer to the natural pH of your hair and skin.

Once upon a time, this was probably true. But in our modern industrial world, to find this kind of pure clean water you would have to collect your rain in a place where the air is free of chemicals, soot and other floating debris. And if you were lucky enough to find such a haven, you would still not be able to store your rainwater for future use. The old rainwater barrel was romantic but hardly clean and pure. Without chlorine, the water in the barrel was a perfect host to bacteria, which often thrived in a characteristic slimy scum on top. You could hardly count on water like that to keep your hair shiny clean.

REDHEADS

Redheads have terrible tempers. Not necessarily. But they almost always have thin, fair or freckled skin that makes it easy to tell when they are blushing or flushing with emotion.

When a person is angry or excited, the tiny blood vessels just under the skin expand and more blood flows into the area. Among brunettes with dark skin or blondes with skin that tans easily, the only evidence of this physical phenomenon is likely to be a faint flushing. But in a redhead with pale, thin skin, the blood-filled vessels can actually make the skin look "purple" or "red" with rage.

If that happens often enough, people accustomed to associating this flush with anger are likely to think that redheads have perfectly horrible tempers. Or are at the very least, awfully emotional.

REGULARITY

Being regular means moving your bowels every day. Not necessarily. In this, as in virtually everything else, people differ. One person's normal pattern may be several movements a day. Another's may be three movements a week. The rest of us may be anywhere in-between. Basically that means that there is no such thing as a normal pattern except what's normal for you. If that pattern changes suddenly or radically, check with your doctor to rule out a medical problem such as an underactive thyroid (which can slow down body functions) or a cancer of the colon (which might block the digestive tract),

The older you get, the less regular you will be. Not necessarily. Food is pushed through the digestive tract by rhythmical, regular intestinal contractions known as peristalsis. As we get older, these contractions may become less forceful, and food may take longer to move along. The result: "irregularity."

See also GAS, WATER.

RINGWORM

You can get ringworm from your dog. Yes, you can. Many illnesses occur only in animals other than man. For example, human beings cannot catch distemper from their pets; dogs cannot catch the common cold from their masters. Ringworm, however, is a zoonose, a disease that can be passed from animals to to human beings, and vice versa. In fact, according to *The Merck Veterinary Manual,* the most important reason to treat canine ringworm is not to protect the pet, who will eventually heal on his own, but to protect his owner.

Other zoonoses are anthrax (which we may acquire from warm-blooded animals), brucellosis (from cattle, sheep, swine, goats and dogs), cat scratch fever (from cats, dogs, others), glanders (acquired from horses), Lyme disease (from dogs, deer, rodents and other wild animals), plague (from cats, dogs, rodents and others), psittacosis (from parrots and related birds), and tuberculosis (from monkeys, apes and cattle).

ROSEMARY

To cure a cold, rub rosemary leaves on your chest. Rosemary leaves contain astringent chemicals called tannins that can irritate the skin, causing the small blood vessels underneath to expand so that more blood flows into the area, which makes the skin tingle and feel warmer.

This reaction also occurs when a mustard plaster is applied to the chest to ease a cold and when hot pepper or wintergreen poultices are used to relieve arthritic aches and pain. Although all these dressings make the skin feel warm and may provide some comfort, none has any real curative effect on the underlying disease.

Rub rosemary leaves on your scalp to cure (or prevent) baldness. Another use for an astringent herb, this time in a fruitless attempt to "stimulate" the scalp and thus increase hair growth.

See also COLDS, MUSTARD, PEPPER.

RUBELLA

See GERMAN MEASLES.

S

SALT

Don't pour salt on an open wound. Good advice. Pouring salt on an open wound makes the bloody liquid on top of the wound more dense than the liquid in the cells underneath, immediately next to the wound. This leads to the physical phenomenon called osmosis. In osmosis, solutions flow across a permeable (passable) membrane from the side where the solution is less concentrated to the side where it is more concentrated. In the case of the salted wound, liquid flows out across the membranes of the cells directly around the wound towards the more concentrated salty liquid solution on top of the wound. As a result, the tissues around the wound shrink and pull. And that's why it hurts if you pour salt on an open wound.

SEEDS

If you eat fruit seeds, a tree will grow in your stomach. No. Fruit seeds are made of indigestible fiber. If you swallow small seeds, they will move, like other indigestible fiber, straight through your digestive tract.

But that does not mean that it is safe to swallow seeds and pits. Large pits, such as peach pits, might block the throat or cause an intestinal obstruction, and some small seeds contain poisonous chemicals. Apple, apricot, cherry, peach, pear, plum and quince seeds and pits all contain amygdalin, a naturally occurring sugar/cyanide compound that breaks down into hydrogen cyanide in your stomach. Amygdalin poisoning is rare, but not unknown, and there has been at least one report of a young girl who died after eating apricot pits.

SEX DETERMINATION

The day of the menstrual cycle on which you have intercourse can determine the sex of the child you conceive. Modern theories about how to pick the sex of your baby in advance are based on the known differences between male sperm (those that carry a Y chromosome) and female sperm (those that carry an X chromosome).

Female sperm are bigger, move more slowly, seem to live longer in the female reproductive tract than the male sperm, and thrive in the acidic environment of the vagina before ovulation occurs. Given that, it seems sensible to say that if you want a baby girl, you should have intercourse several days before ovulation. By the time the egg is released, the male sperm will presumably have given up the ghost, but the female sperm will presumably still be alive to fertilize the egg. On the other hand, if you want a baby boy, theoretically you should have intercourse just as ovulation occurs. That way, the fast-moving male sperm, which thrive in the more alkaline environment of the vagina at ovulation, can reach the egg first.

In theory, this system sounds just dandy. In practice, it has yet to be proven reliable.

What you eat can influence the sex of the child you conceive. In the 1970s, French researcher Joseph Stolkowski and his Canadian colleague Jacques Lorrain put 281 European and North American women who wanted baby boys on a specially designed high salt and potassium, low calcium and magnesium diet. Women who wanted girls got the reverse: low salt and potassium, high calcium and magnesium. About 83% of the patients gave birth to babies of the "right" sex, but you can never rule out the possibility that it was all due to pure chance because there have not been any serious follow-up studies.

Tying off the (right) (left) testicle before or during intercourse guarantees that the baby you conceive will be (a boy) (a girl). This superstition dates all the way back to Hippocrates who, like lots of his contemporaries, believed that boys were produced by sperm from one testicle and girls from the other. He was wrong on that one, but ahead of his time in attributing the child's sex to its father. Most early sex theorists took the simple way out, blaming mothers for giving birth to girls and praising fathers for producing boys.

Carrying a baby (high) (low) shows that it is a (boy) (girl). There is absolutely no known relationship between the fetus's sex and the position it occupies in its mother's womb.

You can tell a fetus's sex by listening to its heartbeat. Maybe. The heartbeat of a female fetus is almost always just a little faster than the heartbeat of a male fetus, but, needless to say, this method is not foolproof.

The only absolutely certain way to determine gender before birth is to examine cells obtained from the fluid surrounding the fetus in the womb (amniocentesis) or cells from the outermost membrane surrounding the fetus (chorionic villus sampling). These tests are used to detect birth defects and genetic malformations prior to birth.

SEX ORGANS

You can tell the size of a man's sex organs by the size of his (nose) (hands) (feet). No.

You can tell the size of a woman's sex organs by the size of her mouth. No.

For a woman, having sex with a man who has a large sex organ is more satisfying than having sex with a man who has a small one. Whether or not sex is successful depends on the people involved, not their organs. Within normal limits, the vagina can widen to accommodate a large penis or tighten to accommodate a smaller one. What makes sex rewarding is the emotions that accompany it. The size of your various body parts is generally irrelevant.

SEXUAL INTERCOURSE

Athletes should avoid sex for a specific period before competing. Stripped of its magic or romantic aura, sexual intercourse is really nothing more than an athletic exercise. The same common sense that dictates against playing tennis or running right before an athletic competition would also rule out sex before a match or game. But there's no scientific or physiological reason that athletes should avoid sex while in training.

Frequent sexual intercourse cures infertility. False. In fact, having intercourse too frequently may make conception even less likely. It takes about 40 hours for a man's sperm count to return to normal after each act of intercourse, so having intercourse more frequently than that may reduce the possibility of conception. (Of course, frequent intercourse is definitely not a reliable form of birth control.

Couples who do not wish to conceive must continue to use contraception each time they have sexual intercourse.)

Having sex cures acne. This piece of medical folklore may have seemed to be true in the days when most people became sexually active in their early 20s, just as their adolescent acne began to fade, but it was always coincidence, not science. Sexually active or not, teen-agers will still get acne triggered by the inevitable increase in hormone production that comes with adolescence.

Sex is dangerous for people who have had heart attacks. According to a University of Florida study reported in *Medical Aspects of Human Sexuality* in 1990, having sex puts the same stress on your heart as walking briskly or climbing up two flights of stairs. The researchers concluded, therefore, that any heart patient who could walk a treadmill running more than 2 miles an hour at a 10% incline without showing any serious increase in blood pressure or any unusual blips on an electrocardiogram, could consider it safe to have sex with his/her usual partner.

The important word here may be "usual." Twenty years ago, in a landmark study on this slightly quirky subject, a team of researchers at the Veterans Administration Hospital in Seattle reported that when middle-aged men with heart disease volunteered to monitor themselves via electrocardiogram leads on their chests and blood pressure cuffs on their arms while having sex in a familiar setting (their own homes) with a familiar partner (their wives), the exertion did not raise their blood pressure or heart rate to levels that might be hazardous to their health. None of the researchers would say whether sex between unmarried people or in strange settings would be equally safe.

Caution: It goes without saying that this is the kind of activity anyone who has heart problems should discuss with his or her own physician.

SEXUAL POTENCY

All men become impotent as they grow older. Emphatically, no. This myth is the male counterpart of the mistaken idea that menopausal women are no longer interested in sex. For a man, sexual potency is defined as the ability to attain and maintain an erection. It is true that as men grow older, the amount of seminal fluid ejaculated at orgasm and the force with which the fluid is emitted may decline, but older men in good health (and sufficiently interested in their sexual partners) can retain their ability to achieve an erection well into old age. According to *The Merck Manual*, this is not uncommon among men in their 70s and 80s.

Having sex too often can make a man impotent. No. But it may make him temporarily less fertile (See SEXUAL INTERCOURSE, above.)

SEXUALLY TRANSMITTED DISEASES (STDs)

You can catch an STD from a toilet seat. It would be a rare but not impossible occurrence. Many of the microorganisms that cause sexually transmitted diseases can remain alive for some time in body fluids (blood, urine, seminal fluid) or discharges left on a toilet seat. Should these fluids or discharges come in contact with the mucous membranes of the anus or vagina or enter the body through a break in the skin, they may carry the STD to a new host.

Contraceptives protect you against STDs. Some do. According to the American Social Health Association (ASHA), using a nonoxynol-9 chemical spermicide (cream, gel, foam) in tandem with a condom and holding the condom in place on the penis until the penis is withdrawn from the vagina appears to offer a degree of protection against a number of microorganisms, including the ones that cause AIDS, chlamydia, herpes and gonorrhea.

Caution #1: Condoms are not guaranteed against tearing. Handle them with care. *Caution #2:* Because the vaginal barrier contraceptives (diaphragm, cervical cap) allow seminal fluid to come in contact with the mucous membranes of the vagina, they are not protective. *Caution #3:* Using oral contraceptives (The Pill) can make the tissues of the vagina more susceptible to invasion by STD organisms. *Caution #4:* The only absolute protection against sexually transmitted disease is sexual abstinence. Next best: a long-term monogamous relationship.

STDs are hereditary. An hereditary disease is one that passes from parent to child through the genes. No STD is transmitted this way. If an STD does pass from mother to child, it is by infection *in utero* or through the baby's contact with infected tissues in the birth canal during delivery. A father may pass his STD on to the child by transmitting it first to the mother through unprotected intercourse during pregnancy. Babies who are born with an STD acquired in one of these ways are said to have a congenital disease, that is, one with which they were born.

Being pregnant protects a woman against STDs. This dangerous myth, less widely accepted now than in the past, is based on the mistaken belief that the cervix (the opening from the uterus into the vagina) closes tightly during pregnancy to "keep the baby from falling out" and that it (the tightly closed cervix) will keep out the microorganisms that cause STD. But the assumption is false. Pregnant women are as vulnerable as everyone else to STDs. So is the fetus in the womb. (See above.)

SHELLFISH

Eating shellfish can make your skin break out. Only in special cases. Folklore aside, most people with acne find little, if any, interaction between what they eat and how their skin behaves. However, it is true that iodides (a form of iodine) can cause acne-like eruptions. In 1990, for example, the *New England Journal of Medicine* reported food prepared and served in processing plants and fast food restaurants where iodine solutions are used to sanitize the equipment may contain as much as 30 times the daily recommended dose of iodine, contributing to skin rashes and episodes of acne, particularly in young people.

Shellfish are high in iodides. For some, but by no means all, people with acne, that might be enough to set off an acne-like reaction.

Never consume alcoholic beverages and shellfish at the same meal. This is a good rule of thumb for people who are allergic and/or sensitive to shellfish. Consuming alcoholic beverages increases sensitivity to allergens. People who are sensitive to shellfish may experience a more intense reaction if they wash the shellfish down with an alcoholic beverage.

Note: The reaction between alcohol and an allergen is not limited to shellfish or seafood. It may occur with other foods as well.

SHINGLES

If a shingles infection goes all around your body, you will die. Shingles is a viral infection that can only occur in people who once had chicken pox. Here's why: After the chicken pox infection runs its course, the virus that caused it retreats up along various nerve pathways and will remain dormant in the body for years. Decades later, the virus can be reactivated by any illness or drug that weakens the immune system. When this happens, the result is shingles, a localized case of chicken pox that usually occurs in a small spot, on one side of the body.

Uncommonly, shingles may occur on both sides of the body or in a circle around the waist. If that happens, the shingles will be more painful than normal, but unless the patient is seriously weakened by another condition such as AIDS, the infection is still self-limiting. It will heal by itself in a week or two.

Shingles is a herpes infection. No. Although the virus that causes chicken pox and shingles is called *Herpes zoster* and the shingles infection is characterized by the kind of painful small blisters we sometimes associate with a herpes infection, shingles has absolutely no relation to herpes.

Shingles is contagious. No. But someone who has never had chicken pox can catch that from someone who has an active case of shingles.

SHOWERS, COLD

A cold shower kills sexual desire. You bet. Anything that takes one's mind off the matter at hand can interfere with sexual desire. What's more, the cold water may constrict blood vessels and temporarily slow the flow of blood a man needs to sustain tumescence. But the interruption is temporary. Turn off the cold water, and the body can turn on again.

A cold shower is stimulating first thing in the morning. Actually, shocking might be a better way to put it. Stepping into a really cold shower when you are just up from a warm bed can constrict surface blood vessels, lower internal temperature, raise blood pressure and increase the load on the heart.

A cold shower can sober you up in a hurry. Like the stimulating caffeine in a cup of coffee, a cold shower may wake you up, turning you into what some alcohol experts call "a wide awake drunk." But it won't hasten the elimination of alcohol from your body, which can only be accomplished by allowing the body enough time to manufacture the enzymes it needs to metabolize the alcohol.

See also ALCOHOLIC BEVERAGES, HANGOVER.

SILENCE

Silence is golden. In a sense, it certainly can be. There is literally no end to the potentially malignant effects of exposure to continuous loud noise. A sudden loud boom can make you jump, and, if it's loud enough, deafen you temporarily. But the real villain is loud noise that goes on and on. Studies on both animals and human beings have shown that continued exposure to loud noise can constrict blood vessels, tighten muscles, raise blood pressure and cause swelling of the inner ear membranes that leads to deafness. One animal study has even suggested that continued exposure to loud noise can cause impotence or infertility.

The question, of course, is how much is too much? We measure sounds in units called decibels (dB). The lowest sound the human ear can hear without help is measured at 1 decibel. A lover's whisper, heard from a distance of about 5 feet, registers about 30 dB. Normal conversation is 60 dB; a rock concert, 115 dB; a modern jet engine or the noise from a gun muzzle, 149 dB. Anyone exposed to sounds higher than 85 dB for prolonged periods of time can expect to lose some hearing acuity.

SINUSES

(Cold and damp) (cold and dry) (warm and wet) (hot and dry) (changeable) weather causes sinus trouble. True. A sinus is a natural, expected hollow space or cavity in a bone. The sinuses most people are referring to when they talk about "sinus trouble" are the ones in the skull, right around the nose and eyes.

Each of these sinuses is lined with mucous membrane. Like the mucous membranes in mouth, nose and throat, the membranes in the sinuses continually secrete sticky mucous. Ordinarily, these secretions drain through a narrow passage to your nose. If this passage is blocked, the mucous may back up into the sinus, where it can irritate the mucous membrane, cause painful pressure in the sinus and perhaps trigger an infection.

A change in barometric pressure is one of the many things that can set off this chain of events. Hot, cold, damp, dry—whatever the weather change, it may irritate your sinuses.

Air-conditioning causes sinus trouble. It may. For some people, cold air causes a reaction called vasomotor rhinitis, an expansion of small blood vessels inside the nasal passages that makes the mucous membrane there swell. The swollen membrane can, in turn, make the sinuses throb.

Steam heat sets off your sinuses. It could. Like cold air from an air conditioner, hot, dry air from a radiator may irritate the mucous membrane lining of the nose, throat and sinuses. One way to avoid this problem is to humidify the warm air by setting a shallow pan of water on the radiator. If you do, make sure to wash the pan out with hot soapy water every evening to prevent bacteria and mold from collecting on the surface of the water.

Smoking causes sinus trouble. Tobacco smoke contains chemicals that paralyze the tiny cilia (hairs) in your nose that ordinarily beat furiously back and forth to keep bacteria, viruses and tiny particles of airborne debris out of your throat and lungs. If these cilia are inactivated, the bugs and debris can get past the nose to irritate the mucous membranes of the sinuses. The result: sinus trouble.

SKIN COLOR

Two white-skinned people who carry a hidden 'black gene' in their genetic makeup can produce a black child. No. Skin color is determined by more than one gene. All human beings carry a variety of genes for lighter and darker skin color in their chromosomes. It is possible for two people with relatively light skin to pass on their darker genes to a child and produce a baby who is relatively darker than they are, but still within the same skin tone scale. But it is impossible for very light-skinned people, such as two blonde, blue-eyed Swedes, to have a dark-eyed, dark-haired, very dark-skinned baby. Or vice versa.

Pale skin is a sign of anemia. It depends. While anemic people are likely to be pale, the reverse is not always true. Frequently, very pale people either have naturally pale skin or skin so thick it does not show the flush of blood just underneath. A more reliable guide to anemia regardless of one's natural skin color is the absence of rosy color on the inside of the eyelid, under the nails or in the creases of the palms.

See also FINGERNAILS.

SLEEP

Most people need eight hours' sleep a night. How much sleep a person needs is a highly individual trait. Some of us can get by on less than eight hours a day; some of us need more. On average, however, most of us do need at least eight hours' sleep a night in order to be alert and up to snuff the following day.

The older you get, the less sleep you need. Not necessarily. Like hair color, skin color and the shape of the body, the amount of sleep we need is determined by our genes. That means we are likely to need the same amount of sleep each night when we are 40 or 70 as we did when we were teenagers.

The real difference may lie in how well we sleep once we are in bed. As we get older, we may develop aches and pains or sleep disorders or simply take on mental burdens that interfere with our ability to sleep well. We may end up staying in bed longer and longer without getting the same period of interrupted sleep we got when we were younger or healthier or more care-free.

People who need only six or seven hours' sleep a night may never notice the difference. But those who need eight or nine hours' sleep a night in order to feel really rested may find themselves staying in bed later in the morning with their sleep time inching over into day-time hours.

One hour's sleep before midnight is worth two after. What time you go to sleep (before midnight or after) has very little to do with how well you sleep, as long as you maintain a reasonably regular sleep schedule. In other words, people who normally go to sleep each night at 1 A.M. can sleep as well as people who normally go to sleep at 10 P.M. Regardless of when we go to bed, we all get our deepest rest in the first three or four hours of sleep. After this, the night is given over to lighter sleep, including the REM (rapid eye movement) sleep, during which we are most likely to dream. When we miss a night's sleep, the next night we make up our deficit of deep sleep first, then our deficit of REM sleep.

'Early to bed, early to rise, makes a man healthy and wealthy and wise.' Maybe in the good old days, when most people worked on farms, getting to bed early made sense because it let you get up early with the animals. Today there is more leeway for personal style. So you can choose an occupation that lets you get up later if that is

what pleases you. What keeps you healthy is getting enough sleep. When you get it, so long as you maintain a regular schedule, is a matter of personal choice.

Count sheep to fall asleep. It's worth a try. A visual ritual or a mantra helps to separate you from the day's distraction and relax you into sleep. If counting sheep turns out to be energizing rather than relaxing because your sheep trip as they hit the fence, jarring you back into reality, try visualizing a candle flame that you try to keep upright against a strong current of air. Other effective ways to relax: Breathing exercises to increase skin temperatures in hands, feet and legs, or attempting to create a feeling of heaviness that moves down from your head to your shoulders and down your body to your feet.

'I never sleep a wink at night.' Unlikely. A truly sleepless night is a remarkable exception, usually brought on by illness or worry or a combination of the two. When observed under scientific conditions in a sleep laboratory or even in their own homes, chronic insomniacs who complain that they never sleep almost always fall asleep, usually within an hour of getting into bed.

You sleep best in a (cold) (warm) room. Take your pick. There is no rule on this one other than your own comfort. As long as the room is not so cold that your shivering shakes you awake or so warm that you are bathed in perspiration, any temperature at which you sleep well is fine.

The fact is that your own internal temperature is more important to your getting a good night's sleep than the room temperature. Each of us has a well-defined individual pattern by which our body temperature rises and falls in a regular cycle every day. We may fall asleep at any point along this cycle, but we are most likely to wake at a point when our temperature is starting to rise. That is why "day people" (people whose temperature begins to rise early in the day) are likely to wake up early in the morning even when they go to sleep very late at night.

Leave the windows open at night when you sleep so there will be enough oxygen in the room. Fresh air seeps in around the edges of windows and doors even when they are shut tight or sealed with tape to prevent the loss of warm air in winter or cooled air in summer. Modern "energy efficient" homes may feel stuffy when the windows and doors are closed, but they are never completely air tight.

However, the Consumer Product Safety Commission and the Environmental Protection Agency, among others, have made it clear that energy efficient windows and doors can raise the level of indoor air pollution: formaldehyde vapors from the carpeting and draperies, nitrogen oxide from a gas stove, carbon monoxide from a gas heater, and other chemicals used in furniture and appliance cleaners. The obvious solution is to open the windows and let some fresh air in.

SLEEPWALKING

Never wake a sleepwalker. It will drive him mad. Waking a sleepwalker can leave him confused and disoriented as he tries to figure out where he is and how he got there, but it certainly won't drive him mad, nor will his confusion persist once he is thoroughly awake. Nonetheless, if possible, it certainly makes more sense to guide the sleeper right back to bed instead of waking him. Once nestled in, he is unlikely to rise again that night. Wake him, and he may spend hours puzzling over what happened.

Boys sleepwalk more frequently than girls do. True. The difference is not enormous, but it is real, say scientists who specialize in sleep disorders. In study after study, when researchers simply ask parents whether their children sleepwalk, they get the same numbers for boys and girls. But if the scientists ask a second question ("Who sleepwalks more often?"), the answer is always, the boys.

Among children, sleepwalking is often thought to be a sign of immaturity. It may occur more often among boys than among girls because girls are likely to mature sooner. Other childhood sleep disorders such as night terrors and bed-wetting are also more common among boys. A small gender difference persists into adulthood, when slightly more men than women are likely to visit sleep clinics complaining of sleepwalking, but this may simply mean that men are more annoyed by sleepwalking, not that they sleepwalk more often.

SMOKING

Smoking stunts your growth. To date, there is no scientific evidence to show that adolescents who smoke grow at a slower rate than do adolescents who are not smokers. However, there is a definite relationship between a pregnant woman's smoking and the growth rate of the fetus she is carrying. Babies born to women who smoke while pregnant are clearly at increased risk of being low birth weight or premature.

Smoking keeps you thin. It may. The idea that smoking can keep you trim dates back as far as the 1930s when one brand of cigarettes ran advertisements suggesting that dieters "reach for a Lucky instead of a sweet."

Over the years, numerous studies have shown that people who smoke are likely to weigh five to 10 pounds less than non-smokers of the same age and height. Today, as more and more of us stop smoking, it has become perfectly clear that most people do gain some weight when they give up tobacco. Smoking speeds up metabolism (the rate at which we use energy). When we stop smoking, we burn less energy (fewer calories), so almost every ex-smoker will gain a few pounds even if he does not increase his food intake. In time, the ex-smoker's metabolism stabilizes and so does his weight, but usually a few pounds higher than it was while he was smoking.

Smoking is less dangerous for women than for men. This myth was prevalent in the 1960s and 1970s when American women were less likely than American men to develop lung cancer or emphysema, two major consequences of long-term smoking. Now that many women have been smoking as long as their male counterparts, lung cancer is the leading cause of cancer death among women as well as men. There is no gender difference.

As long as you haven't got a cigarette cough, smoking isn't dangerous. Wrong. Smoking can damage cells in your mouth, throat and lungs long before it causes a characteristic hacking "smoker's cough." And non-respiratory smoking-linked cancers such as cancer of the bladder, cancer of the cervix and cancer of the pancreas can prove fatal without ever having made you cough.

Smoking isn't dangerous if you don't inhale. False. Nicotine can be absorbed into the body through the mucous membrane lining of the mouth. The nicotine you get this way is just as likely as the nicotine you get from inhaling to increase your risk of heart disease by narrowing your blood vessels, making your blood clot more quickly and raising your ratio of low-density lipoproteins (LDLs), the fat and protein particles that carry cholesterol into your arteries.

Filtered cigarettes are safer than cigarettes without a filter. There is no measurable difference between the two in their ability to make you sick.

Cigars and pipes are safer than cigarettes because you don't inhale the smoke. False. Smoking a pipe or a cigar, even without inhaling the smoke, dramatically increases the risk of cancer of the lip, mouth and tongue.

Smokeless tobacco is safer than smoking tobacco. False. According to the American Academy of Otolaryngology—Head and Neck Surgery, the smokeless tobaccos (chewing tobacco and snuff) are as addictive and carcinogenic as the tobacco in cigarettes, cigars and pipes. Their nicotine and carcinogens are efficiently absorbed through the mucous membrane lining of the nose and cheek. As a result, in the period from 1970 to 1986, as the number of young people who chew tobacco quadrupled and the number who use snuff rose 15 times, the incidence of oral cancers among young people also rose dramatically.

SNAKEBITE

Whiskey is an antidote for snakebite. No. Like snake venom, alcohol lowers blood pressure. Giving whiskey to someone who has been bitten by a snake will only increase the chances of shock.

If you move quickly or get excited after being bitten by a snake, the venom will spread faster. It is true that anything that increases the circulation of blood to your muscles may hasten the spread of the venom injected when a poisonous snake bites. Staying calm enough to get medical help in a hurry definitely goes a long way towards reducing the ultimate effects of any bite by a poisonous snake.

To reduce the severity of a snakebite, make an x-shape incision in the wound and suck out the venom. A bad idea. Although medical treatment for snakebite may involve cutting into the wound and mechanically suctioning the venom, an amateur who crosscuts a snakebite can cause serious damage to nerves and tendons close to the surface of the skin. Sucking the wound increases the chance of infection by transferring bacteria from the mouth to the open wound. The best treatment for a poisonous snake bite is a fast trip to the hospital. For first aid, people traveling in an area far from a hospital should carry and learn to use a snakebite kit.

SNEEZING

Saying 'God bless you' when someone sneezes can stop him from sneezing again. Anthropologists and folklorists know that sneezing has definite magical overtones. In culture after culture, people have believed that the soul can escape from the body in the breath that rushes out from your nose and mouth when you sneeze. Blessing the sneezer is a way to "protect him until his soul returns." But it won't stop the sneezing.

See also BIRTH CONTROL, HICCUPS.

SNORING

Sleep on your stomach to prevent snoring. It just might work. When you sleep on your back, your tongue can drift backward and partially block the air passage into your throat. The sound you get when you breathe and air tries to make its way through this narrowed passage is a snore.

When you sleep on your stomach, gravity pulls your tongue forward and down, leaving enough room for air to get through without noise. If you cannot sleep comfortably on your stomach, try raising the head of the bed by putting a pillow under the mattress. This maneuver may keep your tongue forward, your throat clear and your sleep soundless.

To keep a person from snoring, tie tennis balls to the back of his pajamas. The idea is to get him to turn over on his stomach. (See above.)

Snoring is no big deal, healthwise. Ordinarily, snoring once in a while is nothing to worry about, but if you snore all the time, check with your doctor to be sure your problem isn't swollen adenoids or tonsils, or perhaps an allergy.

SOAP

Wash your hands with soap and water every time you use the bathroom. Using soap rather than plain water is not an affectation. Soap makes your skin more slippery and increases the ability of water to rinse bacteria and microorganisms off your skin. Washing your hands after blowing your nose or using the bathroom or playing with the dog does get rid of bacteria and viruses you might otherwise pass along to someone else. Washing your hands before handling food is basic kitchen hygiene.

You can pick up germs from soap in public washrooms. True. That's why most modern public washrooms have those glass or metal containers over the sink to dispense a measured dose of soap or detergent.

Soap is gentler than detergents to the skin. It depends on the detergent. Obviously a laundry detergent loaded with bleaches, brighteners and water softeners is too strong to use on your skin. In fact, it probably says so right on the box.

SORE THROAT

Gargle with warm salt water to relieve a sore throat. True. The warm, alkaline saltwater solution acts as a detergent, washing away irritating mucous on the surface of the membranes of the throat, giving you real, though temporary, relief. To make a saltwater gargle, the American Academy of Otolaryngology—Head and Neck Surgery recommends dissolving one-quarter teaspoon salt in one cup of warm water.

Gargle with aspirin dissolved in hot water to ease a sore throat. Gargling with this solution will relieve the dryness in your throat and wash away secretions. But you cannot absorb enough aspirin through the membrane lining of your mouth and throat to relieve the pain. The warm water is fine, but for pain relief, it is more effective to swallow two aspirin with a glass of plain water.

Caution: Children who take aspirin while they have a viral illness may be at risk for developing Reye's Syndrome, a relatively uncommon but serious condition that can cause brain damage. Always check with your doctor before giving aspirin to a child who is ill.

Drink honeyed tea to soothe an aching throat. True. Sweet foods stimulate the brain's production of natural painkillers called endorphins. According to researchers at the Taste and Smell Clinic at the Center for Molecular Nutrition and Sensory Disorders in Washington, D.C., recent research suggests that the reaction may be virtually instantaneous, so that your sore throat feels better as soon as you swallow the sweetened tea. The sweet liquid will also stimulate the production of saliva that soothes your dry and irritated throat; the hot water helps loosen and wash away mucous secretions in your throat.

Wrap flannel soaked in turpentine around your throat to cure a sore throat (or a cold). The flannel is okay. Even though it will not cure your sore throat or your cold, it can make you feel cozy and relaxed. But the turpentine's a terrible idea. This common solvent is an irritant that can cause contact dermatitis. It is also a poison that can cause gastric upset, kidney damage, disorientation and coma if absorbed through skin. Inhaling its fumes can cause chest pains and irregular heartbeat, irritate the lining of the bronchi (air passages), and damage your kidneys.

See also COLDS.

SPANISH FLY

Consuming 'Spanish fly' makes you sexy. Spanish fly, also known as blistering fly or cantharides, is a powder made of the crushed dried bodies of a beetle whose proper name is *Cantharis vesicatoria*. The powder is a powerful irritant sometimes swallowed or applied to skin and mucous membranes as an aphrodisiac.

Both are bad ideas. If swallowed, Spanish fly can cause an itching, burning sensation in the urinary tract that may stimulate an erection. Applied to the skin, it may be strong enough to blister skin; it can be absorbed through skin and mucous membranes. Whether swallowed or absorbed, Spanish fly is potentially an extremely toxic substance that can cause severe gastroenteritis, kidney damage, collapse and even death.

SPINACH

Eating spinach makes you strong. False. Spinach is an extraordinarily good source of vitamins A and C. A single 3.5 ounces/100 gram serving will provide 6,700 IU vitamin A, 134% of the RDA for a man and 166% of the RDA for a woman. Spinach is high in calcium and iron, but it also contains oxalic acid, which forms chemical complexes ("binds") with these minerals so that your body cannot absorb them. In fact, the oxalic acid in spinach binds the iron so efficiently that you can absorb only 2% to 5% of the iron in fresh or cooked spinach leaves. Oxalic acid may also concentrate in urine, increasing the risk of kidney stones.

And, like beets, celery, eggplant, lettuce, radishes, collard and turnip greens, spinach contains nitrites that are converted naturally to nitrites in your stomach. Nitrites react with the amino acids in proteins to form nitrosamines. There is no evidence that this natural conversion process causes any problems for a healthy adult. But when spinach and other high-nitrate vegetables are cooked and left to sit at room temperature for some time, natural bacterial and enzyme action will convert the nitrates to nitrites much more quickly. These high-nitrite foods may be hazardous for small children. Occasionally, cases of "spinach poisoning" have been reported among young children fed cooked spinach that had been standing at room temperature before being served.

SPRAINS AND STRAINS

Put a (hot) (cold) compress on a sprain or strain. Yes. A strain is an injury to a muscle; a sprain is an injury to a ligament. The trick to treating them is to pick the right compress at the right time. Ordinarily, the cold compress should come first, to reduce the loss of fluids from torn cells and swelling at the site of the injury and to constrict small blood vessels there so as to slow bleeding under the skin and prevent a black and blue mark.

Later, after a day or so, you can switch to hot compresses to relieve the residual pain. If you used the hot compress first, it would dilate those small blood vessels (which means more bleeding) and increase the flow of liquids from torn cells (which means more swelling).

See also LARD.

SPRING

'In the spring a young man's fancy lightly turns to thoughts of love.' Alfred, Lord Tennyson must have been commenting on the English reaction to spring sunlight after a long wet and foggy winter. Or he may have been referring to the traditional month for marriage, June, named for Juno, wife of Jupiter and protector of marriage.

But is there science to back up a supposed rise in erotic involvement in the spring? No. In fact, what science there is on this arcane subject may support a belief in the opposite situation, a lack of lust in warm weather.

In 1990, epidemiologists at the Chemical Industry Institute of Toxicology, Research Triangle Park, N.C., published a report in the *New England Journal of Medicine* showing that both the density of seminal fluid and sperm counts are lower in the summer than in the winter. This may account for the previously reported hot weather decline in fertility among American, French and British men.

SPRING TONIC

Like your house, your body needs a 'spring cleaning.' It is stretching things, but here's a possible explanation for the myth. In your grandmother's day, when fresh fruits and vegetables were not readily available in the winter, people may well have been starved for the fiber that keeps the digestive system moving along at top speed.

With spring came the flood of high-fiber fresh fruits and vegetables to unblock digestive tracts supposedly plugged up with the winter's "poisons." If it did not work, you could always move on to sulfur and molasses (see below).

Sulfur and molasses cure spring fever. If the lassitude and dreaminess of spring fever were really anemia in disguise, sulfur and molasses might have had a minimally beneficial effect. Molasses is a good source of iron, calcium and chromium (a trace metal essential to the metabolism of carbohydrates). It also contains some sulfur, also needed to metabolize carbohydrates.

What the sulfur did was make the molasses taste vile (bolstering the old idea that medicine has to taste bad in order to work well) and act as a laxative (sulfur is still used as a laxative in veterinary medicine), thus helping to purge those imaginary winter "toxins."

STOMACH, UPSET

Drinking milk soothes an upset stomach. Scientifically, it should not, but in practice it often seems to.

Although milk looks and sometimes tastes like the blandest of foods, studies in the early 1980s at two California research centers showed that rather than acting as an antidote, drinking milk actually increased the production of stomach acid.

At the University of California, San Diego, volunteers were fed an assortment of liquids, including milk, beer, plain and decaffeinated coffee, and regular and decaffeinated soft drinks. Contrary to expectations, milk and beer turned out to be the drinks most likely to stimulate the production of stomach acid.

At the Veterans Administration Hospital in Los Angeles, another team of researchers discovered that drinking milk (regular, low-fat, or skim) did not neutralize stomach acid. All of which conflicts with the experience of people who, ignoring the research, just go on insisting their tummies feel better when they drink milk. In other words, on this one, the jury's still out.

Cola drinks quiet a raging stomach. Generations of doctors once recommended cola drinks to replace the fluids lost during a bout of vomiting or diarrhea. One reason they did this was because they thought that cola drinks were high in potassium, an important mineral lost during this kind of stomach upset. It is now known, however, that while these sweetened liquids can replace fluids, they cannot replace potassium because they contain virtually none.

See also ASPIRIN, LICORICE, TURISTA.

STUTTERING

Boys are more likely than girls to suffer from stuttering. True. When people are under stress, they tend to focus their tension on the muscles at one specific point in the body. This point is called a target area. The best-known target areas are the muscles in the wall of the abdomen, the shoulders, the lower back, the face and the vocal cords.

The target area we pick seems to be related to our gender. Three times as many females as males suffer from spasms in the muscles in the wall of the abdomen when they are under stress (a "nervous stomach"). Women are also more likely than men to suffer from temporomandibular joint disorder (TMD), spasms in the muscles on the side of the face that cause pain in the hinge that opens and closes the lower jaw. But five times as many boys as girls may suffer from spasms that lock the vocal cords. The effort to relax the cords and speak produces the speech problem we call stuttering.

Forcing a left-handed child to switch to the right hand will make him stutter. It may. The link between tension and stuttering is one way to explain the old wives' tale that forcing a left-handed person to write with his right hand can make him stutter, says Dr.

Martin F. Schwartz, executive director of the National Center for Stuttering in New York.

The left side of the brain controls speech. It also controls movement on the right side of the body. The right side of the brain controls movement on the left side of the body. A right-handed person uses the left side of his brain for speaking and writing. A left-handed person also uses the left side of his brain for speaking, but he uses the right side of his brain for writing.

This is the natural way for a left-handed person to behave. He or she does it instinctively, without thinking. Forcing a change to the right hand means forcing the person to stop and think before picking up a pencil. Although some people may make the switch without a hitch, other will translate the stress into TMD or lower back pain, or spasms of the vocal cords that turn a normal happy lefty into a tense, right-handed stutterer.

Cut the tongue to cure a stutter. Absolutely not. This once-accepted "remedy" is a cruel and totally useless treatment performed in the mistaken belief that stuttering was caused by a person's being "tongue-tied," that is, that the membrane connecting his tongue to the floor of the mouth is too tight and that cutting it would cure the stutter.

Children who stutter will outgrow the problem naturally. Sometimes, yes; sometimes, no. There is no hard and fast rule.

Tickling a baby's feet will make him stutter. It's hard to talk when you are laughing, so a laughing child may seem to stutter, but unless the child is already a stutterer, this effect is strictly temporary and will disappear as soon as the tickling stops.

STYES

To heal a stye, bathe it in milk. A stye is an infection of a small gland at the base of an eyelash. The infection makes the gland swell into a painful little lump. While bathing it in warm liquid can open and drain the infection, milk is the wrong liquid to choose since it can leave the eyelid sticky and uncomfortable.

To cure a stye, rub it with a golden wedding ring. A bad idea. The magic of the wedding ring is twofold. First there's the charm of an unbroken circle, believed to keep evil spirits at bay. Second there's the gold, a rare and expensive precious metal. But its medical power to heal a stye is zilch. Rubbing a stye may physically break open the infection, but this may also spread to the surrounding tissue.

SUGAR

Sugar is quick energy food. All carbohydrates contain sugars. All sugars are classified into one of several groups, depending on their molecular structure.

Monosaccharides ("simple sugars") are sugars consisting of one molecule of a sugar. Examples are glucose and fructose. Disaccharides ("double sugars") are composed of two molecules, one each of a different sugar. The best-known example is sucrose (table sugar), which is composed of one molecule of glucose and one molecule of fructose. Polysacchides ("many sugars") are sugars consisting of many sugar molecules. Polysaccharides such as dextrin are composed of several molecules of the same sugar (glucose). Many plant starches and fibers such as amylose, amylopectin and cellulose are polysaccharides.

When we consume carbohydrates, our bodies break them down (metabolize them) into their simpler constituents: glucose, fructose, galactose. Glucose can be converted to glycogen, the form of sugar stored in the liver. When we need energy, the glycogen is reconverted to glucose and released into the bloodstream on demand.

The simpler the structure of a carbohydrate food, the easier it is for our bodies to metabolize it to glucose. That's why sugars are considered "fast energy foods."

Sugar is empty calories. If by "empty calories" you mean that sugar supplies energy (calories) but is totally devoid of other nutrients, you are wrong. It may not be a powerhouse of vitamins and minerals, but according to the U.S. Department of Agriculture (USDA), one tablespoon of granulated white table sugar provides 45 calories from 12 grams carbohydrates, plus a trace of calcium, phosphorous, iron, potassium and sodium.

Brown sugar is more healthful than white sugar. Brown sugar, which is nothing more mysterious than plain white sugar sprayed with molasses, contains 60 times as much calcium as an equal amount of white sugar, 56 times as much phosphorus, 48 times as much iron, 108 times as much potassium, 19 times as much sodium, plus very small amounts of the B vitamins thiamine (vitamin B1), riboflavin (vitamin B2) and niacin. But those numbers are deceiving. Given the small amounts of pure sugar we use in food, such as the 1 teaspoon we normally add to coffee, there is no meaningful nutritional difference between white sugar and brown sugar.

The sugar in fruit is more healthful and natural than refined table sugar. Eventually, the fructose in fruit is metabolized to glucose (see above) just like all other sugars, but the sugar in fruit does come in a "package" with vitamins, minerals and food fiber.

Eating too much sugar causes diabetes. No. People with diabetes have an inability to produce or use the insulin needed to metabolize and maintain normal levels of blood sugar. As a result, unmetabolized sugar circulates in their blood and is eventually excreted in the urine (which is why an abnormally high level of sugar in the urine may be a symptom of diabetes).

Although people with diabetes usually must limit their intake of sugar, it is the inability to produce or use insulin, not the amount of sugar they consume, that causes their disease.

Eating sugar causes cavities. It may. The bacteria that cause tooth decay thrive on the material that piles up on your teeth when carbohydrates you have eaten ferment in your mouth.

Sugary foods that leave your mouth quickly are less likely than foods that stay in your mouth to cause a buildup of the material that nourishes bacteria. Sometimes this can lead to apparently paradoxical situations. For example, healthful, low-fat raisins that stick to your teeth or totally fat-free, high-sugar hard candies that dissolve slowly in your mouth are more likely to cause cavities than are rich and creamy chocolates that are gone from your mouth in minutes.

Sugar makes your cavities ache. True. When sugar enters a cavity in your tooth, like salt on an open wound, it makes the liquid in cells on top of the cavity more dense than the liquid in the cells around it. This leads to the physical phenomenon called osmosis. In osmosis, solutions flow across a permeable membrane from the side where the solution is less concentrated to the side where it is more concentrated. In the case of the sugared cavity, that means that liquid flows out across the membranes of the cells directly around the cavity towards the more concentrated sugary solution on top. As a result, the tissues around the cavity shrink and pull. And that's why it hurts when you get sugar in your cavities.

See SALT.

SUICIDE

People who threaten suicide never go through with it. A dangerous and misleading myth. People who threaten or plan a suicide mean what they say. The fact that they may sometimes fail in their attempt in no way invalidates their warning. We 'measure the number of suicides in this country based on the cause of death listed on death certificates. This may underestimate the true incidence of suicide, which now ranks among the top 10 causes of death among adults in urban America, and accounts for nearly one-third of the deaths among American college students and 10% of the deaths among Americans age 25 to 34.

Our refusal to take threats of suicide seriously, therefore, may say more about our own inability to deal with the subject than it does about the seriousness of these threats.

SUNBURN

A healthy tan is good for your skin. The phrase "a healthy tan" is an oxymoron, a contradiction in terms. Every sunburn damages skin, forcing it to increase the production of melanin, the dark pigment that gives dark skin its color and makes lighter skin look "tan." Increased melanin production is a self-defense mechanism to protect against the sun's burning rays. It is always a sign of skin damage; never a sign of skin health.

You can't get sunburned on a cloudy day. Wrong. According to *The Medical Letter,* a newsletter for health professionals, even when the sky is masked by a cloudy cover, 60 to 80% of the sun's burning ultraviolet (UV) rays will slip through to you.

You can't get sunburned if you stay in the shade. Wrong again. Even if you stay out of direct sunlight, on a bright day ultraviolet rays reflected up from the ground or scattered through the air can burn your skin. This is particularly true on or near the water. Both water and sand are efficient reflectors of the sun's rays.

Vegetable oils or mineral oil will protect you against a sunburn. No. Neither provides any barrier against the ultraviolent rays that damage your skin.

To soothe a sunburn, smooth on sweet cream or yogurt. True. At first, mildly sunburned skin is red and slightly swollen. At this stage, the cool sweet cream or yogurt dressing can ease the pain. Later, as the sun-injured skin begins to heal, it will shrink, dry and ultimately peel. At this stage, sweet cream and yogurt, which are natural oil-and-water emulsions, can relieve the dryness.

Caution: If you use these folk remedies, be absolutely sure to rinse them off thoroughly with lots of tepid water. If you leave them to dry on your skin, they will only make you itchy and uncomfortable. And remember, a serious, truly painful, major sunburn is a burn. Like any serious burn, it requires immediate medical attention.

SUNGLASSES

Wearing sunglasses indoors will weaken your eyes. False. Wearing very dark glasses all the time, indoors and out, may temporarily increase your sensitivity to bright lights enough to make you uncomfortable for a while if you stop wearing the shades, but healthy eyes will readjust quickly and there are some situations in which wearing tinted lenses indoors can make you much more comfortable.

If you work all day in an office with fluorescent lighting, you may feel better and possibly even see better if you wear very lightly tinted lenses. Fluorescent lighting operates in the blue-green part of the spectrum, a harsh and disconcerting light by which to read. In addition, fluorescent bulbs provide an unsteady, flickering kind of illumination. This flutter is too rapid to be perceived consciously by the human eye, but it is irritating nonetheless. Some sensitive people may even find that it triggers repeated headaches. Tinted glasses may make the blue-green light and the fluorescent flutter less irritating.

SUNLIGHT

To cure a case of athlete's foot, take off your shoes and socks and expose your feet to the sunlight. Walking around with your naked feet out in the warm, sunny air does help keep feet dry, and that, in turn, may reduce the risk of an infection caused by *Tinea pedis,* the moisture-loving athlete's foot fungus. But it isn't enough to guarantee protection against athlete's foot if you spend the rest of the day in sweaty socks and sneakers or walk around unprotected on damp floors where the fungus is lurking or dry your feet with a towel used by someone who has athlete's foot. Your best line of defense is the same old boring advice your mother gave you: Wear clean, dry shoes and socks and keep your feet clean and dry, as well.

Note: It is safer to wear open sandals than to walk entirely bare-foot. The sole protects your foot from cuts and bruises while the open top lets in the air and sunlight.

See also ATHLETE'S FOOT, DIAPER RASH, TUBERCULOSIS.

SWIMMER'S EAR

A drop of vinegar prevents/cures 'swimmer's ear.' Swimmer's ear is an itchy infection caused by bacteria in water that gets into your ear while you are swimming. A few drops of a vinegar-and-water solution may act as a mild antiseptic.

Caution: Never use this home remedy except on the advice of your doctor. Vinegar and water will not cure an earache or an ear infection. It may cause complications (including infection) if used by anyone who has a ruptured eardrum or has had ear surgery or has a tube implanted in his ear.

SWIMMING

Wait an hour after eating before going in for a swim. Not a bad idea. After you eat, your stomach muscles go to work on the food you've just taken in. To do this, they need an adequate supply of oxygen-rich blood. If you begin strenuous exercise, such as a 40–yard dash across a pool or a plunge into an icy ocean right after eating, your heart may not be able to supply both stomach and skeletal muscles at the same time. Blood will flow away from your stomach to your arms and legs, and your stomach muscles, deprived of blood, may cramp.

This is less likely to happen to healthy people who eat a light meal and then wade into the water for a sedate paddle than it is to someone who downs a trencherman's lunch or is in poor health, perhaps with heart disease, and dives into a heart-thumping dash across the pool right after eating. But either way, waiting an hour gives your digestive tract time to get its work done so that its need for blood returns to normal.

So is it better to go swimming before you eat, when you're still hungry? No. When you feel hungry, your muscles are hungry, too, starved for glycogen, the fuel on which they run. As every serious athlete knows, glycogen-starved muscles are much more likely to cramp. The idea that you should wait an hour after eating seems to be a compromise that allows time for digestion and an increase in the availability of muscle-powering glycogen.

SWIMMING POOLS

Women can get pregnant by swimming in a coed swimming pool. Only if they do in a pool what most people do in more private surroundings.

The water in swimming pools turns blonde hair green. If the hair is blonde because it's been bleached, it is possible that the chlorine in the pool water will turn it faintly greenish. In one case, reported in the *New England Journal of Medicine* in 1975, you didn't even have to go swimming to have your hair turn green. The culprit turned out to be ordinary fluoridated tap water. The fluoride in the water system in Framingham, Massachusetts, changed the pH (acid/alkaline balance) of the city's water so that it leeched out traces of copper from the water pipes. The coppery water produced an epidemic of green hair among the students at Framingham State College, with blondes developing the brightest tint.

See also ATHLETE'S FOOT.

T

TEA

A cup of tea has less caffeine than a cup of coffee. If what we are talking about is regular tea vs. regular coffee, the answer is almost certainly, yes. According to the American Dietetic Association, a cup of regular, drip brew coffee has, on average, 139 mg caffeine. A cup of tea brewed from a regular tea bag has 47 mg caffeine if brewed for five minutes. Brewed for one minute, it has 29 mg caffeine. A cup of Japanese green tea brewed for five minutes from loose tea has 21 mg caffeine.

A cup of tea soothes an upset stomach. It depends on what is causing the upset. If the culprit were caffeine, then switching from moderate amounts of coffee to moderate amounts of tea might help. But both tea leaves and coffee beans contain oils that may irritate the lining of the stomach. That's why people with ulcers and some other stomach or intestinal disorders are warned off tea as well as coffee.

TEA BAGS

A wet tea bag or compresses of cool tea can soothe itchy, burned or irritated skin. Tea leaves contain tannic acid, a substance that causes proteins on the surface of the skin to coagulate, forming a scab or crust. As a result, tannic acid was once used as standard treatment for serious burns, to create a temporary protective sheath that would hold in the body seeping out when the top layers of skin are burned away. However, tannic acid is now known to be poisonous when absorbed in large amounts over large areas of burned or broken skin. Today, neither tea nor tannic acid dressings are used to treat burned skin.

Chewing on a wet tea bag eases the pain of a toothache. False. There's no natural painkiller in tea leaves.

Biting on a tea bag after an extraction stops the wound from bleeding. It might help. Pressure against a wound constricts torn blood vessels and helps slow the flow of blood. In addition, according to the National Institute for Dental Research, the tannic acid in tea leaves is a mild coagulant (an agent that accelerates blood clotting). Biting on a wet tea bag just might slow and stop the bleeding after you've had a tooth pulled. Check with your dentist to be sure.

TEETH

Healthy teeth are white. Although teeth may look white against tanned or naturally dark skin, their natural color is yellowish, or to put it more kindly, ivory. Well-made good dentures reflect this fact. If you scrutinize them carefully, you will see that they, too, are ivory, not white.

Nonetheless, many people persist in thinking their teeth should be pristine white, thus contributing to the coffers of the makers of toothpastes and powders whose claim to fame is that they "whiten" your teeth. Anything that really does change the color of your teeth is likely to be either a kind of white "paint" that covers up the stains on your tooth or an abrasive such as baking soda that rubs them away.

Everyone's teeth turn yellow with age. Some yellowing does occur naturally as a tooth matures and its pulp (which contains the blood vessels and fibrous tissue that makes the tooth a living thing) shrinks, leaving layers of dentin behind on the inner surface of the tooth. Dentin is more yellow than dental enamel, the coating on the surface of the tooth above the gum line. As the dentin builds up inside the tooth, it makes the tooth more opaque and keeps light from shining through, which is why the tooth looks darker. The same thing happens when you have root canal work that removes the nerve and puts an opaque filling in its place.

If your teeth get so dark that you think they are unsightly, you can have them bleached. A "dead" tooth (one with the nerve and pulp removed) can be bleached permanently from the inside. A living tooth must be bleached on the outside. It will be lighter for a while, but will eventually darken again as the pulp inside continues to shrink.

(The superficial yellow or brown stains caused by coffee, tea and tobacco are definitely not the normal results of aging. These stains can be easily removed either by a professional cleaning or by your brushing with a mildly abrasive mush made from baking soda and water.)

Caution: Check with your dentist or periodontist before brushing with baking soda. If you have extensive gum recession, the baking soda mixture may be too abrasive. Never use baking soda to brush dentures; the abrasive can damage the surface of the false teeth.

Some people have soft teeth. This is a nonsensical statement, once used to explain why some people have more cavities than others.

Except for those rare individuals who inherit an uncommon inability to form the enamel covering for the teeth, nobody has "soft teeth." Dental enamel, the substance that forms the outer surface of every tooth, is composed of crystalline calcium salts, an extraordinarily tough substance made to withstand normal use during your lifetime. Some more reasonable explanations for excessive tooth decay might be poor dentistry, poor dental home care or perhaps an inherited vulnerability to the bacteria known to cause tooth decay.

See also AGING, APPLES, BAKING SODA, PREGNANCY.

TEMPERATURE

The normal body temperature for a human being is 98.6° F. That figure is more an average than an absolute. The normal internal temperature of a healthy human body varies considerably with age, sex, day of the month and time of day.

For example, infants and young children have an average normal body temperature of 99° F or even slightly higher. They may run a fever as high as 104° F during a serious illness without showing any serious lingering effects afterwards. Older people, on the other hand, may run an average normal temperature around 97° F, and in the course of a menstrual cycle, the body temperature for a woman of child-bearing age varies with her hormone status, rising about a degree right after ovulation.

The most accurate way to take your temperature is with a thermometer under your tongue. Well, at least it's the most accurate way to take the temperature inside your mouth. If you measure your temperature by mouth, it will run 0.5°–1.0° F lower than your temperature measured by a thermometer inserted in the rectum.

Caution: Whether you take your temperature orally or rectally, use only the thermometer designed specifically for that purpose. An oral thermometer is too fragile to be inserted into the rectum.

See also HANDS, HOT WEATHER.

TETANUS

Stepping on a rusty nail causes tetanus. It isn't the nail, it's the tetanus spores. Tetanus is an acute illness caused by the neurotoxin (nerve poison) produced by the bacteria *Clostridium tetani.* The spores (resting stage) of this bacteria are anaerobic, which means they live most comfortably in places where there is very little oxygen, such as a puncture wound deep into body tissue.

Tetanus spores are most often found in soil and in feces, insect as well as animal, so the risk of tetanus from a puncture wound is greatest out of doors, which is where you are most likely to step on that legendary rusty nail. However, tetanus spores are ubiquitous. They can live indoors, too, and because they may infect even in a small puncture wound, prudence dictates that any such injury get immediate medical attention.

You need a tetanus booster every two years. This is about the time span between the first immunization and follow-up shots for young children. Adults who were immunized as children are believed to be protected with a tetanus booster every 10 years or immediately after possible exposure to the tetanus organism.

THINKING

Deep thinking makes you thin. Sorry, no. Your brain burns calories all the time, but not enough to make a noticeable difference in your weight.

According to Dr. Louis Sokoloff, M.D., chief of the laboratory of cerebral metabolism of the National Institutes of Mental Health, the average brain uses no more energy when solving puzzles, such as math problems, as it does when simply looking at a nifty sunset— one quarter of a calorie a minute, just about the amount of energy it takes to burn a 20-watt bulb.

So, how come you feel totally drained after an hour spent balancing your checkbook? Simple. While you are working, your muscles may tense and your heartbeat may rise as your whole body (not just your brain) gets into the act. The result may be exhaustion, but no measurable weight loss.

THROAT, DRY

Keep a pan of water on the radiator to prevent your throat from turning dry in the winter. Water evaporating from an open bowl is a simple and effective humidifier that moistens the room air and soothes dry membranes in your nose and throat. To lower the risk of the water's being contaminated with mold and other microorganisms that float naturally through the indoor air, wash the bowl every night with hot, soapy water.

See SORE THROAT.

THUNDERSTORMS

Thunderstorms can make you feel edgy or even sexy. True. As a thunderhead (the cloud associated with thunderstorms) develops, a large electrical field grows inside the cloud. According to the National Oceanographic and Atmospheric Administration, the particles in the upper part of the cloud are usually positively charged. In the lower part of the cloud, a large negative charge grows around a positively charged center. Normally, earth's atmosphere is negatively charged, but the approaching thunderstorm builds up a positive charge on the ground below and for several miles around. The attraction between the positive charge under the storm cloud and the normal negative charge in the cloud can make the air in-between crackle.

With the storm coming closer, the barometer drops, reducing the pressure of the air against your skin. This adds to the tension. With the pressure of the air against your skin lower than the pressure of your body pushing outward, your tissues begin to absorb more moisture, swelling slightly. That makes you feel slightly out of sorts, maybe even edgy. Some people think this feels sexy.

Being in a thunderstorm can make your hair stand on end. Yes, it can. The crackling interaction between the negatively charged air and the positively charged storm cloud can make individual strands of hair stand up. How straight depends on how short they are. The very short hair on your arms may stand straight up, while the longer hair on your head merely ripples.

This phenomenon is generally so well documented that meteorologists routinely warn that if you are outdoors in the open and your scalp begins to feel tingly, you should immediately get down flat on the ground. The tingle may be a warning that a bolt of lightning is about to strike in your vicinity. Lightning is likely to strike the tallest object; your aim, therefore, is to lie as low as possible.

Thunderstorms turn milk sour. It's certainly possible (some say, possibly certain) that milk left standing at room temperature during a thunderstorm will sour, but it has nothing to do with the noise of the thunder or the random electricity displayed in every lightning strike. If the milk sours it is probably because the hot and humid weather associated with thunderstorms encourages the bacteria that spoil milk to multiply like microscopic rabbits. To prevent this from happening, store the milk in the refrigerator.

See also LIGHTNING.

TICKS

To remove a tick, paint it with nail polish. Putting a drop of polish on a tick suffocates the bug so that it stops wriggling, which is helpful but unnecessary. All you really need to remove a tick is a pair of tweezers and a steady hand. Grasp the tick securely with the tweezers and pull steadily so that you remove the tick's head along with its body. If you live in an area where tick-borne illnesses such as Lyme disease or Rocky Mountain spotted fever are endemic, save the tick and show it to your doctor to aid in her diagnosis.

Put a drop of olive oil, mineral oil or petroleum jelly on a tick to make it let go. Doing this will kill the tick, but, once again, it's overkill. See above.

TOENAILS

When you trim your toenails, always cut them straight across. True, but remember to smooth down the sharp corners with an emery board so the edges do not snag your socks or stockings or bend into the skin at the side of the toes when you put on your shoes.

People with diabetes are more likely than others to have ingrown toenails. No, but they are more likely to suffer from foot infections because people with diabetes often have impaired circulation and/or nerve damage in the feet and lower legs. Damaged nerves make the feet less sensitive to pain so that ordinarily minor irritation caused by poorly fitted shoes may escalate into major problems. At the same time, impaired circulation reduces the supply of oxygen to the feet, which slows the healing process and increases the growth of microorganisms that thrive in an oxygen-starved environment.

See also FINGERNAILS.

TONSILS

Tonsils are useless organs that should always be surgically removed. Actually, in infancy, one's tonsils are very useful. They start out as protective filters that catch and hold bacteria, viruses and particles of airborne dust and dirt that might otherwise make an infant ill. By the time a child is three, however, the tonsils begin to shrink and lose their protective power. But they never disappear entirely unless they are surgically removed, and the small tonsils that remain may become infected if overwhelmed by pathogenic organisms.

Before the introduction of antibiotics, infected tonsils were always taken out. Often, healthy tonsils were removed to prevent infection. According to the *Columbia University College of Physicians and Surgeons Complete Home Medical Guide,* the modern rule of thumb is that any tonsils that cause three or more bouts of tonsillitis (infected tonsils) with high fever in one year should be removed.

Even if you take them out, tonsils can grow back. No. Once removed by surgery, your tonsils will never grow back. The confusion here may stem from the fact that adenoids, which are swollen lymph glands in the nose and throat, are difficult to remove entirely by surgery. A small piece left in place may enlarge again, thus giving rise to the belief that tonsils, like adenoids, can "grow back again."

See also OPERATIONS, SURGICAL.

TOOTHACHE

To soothe a toothache, hold an aspirin against your gum. Don't do it. Aspirin is caustic; it can burn your gum. In addition, the painkiller is not efficiently absorbed through mucous membranes. Better to take two aspirin (or acetaminophen) with a glass of water, and call your dentist in the morning. Or right then, if you are really in pain.

Oil of cloves will heal an aching tooth. Oil of cloves contains eugenol, a topical anesthetic that does relieve nerve pain. Dentists often pack a clean open cavity with a tiny piece of cotton saturated with a drop of eugenol to relieve the pain or mix eugenol with zinc oxide the make a soothing temporary dressing for use in the early stages of root canal therapy.

Caution: Eugenol is serious medicine, not a harmless home remedy for amateurs. Like many other essential plant oils, it is potentially poisonous, and according to the Poison Control Center in New York, it may be lethal if swallowed or absorbed through skin or mucous membranes.

See also ASPIRIN, TEA BAGS.

TRENCH MOUTH

'Trench mouth' is catching. No. Trench mouth is a form of periodonditis (an infection of the gum) that got its folksy name during World War I when its symptoms—bleeding gums, loose teeth, bad breath—were common among soldiers in the trenches in France. Because there were so many soldiers packed in so close together, it seemed logical to assume they were catching whatever it was they had from each other. But they weren't. Trench mouth is brought on by an individual's susceptibility to poor diet, poor dental hygiene and poor living conditions.

TUBERCULOSIS

A positive reaction to a tuberculin skin test proves you have tuberculosis. Not necessarily. What it does prove is that you have been infected with the tuberculosis (TB) bacilli at one time. After exposure, the TB bacilli may remain dormant in your body and on your skin for years without your ever developing the disease or being in danger of passing it on to someone else. However, to forestall the possibility of their developing TB later on, people who have a positive reaction to a skin test (an injection of protein from the tuberculosis organism into the skin of the forearm) may be advised to take a six-month course of an anti-tuberculosis drug such as isoniazid (brand names: INH, Laniazid, Nydrazid, Rifamate, Rimactane/INH, Teebaconin).

Sunbathing cures tuberculosis. Tuberculosis is a disease that flourishes among poorly nourished or immuno-deficient people living in crowded conditions. At the beginning of the 20th century, it was common among immigrants in the inner cities. The introduction of effective anti-tuberculosis drugs sent the incidence of TB in the United States spiraling downward in the 1970s and early 1980s, but it is now on the rise among urban ghetto dwellers and people with AIDS.

People who have TB can't be cured by sunbathing, but sunlight can reduce transmission of the disease. According to experts from the National Jewish Center for Immunology and Respiratory Medicine in Denver, the sun's ultraviolet (UVA/UVB) rays do kill the tuberculosis bacterium. The instinctive recognition of this scientific fact by people who did not differentiate among respiratory illnesses may have been what energized the folk belief that sunbathing cured a cold.

See also COLDS.

TUNA FISH

Eating tuna fish gives you acne. Tuna fish is high in iodine, which in excessive amounts can trigger acne-like eruptions in sensitive persons. For most of us, however, what we eat has little or no connection with whether or not we get acne.

Mixing tuna fish with mayonnaise makes the tuna fish more likely to spoil quickly. It may depend on the mayonnaise. Homemade mayonnaise, a blend of raw eggs and oil, is a perfect growth medium for bacteria, including those that spoil food. Commercial mayonnaises, however, contain vinegar or lemon juice, acids that act as natural preservatives, slowing the growth of the *Salmonella* and *Staphylococcus* organisms that are the most frequent cause of food spoilage leading to food poisoning.

Be warned, though, that the University of Wisconsin Food Research Institute researchers who confirmed the preservative benefits of mayonnaise back in 1982 also added a caveat. Mixing food with mayonnaise does not eliminate the need for refrigeration. Mayonnaise may slow bacterial growth, they stressed, but it will not stop it entirely. The best way to keep food safe is to keep it cold enough or hot enough to reduce bacterial growth to safe levels.

See also FOOD POISONING.

TURISTA

You only get turista in tropical countries. Not true. Turista, which is more properly known as "traveler's diarrhea" (TD), is more common in tropical countries than in temperate ones, but you can acquire it in either location.

Traveler's diarrhea may be triggered by a viral infection. More commonly, it is caused by *Escherichia coli (E. coli)*, a bacterium found in feces and thus in food and water contaminated with feces. When the bacteria reach your intestinal tract, they begin to release the toxins that cause gastric distress.

According to the Hoffman-LaRoche company, which makes drugs to combat traveler's diarrhea, the disease can show up anywhere sanitation is poor. It is most common in Asia, and southern Europe and Africa, as well as Latin America. As many as half of the 8 million Americans who travel to these places each year may end up with vomiting, diarrhea and fever attributable to TD.

Drinking bottled water will prevent traveler's diarrhea. It is one step in the right direction, but it will only protect you if the water was boiled before it was bottled. Contaminated water must be boiled vigorously for at least 15 minutes to destroy pathogens; if this is not done, bottling itself confers no particular protection.

The same thing goes for bottled carbonated beverages or beer. Carbonation alone will not purify contaminated water, nor will brewing alone. To be considered safe to drink, local beers made from potentially contaminated water must be pasteurized after brewing.

If you find yourself in an area where traveler's diarrhea is common, always peel fresh fruit before eating to get rid of bacteria on the skin. If the fruit is contaminated with turista organisms, peeling will not protect you from traveler's diarrhea. Why? Because as soon as you slice into the fruit to cut the skin, you transfer organisms from the surface to the flesh of the fruit inside. It is immeasurably safer to stick to fruits and vegetables that have been thoroughly cooked in vigorously boiling water for at least 15 minutes.

To replace fluids lost through traveler's diarrhea, drink a solution of sugar or honey and water. The major danger posed by serious diarrhea is dehydration accompanied by an imbalance in electrolytes, the chemicals that regulate impulses between cells in our bodies and make it possible for us to maintain the fluid balance that sustains life.

Solutions made of sugar, honey or corn syrup, salt, and water are common folk prescriptions to replace the fluids and electrolytes and keep our fluid balance in trim. In fact, these remedies are so effective that the World Health Organization (WHO) has created its own standard stomach-soothing recipe: Pour 8 ounces of orange juice into a drinking glass. Add a pinch of salt and ½ teaspoon honey or corn syrup. Fill another drinking glass with 8 ounces distilled water and add ¼ teaspoon baking soda. Drink alternately from each glass.

Caution #1: Your drinking glass should be scrupulously clean, washed only in pure, bottled water. If that's not possible, stick to disposable cups. *Caution #2:* The WHO formula is for an older child or an adult. If you are preparing it for a young child, check the quantities with your doctor. *Caution #3:* If you are preparing this formula for an infant, use sugar or corn syrup, not honey. Honey is considered hazardous for infants because it can transmit spores that may cause infant botulism.

See also HONEY, YOGURT.

TWINS

Twins run in families. Fraternal twins, yes. Identical twins, no.

Identical twins are individuals whose birth is the result of the accidental separation of a single fertilized egg into two distinct individuals. (Incomplete or partial separation of the fertilized egg produces the individuals we call "Siamese" twins.)

Fraternal twins, on the other hand, are two separate and distinct people created when two separate eggs are fertilized by two separate sperm. Because most women release only one mature egg each month at ovulation, the unusual tendency to release two mature eggs is assumed to result from a genetic difference. Nobody knows exactly how the trait is transmitted or whether it is inherited from one's mother or father.

Identical twins are identical. Yes. To all intents and purposes, they are biological carbon copies of each other. They have identical blood types, eye color, skin color and fingerprints. Skin grafts or organ transplants from one to the other will be accepted completely without any hint of tissue rejection.

Identical twins are also identical in intelligence potential and they are likely to develop the same chronic illnesses or medical conditions at approximately the same time in their lives even if they are brought up in separate households.

Your chance of having twins goes up as you get older. Yes, for fraternal twins. No, for identical twins.

Among pregnant women younger than 20, the incidence of fraternal twins is roughly six in every 1,000 births. At age 35 to 39, it rises to about 16 in every 1,000 live births. After 40, it declines again. The chance that you will have fraternal twins also rises with the number of pregnancies you experience. Taking a drug to increase fertility also increases the chance of producing multiple fetuses, including fraternal twins.

The likelihood of a woman's giving birth to identical twins does not appear to be affected by her age at the time she becomes pregnant or by her taking fertility drugs. Nor do other factors such as race or ethnicity or the number of previous pregnancies appear to be a factor, although women who have given birth to one set of twins are more likely than other women to produce twins in subsequent pregnancies.

U

ULCERS

People with peptic ulcers should drink plenty of milk and cream. Milk and cream were the twin cornerstones of the Sippy Diet, a high-cholesterol, high-fat diet once prescribed for people with ulcers. The regimen started with hourly feedings of milk and cream, then added eggs, custards and pureed foods.

The Sippy Diet dates from the days when doctors assumed that peptic ulcers (ulcers of the stomach and duodenum) were caused solely by stomach acid. Acting on this assumption, they theorized that dairy foods would suppress the production of stomach acid, thus reducing the incidence of new ulcers and speeding the healing of existing ones.

Today, gastroenterologists believe that when it comes to ulcers what you eat is irrelevant. All foods, bland as well as spicy, stimulate the production of stomach acid. More to the point, it now appears that the prime mover in ulcer disease isn't stomach acid, but a bacteria that attacks the intestinal lining. Exactly what sets off the bacterial attack remains a mystery, but, except for a few specific irritating foods, diet has largely been exonerated as a cause of ulcers, and the American Dietetic Association now rates the milk-and-cream Sippy Diet obsolete.

People with ulcers should stick to a bland diet. Only if they like the food. Despite the folklore linking spicy foods to ulcers, all controlled scientific studies to date show that while the hot and spicy food may singe your tongue, most of it doesn't ulcerate your stomach or affect the rate at which your ulcers heal.

The only exceptions are irritating spices such as pepper, cloves and nutmeg, which are known to inflame the intestinal lining. Of course, if a particular food upsets your stomach, you should avoid it—even if you don't have an ulcer.

People with ulcers should stick to decaffeinated coffee. People with ulcers should almost certainly avoid coffee, period. It is now clear that caffeine isn't the only culprit in coffee. Both regular and decaffeinated coffees contain flavoring and aroma oils that are irritating to the lining of the stomach and intestinal tract.

Ulcers run in families. They may. People who have close blood relatives (mother, father, sister, brother) with ulcers appear to have a higher-than-normal risk of developing ulcers themselves.

Women don't get ulcers. They do, but not in the same numbers men do. Although the incidence of ulcers among men went down and the incidence of ulcers among women went up during the 1970s and 1980s, today there are still approximately two men with ulcers for every woman who has them.

URINE

Urine is an antiseptic. In primitive societies, body wastes or by-products such as urine, feces, hair cuttings and fingernail parings are often credited with magical properties and used as medicine. There is a long history of this sort of thing, and as Anthony Smith, author of *The Body*, points out, medieval Europeans, like their ancestors, used urine to disinfect battlefield wounds.

That may sound unappealing, but it is not as far-fetched as you might think.

In the absence of a urinary infection, the urine of otherwise healthy people is bacteria-free as it comes from the body and might, in certain circumstances, have been cleaner than the water available to ancient and medieval armies in the field.

But stale urine is not. When urine is allowed to sit around, it becomes contaminated with bacteria. In fact, one reason stale urine smells strongly of ammonia is that the bacteria in it have decomposed its urea, the nitrogen-carrying waste compound in urine. (Ammonia is a nitrogen compound.)

A drop of urine in the eye prevents cataracts. No. In fact, putting a drop of urine in your eye might vary well contaminate and infect the eye.

Injections of urine break down fat cells and help you lose weight. Definitely not. There is absolutely no serious scientific study to support this diet fad of the late 1970s and early 1980s.

Eating asparagus can makes your urine smell funny. True. Methyl mercaptan, a smelly sulfur compound produced when our bodies digest asparagus, is excreted in urine, causing a noticeably unpleasant aroma.

Gargling with urine heals a sore throat. Well, it is warm, and it is supposed to taste salty, but the prudent course—especially when you're sick and your urine may be contaminated with bacteria and other organisms—is to avoid body wastes and stick to the conventional gargle: hot salty water.

See also SORE THROAT.

URINE TESTS

Urine tests are an accurate guide to who uses drugs. Not always. What urine tests can do is pinpoint the presence of specific chemicals in urine. Whether or not the presence of these chemicals indicates drug use can be open to serious question.

For example, people who take ordinary over-the-counter allergy and cold remedies containing decongestants may have chemicals similar to amphetamines in their urine, and people who consume foods made with poppy seeds, such as poppy seed bagels, may have morphine- and heroin-like chemicals in their urine. (Poppy seeds come from the plant whose latex yields opium and its constituents, morphine and codeine.)

V

VASELINE

Vaseline is a useful sexual lubricant. Absolutely not. Vaseline is a brand name for petroleum jelly (petrolatum), a hardened oil that will not dissolve in water. That means that it is very hard to wash petroleum jelly off skin or mucous membranes. More important, petroleum jelly dissolves latex, the material used for diaphragms, cervical caps and most condoms. If you use petroleum jelly with one of these forms of birth control, the jelly will quickly eat tiny holes in the latex, allowing sperm to get through.

Vaseline makes hair grow on your skin. Especially your face. No. Neither will any other over-the-counter skin cream, oil or lotion.

VINEGAR

Drinking vinegar cleans out the body. This folk remedy is based on the fact that vinegar irritates the bladder, thus increasing the urge to urinate. For some people this is an (erroneous) sign that the body is "cleansing" itself. Others take it for what it is: a temporary discomfort.

Rinsing your hair with vinegar after you shampoo makes the hair shine. True. Granny's favorite hair rinse made great sense in the days when women washed their hair with soap that was basic (alkaline) and could leave a dulling scum. Vinegar, an acid, dissolves and removes this coating.

Today, however, virtually all shampoos are made of detergents, which are designed to be rinsed off in running water. So is the vinegar rinse still valid? Maybe.

The physical action of washing your hair can ruffle up the tiny scales that form the outer covering of the hair shaft. When your hair dries, the scales are left standing up every which way, reflecting light in hundreds of different directions at once, so that your hair looks dull instead of shiny.

The acid vinegar rinse (typically one tablespoon vinegar in a cup of warm water) will smooth down the ruffled scales so that your hair reflects light evenly and look shiny. Because vinegar can darken blonde hair, blondes should use that other archetypal acid hair rinse, lemon juice and water, instead.

To cleanse the vagina, rinse with a vinegar-and-water douche. It has no colors, no perfumes, no preservatives, and it is an acid solution that encourages the growth of the protective bacteria that live in the vaginal area, so, if used occasionally, the vinegar-and-water douche is generally presumed to be safe. But it is not really necessary. The healthy vagina continually cleans itself by producing natural secretions that wash down its walls. Frequent douching, with or without vinegar, can wash away these natural secretions and dry out the vaginal tissues.

See also LEMONS, MIGRAINE HEADACHES, SWIMMER'S EAR.

VIRGINS

Virgins bleed the first time they have sexual intercourse. Anyone, male or female, who has never had sexual intercourse is considered a virgin. Women who are virgins are presumed to have an intact hymen, a fold of fibrous tissue, skin and mucous membrane at the opening of the vagina. At first intercourse, this covering is likely to be torn, and the torn tissue will, presumably, bleed.

But the absence of bleeding does not necessarily prove that a woman is not a virgin. The hymen may simply have disappeared spontaneously or it may have been torn by different kinds of vigorous exercise such as horseback riding or it may have been stretched sufficiently by the use of tampons to permit blood-free entry of the penis. (This should not be taken to suggest that using tampons destroys virginity. The hymen is a fold, not a solid tissue, across the entrance to the vagina. Inserting a tampon simply stretches a naturally occurring opening.)

Virgins never reach orgasm the first time they have intercourse. Some do, some don't. It's strictly a matter of individual reaction that proves nothing regarding a woman's status as a virgin.

Virgins can't get pregnant. It would be unusual but at least theoretically possible for a girl who has never had sexual intercourse (the insertion of the penis into the vagina) to become pregnant if her partner ejaculates close to the entrance to the vagina and contact between them is so intimate that even without penetration the sperm have access to the vagina.

. Another possibility for virgin pregnancy is purely theoretical insofar as human beings are concerned. Among some species of animals, females may conceive asexually without the participation of a male. This phenomenon, known as parthenogenesis, occurs when an ovum begins to divide and multiply on its own. In laboratory frogs, for example, parthenogenesis has been triggered by electrical impulses.

To date, there is no confirmed case of parthenogenesis among mammals on record, but there have been cases of women who claim to have conceived this way. If such a thing were to occur, the child would be female, an exact genetic copy of its mother, because all its genes and chromosomes would have come solely from her.

VITAMIN A

Vitamin A prevents (or cures) cancer. For years, nutrition writer Adelle Davis, who herself died of bone cancer in 1975, contended that massive doses of vitamin A could stop the growth of malignant tumors in laboratory rats. Ms. Davis also recommended massive daily doses of vitamin A for human beings, despite the fact that continued large doses of this fat soluble vitamin, which is stored in the body's fatty tissues, may be toxic.

By the early 1980s, however, the National Cancer Institute was recommending increased consumption of deep green and yellow fruits and vegetables rich in carotenoids as a way to reduce the risk of certain cancers, including cancers of the respiratory system.

Carotenoids are not vitamin A. They are naturally occurring pigments found in fruits and vegetables, some of which, notably *alpha*-carotene and *beta*-carotene, have "vitamin A-activity," which means that they can be converted to vitamin A in the body. True vitamin A, also known as "pre-formed vitamin A", is found only in certain foods of animal origin, such as liver and dairy products.

Early in the decade, the preferred carotenoids were the ones with vitamin A activity, but by the end of the '80s, it began to seem that other carotenoids, such as lycopene (the red pigment in tomatoes), might be protective even though they do not have vitamin A activity.

As of this writing, the question of whether or not vitamin A is an anti-carcinogen remains unresolved, but people on both sides of the argument agree that it is a good idea to increase our consumption of fresh fruits and vegetables, particularly those rich in red, orange and yellow pigments.

VITAMIN C

Taking vitamin C every day prevents colds. Almost certainly not. Forty years' investigation into the relationship between vitamin C and the common cold has failed to turn up any evidence that taking vitamin C prevents colds. But there *are* several serious studies suggesting that taking vitamin C may make any cold you do catch slightly easier to live with.

In 1975, the *Journal of the American Medical Association* published a review of 14 studies of vitamin C and the common cold conducted from 1942 to 1974. The results showed that people who take 1 gram (1,000 mg) or more vitamin C a day appear to have an average one-tenth of one cold less each year than people who do not take vitamin C, and that their colds last an average one-tenth of one day less.

The article concluded that this difference was too small to warrant taking vitamin C supplements each day, a position shared by the National Research Council, the agency that establishes the Recommended Dietary Allowances (RDAs) for vitamins, minerals and other nutrients.

In 1987, however, cold researchers at the Respiratory Virus Research Laboratory at the University of Wisconsin Medical School published the results of a study suggesting the relief offered by vitamin C might be more significant than that. In this study, 16 healthy people (eight of whom got 500 mg vitamin C four times a day for 3.5 weeks, while the others got a placebo) shared living quarters for a week with eight cold sufferers. At the end of the week, everyone was sent home. The volunteers who had been taking vitamin C were given 2 grams a day for the next two weeks; the others again got placebo.

Taking vitamin C did not prevent colds; all but three of the healthy volunteers got sick. But the volunteers who had taken vitamin C had milder symptoms and, on average, their colds went away not one-tenth but five days sooner. In October 1990, at the annual meeting of the American Society for Microbiology, the Wisconsin researchers announced the results of two follow-up studies confirming these results. It is almost certainly not the last word to be heard on this one.

VITAMINS AND MINERALS

Vitamin and mineral supplements containing 'natural' vitamins and minerals are more healthful than synthetic ones. Whether your supplements are labeled natural or synthetic, the nutrients they contain are exactly the same chemical substances. For example, the ascorbic acid (vitamin C) in orange juice and in "natural" supplements is exactly the same as the ascorbic acid created in a laboratory, a compound with the chemical structure $C_6H_8O_6$. Any change in this formula would create a totally different chemical, no longer identifiable as ascorbic acid. The same is true for all other vitamins and minerals.

The real difference between supplements labeled "natural" and all the others is that in many cases, the "natural" ones are put together without sugar, starch or artificial colors. But this is by no means certain, and the only way to be sure is to check the ingredient label.

It's better to get your vitamins from food than from supplements. This is almost always true. Foods provide a nutritious combination of nutrients (vitamins, minerals, protein, fat and carbohydrates) that may act in concert with each other. For example, dietary protein increases the body's absorption of calcium. Milk foods, an excellent source of calcium, are also good sources of protein. Calcium supplements are not.

Vitamins and minerals are natural substances. That means it's safe to take as much as you want. No. As the famed 16th-century Swiss physician and alchemist Philippus Augustus Paracelsus was first to note, all toxicity depends on dosage.

Some substances that are poisonous in large doses may be life-sustaining in miniscule amounts. For example, arsenic. Minute amounts of this trace element, which occurs naturally in fish and seafood, appear to be essential for life. According to the National Research Council, rats, chickens, goats and other animals grow more slowly and are unable to reproduce when they are arsenic deficient.

Even substances normally considered safe at any dose may be harmful in very large amounts. Consider water. We cannot live without it, but people who drink more than they can eliminate through the kidneys may be at risk for water intoxication, a condition characterized by mental confusion, coma, convulsion and, possibly, death.

Water intoxication is rare to be sure, but it is not unknown among people with conditions such as kidney disease and congestive heart failure.

Like water, vitamins and minerals are essential nutrients generally considered safe. But when taken in amounts far exceeding the recommended dietary allowances (RDAs), they can cause side effects that range from skin disorders to death. Like any other medicine, they should be handled with care.

Some Known Adverse Effects of Excessive Doses of Vitamins and Minerals

Vitamin	RDA*	Adverse effect**	Dose**
Vitamin A	5,000 IU (M)# 4,000 IU (F)	Fetal malformations Headache, vomiting, hair loss, dry skin, bone abnormalities, liver damage	20,000 IU daily during pregnancy 50,000 IU daily long-term
Vitamin D	400 IU	Kidney & heart damage	1,800 IU (children/ adult toxic dose unknown)
Vitamin C	60 mg	Kidney stones in susceptible persons	Unknown
Niacin	15 mg	Dilation of blood vessels, flushing	3 to 9 gm daily
Vitamin B6	2.0 mg (M) 1.6 mg (F)	Disorders of nerves in hands and feet	92+ mg daily for 6 mos
Calcium	800 mg ##	Constipation; urin- ary stones (male); kidney damage	Varying amounts, depending on individual health status
Iron	10 mg (M) 15 mg (F)	Poisoning/death	3 g/lethal dose (children) Adult lethal dose: 200-250 mg/kg body weight

*Recommended dietary allowances for healthy adults
**Unless otherwise noted, effects and dosages are for adults
#(M) = male; (F) = female
##The RDA for men and women to age 24 and women older than 50 is 1,200 mg
Source: National Research Council, *Recommended Dietary Allowances* (Washington, D.C.: National Academy Press, 1989)

W

WARTS

You can cure your warts by covering them with (castor oil) (radish juice) (the juice of marigold flowers) (raw meat) (copper pennies) (the sap from dandelion flowers) (a black snail) (bacon) (the bark of an ash tree) (burying a bag that contains as many stones as you have warts) etc. etc. etc. Yes. Yes. Yes. Yes. Yes. Yes. Yes. Yes. Yes. Yes. No. No. No. No. No. No. No. No. No. No.

Warts are viral infections of the skin whose course can be decidedly erratic. They may disappear completely after a few months or they may hang around for years, recurring at the same site or showing up in other places. If a natural remission occurs around the time the patient is using one of these "cures," the remission is likely to be mistakenly attributed to the cure.

Cast a magic spell to cure a case of warts. Surprise: This one seems to be true so long as you are willing to consider hypnosis the modern medical equivalent of a magic spell.

Warts are viral infections of the skin whose course can be decidedly erratic. They may disappear completely after a few months or they may hang around for years, recurring at the same site or showing up in other places. Like many skin conditions, warts occasionally respond to the power of suggestion implicit in a psychological cure such as post-hypnotic suggestion.

In 1990, a group of psychologists led by Nicholas P. Spanos, Ph.D., professor of psychology at Carleton University in Ottawa, Canada, hypnotized ten patients with warts, told them that the skin around their warts was beginning to "feel tingly and grow warm," instructed them to imagine their warts shrinking and dissolving, and directed them to practice this imagery (imagining their warts shrinking and dissolving) once a day after they "woke up."

A second group of ten wart patients was given the conventional treatment, painting the warts with salicylic acid. A third group of ten was given a placebo. A fourth group of ten served as controls: no hypnosis, no treatment, no placebo.

After six weeks, the 10 patients who had been hypnotized were doing much better than the other 30; six had lost at least one wart. Three of the controls and one of the patients who got a placebo had lost warts. None of the people given salicyclic acid had lost a single wart.

You can catch someone else's warts. True. Warts are contagious viral infections that can be passed from one person to another or spread from site to site on a single body.

See also POTATOES.

WATER

Drink eight glasses of water a day. Water accounts for between 50% and 70% of a healthy adult's total body weight. In an average day, that person loses about 2,400 milliliters (ml) water through urination, defecation, respiration and perspiration.

We replace the water we lose by drinking liquids. We also get water from food. A raw apple, for example, is 84% water; a 100mg/3.5-ounce lean hamburger, 56%. Finally, our bodies make water as a by-product when we digest food.

Figuring out exactly how much water we get from each source can be complicated, but here's a simple calculation about how to replace what we lose. There are about 30 ml water in a fluid ounce. A 10–ounce glass of water delivers about 300 ml. Eight 10–ounce glasses give you 2,400 ml, just about what an average adult body loses on an average day.

Note: When activity increases, so does water loss, which is why people who engage in strenuous activity should increase their consumption of liquids.

Fluoridated drinking water causes cancer. In the more than four decades since Grand Rapids, Michigan, became the first American community to fluoridate its water supply, no controlled scientific study has ever shown that drinking fluoridated water causes cancer in human beings.

In 1990, however, the National Toxicology Program, a division of the U.S. Public Health Service, published the results of a study of laboratory rats and mice given long-term high doses of fluorides. In this study, undertaken at the direction of Congress, four male rats developed osteosarcomas (cancers of the bone).

Because fluorides concentrate in bones, fluoridation opponents point to this as proof that fluoridated water is carcinogenic. Supporters of fluoridation, however, point out that the cancers occurred only in male rats, not in female rats or male or female mice; that the numbers (.03% of the animals in the study) are too small to be meaningful; and that the doses of fluorides were nearly 100 times what we get in our water.

Chlorine purifies drinking water. It does a pretty good job, but it isn't perfect.

Adding chlorine to drinking water eliminates large numbers of bacteria in the water, reducing the bacterial population to levels ordinarily considered harmless. But chlorine cannot eliminate microscopic particles of solid particles in the water, nor will it eliminate potentially hazardous industrial contaminants.

Never drink from the bathroom tap. When the chamber pot was discarded in favor of the flush toilet, there was always the possibility that primitive plumbing systems could allow sewage waste to mix with the water from the bathroom taps. Modern plumbing, however, does not permit any mingling of the water flow and waste drainage systems, so you can drink from any tap you choose. The fact that some people who think it's dangerous to drink from the bathroom tap use water flowing from it to brush their teeth only serves to illustrate the occasionally stunning illogic of the human mind.

It is not safe to drink water from a hot water tap. When water is heated, its oxygen bubbles to the surface and escapes. That is why water from the hot tap or water that has been boiled tastes "flat." But there is no reason not drink it if you want to. It is nutritionally identical to water from the cold tap.

Always let the water run from the tap awhile before you drink it. True. Letting the water run makes it colder and increases its oxygen content, thus making the water taste better.

More important, letting the water run a minute or so until it gets cold can make the water safer. Virtually all the water faucets in this country are made with metals that leech lead into the water, either from lead solder in older pipes or from the brass used to build the faucet itself. (The brass may be covered with chrome or porcelain.) Although experts disagree as to exactly how much lead there actually is in the water, everyone agrees that "first draw" water—the water that comes out right away when you turn on the tap—contains the most lead because it has been sitting in the faucet, perhaps for several hours. For information about tap water safety, call the Environmental Protection Agency's Safe Drinking Water Hotline: 1-800-426-4791.

You can't get clean when you wash in 'hard' water. Hard water is called *hard* because it contains more than 100 parts dissolved minerals such as calcium and magnesium per million parts water. These minerals make the water basic (alkaline). They are hard to rinse off and can leave a scum on your body, hair or clothes. Soft water, on the other hand, is lower in minerals, more acidic and does not leave a scum on anything.

For the record, you may wish to know that the hardest drinking water in the United States comes from underground wells in the West and Midwest; the softest, from surface reservoirs in the Northeast.

See also RAINWATER.

WET FEET

If your feet get wet, you'll get a cold. Maybe. Wet clothing, including wet boots, shoes and socks, conducts heat away from the body so that you feel chilled and the temperature inside your nasal passages drops. Many researchers, including those at the Army Research Institute of Environmental Medicine in Natick, Massachusetts, have confirmed that this drop in temperature can reduce the activity of cells in the nasal mucous membranes that ordinarily release the antibodies that protect you against cold viruses. As a result, you are more susceptible to infection. But it's important to remember that there has to be a virus present; simply having wet feet in cold weather won't cause a cold.

WEIGHT GAIN

People who eat fast gain more weight than people who eat slowly. Only if they eat more food. Which is, of course, a distinct possibility.

It takes a few minutes for the food you eat to reach your stomach and make you feel full. If you eat quickly, you may consume more food than is necessary to quell your hunger pangs.

On the other hand, eating slowly and waiting to see if you're still hungry before you reach for a second helping may enable you to cut back on your calories without feeling deprived. And that can limit weight gain.

See also FAT PEOPLE, OBESITY.

WILLOW BARK

The bark of the willow tree cures fever and pain. The willow tree (Latin name: *Salicaceae*) is rich in salicin, a naturally occurring chemical related to acetyl salicylic acid (aspirin).

Chewing willow leaves or brewing a tea from willow bark is a folk remedy for pain that dates back at least as far as the Romans. Salicylates first came to the attention of organized medicine late in the 18th century when the "doctrine of signatures" was in fashion. This simple theory said that nature had provided a remedy for every disease, and that one only had to look hard to find it. In a paper delivered to the Royal Society of England in 1763, the Reverend Edward Stone modestly allowed as how he had found in a tree that grows in moist, damp areas a cure for the aches and pains associated with that kind of climate. What he had discovered was the willow.

The ability of salicylates extracted from willow to ease pain and reduce fever was first demonstrated around 1850, but the compounds were shelved because they were so irritating to the gastrointestinal tract that taking them triggered miserable gastric upset. By the 1890s, however, scientists had been able to produce acetyl salicylic acid (aspirin), which is much less irritating to the gastric tract than the simpler salicylates.

Aspirin became commercially available in small quantities around the turn of the century. But there was not enough on hand to be of real use when the influenza pandemic struck in 1917. Since one of the most devastating effects of the flu was an extraordinarily high fever, epidemiologists find it morbidly fascinating to speculate as to how an adequate supply of a medicine to reduce fever might have affected the course of the epidemic.

WINE

Drinking red wine strengthens the blood. At first blush, this is the perfect example of the like-causes-like school of medicine and nutrition: Red wine is red, liquid and "strong," so drinking it is presumed to strengthen the blood.

That's the mythology. The medical fact is that drinking red wine, or indeed, any alcoholic beverage, makes some of the body's blood vessels expand. It also seems to decrease blood levels of low-density lipoproteins (LDLs), the "bad" fat/protein particles that carry cholesterol into your blood vessels, while raising blood levels of high-density lipoproteins (HDLs), the "good" particles that speed the exit of cholesterol from your body.

As you might expect, the discovery of this fact has prompted an immediate and continuing debate about whether the HDLs that increase when you drink alcoholic beverages are really good ones. And the debate rages on.

Drinking wine protects you against germs. In 1978, researchers at Health and Welfare Canada and the Food Research Institute of the University of Washington found that wine and grape juice both inactivated (but didn't kill) viruses in laboratory test tubes.

Oenophiles headed righteously for their wine cellars. The scientists went back to their labs, where, alas, they discovered that viruses could be reactivated after 30 minutes to an hour's exposure to "biological systems," a euphemism for stomach tissue from baby pigs or ordinary human blood. In the end, the conclusion seems to be that for living human beings the wineglass offers pleasure but no protection against germs.

WOUNDS

Seawater disinfects an open wound. People who live near the seacoast often say yes, but medical experts disagree because seawater teems with microbes, including, you may be surprised to learn, those that cause tetanus.

See also COBWEBS, JELLYFISH, TETANUS.

WRINKLES

As they get older, women wrinkle more severely than men do. Probably. One reason for this may be a difference in bone density. As they age, both men and women lose bone density, but women lose more and they lose it more quickly. The increased loss of bone in the forehead and cheeks causes a woman's skin to sag and wrinkle more than a man's does.

A second reason why women may tend to wrinkle more is the loss of sex hormones (notably estrogen), which leads to fine wrinkles on the forehead and around the eyes. The same thing occurs in men who lose testosterone. Women also have relatively thinner skin, and estrogen loss accelerates age-related thinning of the dermis, the layer of cells just under the epidermis, the top layer of skin. As we age, the dermis thins, loses elasticity and starts to sag. This happens to both sexes, but because the average woman starts out with skin that is microscopically thinner than the average man's, she is apt to wrinkle more.

See also FACE/FACIAL EXPRESSION.

X

X-RAYS

Dental X-rays are harmless. It's seems to be a question of where and when you get the X-rays.

In 1988, a group of researchers at the University of Southern California (USC) School of Medicine in Los Angeles interviewed 408 patients with tumors of the parotid gland, a salivary gland in your cheek that is directly in the path of radiation exposure for most dental X-rays. The researchers compared these patients' history of radiation exposure with that of 408 people without parotid tumors. What they found was that the people with malignancies of the salivary gland had been exposed to the very high levels of radiation commonly emitted by the old-fashioned machines used to perform dental X-rays in the 1950s.

Does that mean you should avoid all dental X-rays? No. What it does mean is that the early dental X-ray machines were not as safe as the ones in common use today.

Because the damage from ionizing radiation is cumulative, no exposure can ever be considered totally safe, but the amount of radiation delivered in an examination performed by a competent technician using a well-maintained modern dental X-ray machine appears to be well within safe limits, about 1/500th of the minimum average dose associated with an increase in the risk of cancer of the salivary glands for the patients in the USC study.

The USC scientists stressed the fact that even this low rate could be cut even further if all dentists in the United States used a form of X-ray film called "E-speed X-ray film." This extremely sensitive film requires 50% less radiation to register a picture than does the film most often used in American dental offices. In addition, using a machine that delivers X-ray beams in a carefully delineated pattern called "rectangularly columnated" might reduce the amount of radiation to which the patient is exposed by another 50%.

Pregnant women should avoid X-rays. One way to measure the amount and intensity of radiation exposure is in terms of the rad (*r*adiation *a*bsorbed *d*ose). Fewer than one in every 1,000 X-ray examinations performed by a competent technician working with modern, well-maintained equipment delivers more than 1,000 millirads (a millirad = 1/1000th of a rad) ionizing radiation, the amount below which the probability of obvious damage to the developing fetus is so low as to be considered negligible in figuring out whether or not to get the examination.

Another way to measure radiation exposure is in terms of the millisievert. Federal guidelines for radiation exposure current in 1990 set a recommended limit of 5 millisieverts exposure for pregnant women during the entire nine-month period of a normal healthy pregnancy. (In an ordinary chest X-ray, your body absorbs about 0.1 millisieverts, 1/50th of the recommended exposure limit during pregnancy.)

But the question of whether or not a woman who is pregnant should have an X-ray examination is so sensitive, especially during the first three months of the pregnancy, that it should never be decided on statistics alone. This is a decision that requires serious discussion between a pregnant woman and her doctor, the person best equipped to evaluate the risk vs. benefit ratio for her and for her fetus.

Y

YAWNING

You yawn because you need oxygen. Probably not. You may yawn because you are sleepy or because you are bored or because you are anxious, but a need for oxygen does not seem to have anything to do with it.

In 1987, researchers in the department of psychology at the University of Maryland in Catonsville, decided to test the folklore by asking volunteers to breathe in either plain air or air enhanced with CO_2 (carbon dioxide) or air enhanced with pure oxygen.

The result? People breathing in the CO_2 mixture didn't yawn any more frequently than the people breathing plain air, and the people breathing the oxygen-enhanced air didn't yawn any less frequently. Everybody yawned at about the same rate in response to about the same stimuli (see above), which goes a long way towards proving that a need for oxygen isn't what sets off a yawn.

YOGURT

Eating yogurt cures (or prevents) vaginal infections. As they eliminate disease organisms, antibiotics may also decimate the beneficial bacteria that live naturally in various parts of the human body. Women who take antibiotics, for example, are at risk of vaginal yeast infections because antibiotics destroy the beneficial lactobacilli that normally inhabit the vaginal area. The lactobacilli ordinarily keep yeasts and other pathogenic organisms in check. When the lactobacilli are destroyed, the yeasts proliferate. The result: vaginitis.

Because some yogurts contain live lactobacilli, many people wrongly assume that eating the yogurt will prevent a vaginal yeast infection.* Unfortunately, lactobacilli taken by mouth are quickly inactivated by stomach acid. They do not reach the vaginal area alive, and thus they

*Cultured milk products, including yogurt, that are pasteurized after culturing ("ultrapasteurized") do not contain live lactobacilli cultures. Check the label to be sure.

cannot cure an infection by correcting an antibiotic-caused lack of lactobacilli there.

Douching with a yogurt-and-water solution will cure a vaginal infection. No. Douching with a yogurt-and-water solution is a messy and ineffective substitute for medical treatment with antifungal drugs. What's more, several medical conditions, including some sexually transmitted diseases, may causes symptoms similar to those of a yeast infection. In the absence of a specific medical diagnosis, self-treatment with yogurt may be hazardous to your health.

Eating yogurt before you travel abroad can protect you against turista (traveler's diarrhea). This theory, popularized by nutrition guru Adelle Davis in the 1970s when yogurt was the reigning magic food, suggests that by loading up on beneficial bacteria you can defeat the ones that make you ill. Again, the answer is that once the bacteria reach the stomach, they are inactivated and therefore useless in preventing disease. Enjoy the yogurt, but don't depend on it to protect you against the miseries of turista.

Frozen yogurt is more healthful than ice cream because it has less fat. It depends on what kind of milk is used to make the frozen yogurt. If the dessert is made from whole milk (3.5% milk fat), it may turn out to have as many calories derived from fat as ice cream does. On the other hand, if it is made from low-fat (1% milk fat) or skim (fat free) milk, the frozen yogurt has less fat, just about what you would get from ice milk. Don't guess: Always check the nutrition labeling; what you find there may surprise you.

See also ICE CREAM, SUNBURN, TURISTA.

Z

ZINC

Sucking on zinc lozenges cures a cold. There is no evidence to show that this bit of totally modern medical folklore, which zipped in and out during the late 1980s, is true.

More important, downing large numbers of zinc tablets may be harmful. According to the National Research Council, which establishes the recommended dietary allowances (RDAs) for vitamins, minerals and other nutrients, consuming more than 2 grams (2,000 mg) zinc as zinc sulfate can cause acute toxicity characterized by gastrointestinal irritation and vomiting.

In 1989, the National Research Council set the RDA for zinc at 15 mg for a man, 12 mg for a woman. In a 1984 study, healthy adults who were given zinc supplements at 20 times this RDA suffered impairment of the immune system. In a 1978 study, people taking 10 to 30 times this amount developed abnormally low blood levels of copper and blood cell disorders. In a 1980 study, daily doses of zinc supplements five to 13 times the RDA triggered a decline in the blood levels of high-density lipoproteins (HDLs), the protective fat/protein particles that speed cholesterol's exit from your body.

ZINC OXIDE

Smearing zinc oxide ointment on your nose will prevent sunburn. Absolutely. The thick, white ointment is a physical barrier that keeps the suns burning ultraviolet (UV) rays from reaching your skin. The drawback, of course, is that the stuff looks awful, which is why medically protective, cosmetically acceptable sunblock lotions, gels and creams are so popular.

Selected
Bibliography

The American Medical Association Handbook of First Aid and Emergency Care.
New York: Random House, 1990.

The American Dietetic Association. *Handbook of Clinical Dietetics.* New Haven:
Yale University Press, 1981.

American Red Cross Standard First Aid. The American Red Cross, 1988.

Bark, Joseph P. *Skin Secrets.* New York: McGraw-Hill Book Company, 1988.

Barkham Bourroughs Encyclopedia of Astounding Facts and Useful Information 1889.
Westport, Ct.: Brayden Books, 1983.

Berkow, Robert, ed. *The Merck Manual,* 15th edition. Rahway, N.J.: Merck Sharp
& Dohme Research Laboratories, 1987.

Braunwald, Eugene; Isselbacher, Kurt J.; Petersdorf, Robert G.; Wilson, Jean D.;
Martin, Joseph B.; and Fauci, Anthony S., eds. *Harrison's Principles of Internal
Medicine.* New York: McGraw-Hill, 1987.

Briggs, George M., and Callaway, Doris Howes. *Nutrition and Physical Fitness.*
New York: Holt, Rhinehart and Winston, 1984.

Chamberlain, Mary. *Old Wives' Tales.* London: Virago Press, 1981.

Dauncey, Helen. *Is It Poisonous?.* Ambler, Pennsylvania: Medical Business Ser-
vices, 1990.

DiCanio, Margaret. *The Encyclopedia of Marriage, Divorce and the Family.* New
York: Facts On File, 1989.

Duke, James A. *A Handbook of Medicinal Herbs.* Boca Raton, Florida: CRC Press,
1988.

Fernie, W. T. *Meals Medicinal.* Bristol, England: John Wright & Co., 1905.

Ford, Regina Daley. *Diagnostic Tests Handbook.* Springhouse, Pennsylvania:
Springhouse Corporation, 1986

Fraser, Clarence M., ed. *The Merck Veterinary Manual,* 6th edition. Rahway, N.J.:
Merck & Co., 1986.

Griggs, Barbara. *Green Pharmacy.* New York: The Viking Press, 1981.

Handbook of Nonprescription Drugs, 8th edition. Washington D.C.: American Pharmaceutical Assocaition, 1986.

Harris, Marvin. *The Sacred Cow and the Abominable Pig.* New York: Touchstone
Books, 1987.

Hoffman, Mark S., ed. *The World Almanac and Book of Facts 1990.* New York:
World Almanac, 1990.

Kennell, Frances. *Folk Medicine.* London: Marshall Cavendish, 1976.

Knight, James A. *Doctor-to-Be: Coping with the Trials and Triumphs of Medical School.* New York: Appleton-Century Crofts, 1981.

Krupp, Marcus A., Chatton, Milton J., and Tierney, Lawrence M. *Current Medical Diagnosis and Treatment 1986.* Los Altos, California: Lange Medical Publications, 1986.

Levy, Judith S., and Greenhall, Agnes. *The Concise Columbia Encyclopedia.* New York: Columbia University Press. 1983.

Lewis, Walter H., and Elvin-Lewis, Memory P. *Medical Botany.* New York: John Wiley & Sons, 1977.

National Research Council. *Recommended Dietary Allowances,* 10th edition. Washington D.C.: National Academy Press, 1989.

Rinzler, Carol Ann. *The Complete Book of Food.* New York: World Almanac, 1987.

———. *The Complete Book of Herbs, Spices and Condiments.* New York: Facts On File, 1990.

Rose, Kenneth Jon. *The Body in Time.* New York: John Wiley & Sons, 1988.

Sifton, David W., ed. *PDR's Drug Interactions and Side Effects Index.* Oradell, N.J.: Medical Economics, 1988.

Smith, Anthony. *The Body.* New York: Viking Penguin, 1986.

Stedman's Medical Dictionary. Baltimore, Md.: Williams & Wilkins, 1982.

Steiner, Richard P., ed. *Folk Medicine.* Washington D.C.: American Chemical Society, 1986.

Tapley, Donald F.; Weiss, Robert J.; Morris, Thomas, eds. *The Columbia University College of Physicians and Surgeons Complete Home Medical Guide.* New York: Crown Publishers, 1985.

Thomas, Mai. *Grannie's Remedies.* New York: Gramercy Publishing Company, 1965.

Tyler, Varro E., *Hoosier Home Remedies.* West Lafayette, Indiana: Purdue University Press, 1985.

———. *The New Honest Herbal.* Philadelphia: George F. Stickley & Co., 1987.

Windholz, Martha, ed. *The Merck Index,* 10th edition. Rahway, N.J., Merck & Co., 1987.

Wurtman, Judith J. *Managing Your Mind and Mood Through Food.* New York: Rawson Associates, 1986.

Zimmerman, David R. *The Essential Guide to Nonprescription Drugs.* New York: Harper & Row, 1983.

In addition to the general and specific reference books listed above, the sources for information in *The Dictionary of Medical Folklore* included material published in the following periodicals:

American Health
Hippocrates
The Journal of the American Medical Association
Mayo Clinic Healthletter
Mayo Clinic Nutrition Letter
The New England Journal of Medicine
The New York Times
Newsday
Newsweek

Science
Science Digest
Science News
Time
Tufts University Diet & Nutrition Letter

and publications of the American Academy of Otolaryngology—Head and Neck Surgery, American Cancer Society, American Diabetes Association, American Heart Association, U.S. Department of Agriculture and U.S. Department of Commerce.

Index